Kareem Abdul-Jabbar

MYCROFT HOLMES

WRITERS:
Kareem Abdul-Jabbar & Raymond Obstfeld

ART:
Joshua Cassara

COLORS:
Luis Guerrero

LETTERS:
Simon Bowland

TITAN
COMICS

TITAN COMICS
EDITORIAL

SENIOR EDITOR
ANDREW JAMES

DESIGNER
DAN BURA

ASSISTANT EDITORS
Lauren Bowes, Lauren McPhee

PRODUCTION ASSISTANT
Natalie Bolger

PRODUCTION SUPERVISOR
Maria Pearson

PRODUCTION CONTROLLER
Peter James

SENIOR PRODUCTION CONTROLLER
Jackie Flook

ART DIRECTOR
Oz Browne

SENIOR SALES MANAGER
Steve Tothill

PRESS OFFICER
Will O'Mullane

BRAND MANAGER
Chris Thompson

ADS & MARKETING ASSISTANT
Tom Miller

DIRECT SALES & MARKETING MANAGER
Ricky Claydon

COMMERCIAL MANAGER
Michelle Fairlamb

HEAD OF RIGHTS
Jenny Boyce

PUBLISHING MANAGER
Darryl Tothill

PUBLISHING DIRECTOR
Chris Teather

OPERATIONS DIRECTOR
Leigh Baulch

EXECUTIVE DIRECTOR
Vivian Cheung

PUBLISHER
Nick Landau

@COMICSTITAN   TITAN COMICS   FACEBOOK.COM/
                                            COMICSTITAN

MYCROFT HOLMES AND THE APOCALYPSE HANDBOOK
ISBN: 9781785853005

10 9 8 7 6 5 4 3 2 1

Printed in China.

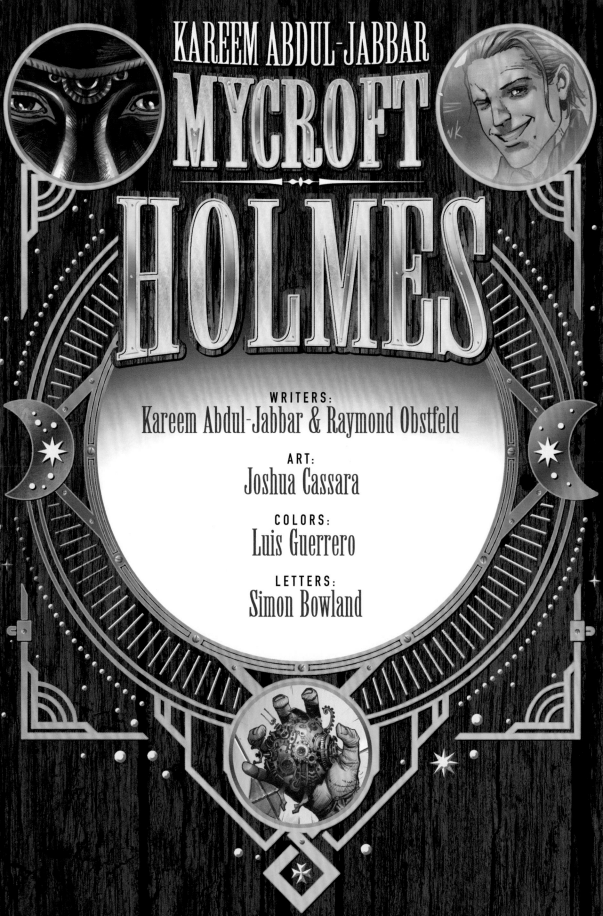

KAREEM ABDUL-JABBAR
MYCROFT HOLMES

WRITERS:
Kareem Abdul-Jabbar & Raymond Obstfeld

ART:
Joshua Cassara

COLORS:
Luis Guerrero

LETTERS:
Simon Bowland

TO FIND OUT MORE ABOUT OUR GREAT COMICS TITLES, VISIT
WWW.TITAN-COMICS.COM

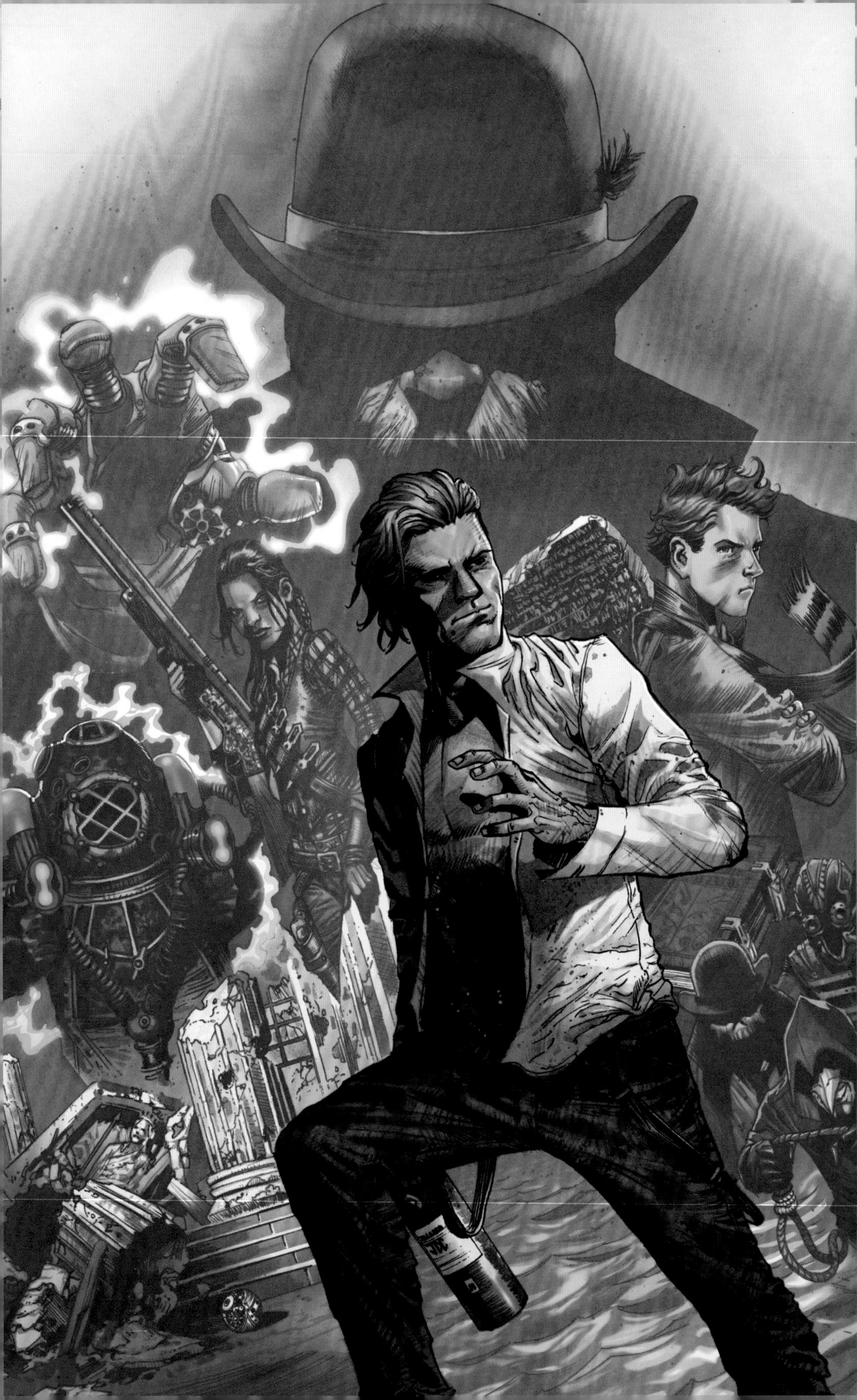

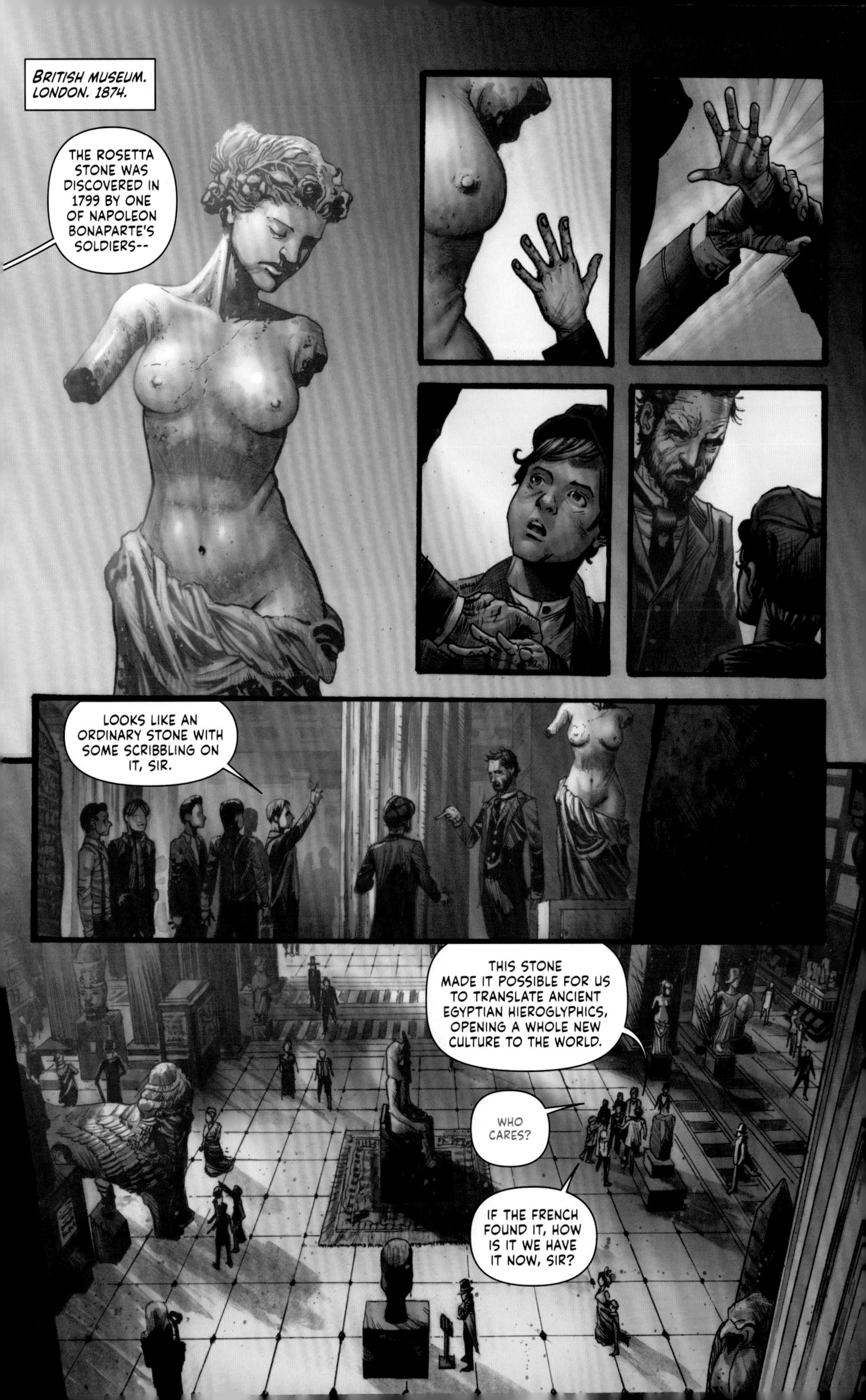
BRITISH MUSEUM. LONDON. 1874.
THE ROSETTA STONE WAS DISCOVERED IN 1799 BY ONE OF NAPOLEON BONAPARTE'S SOLDIERS--
LOOKS LIKE AN ORDINARY STONE WITH SOME SCRIBBLING ON IT, SIR.
THIS STONE MADE IT POSSIBLE FOR US TO TRANSLATE ANCIENT EGYPTIAN HIEROGLYPHICS, OPENING A WHOLE NEW CULTURE TO THE WORLD.
WHO CARES?
IF THE FRENCH FOUND IT, HOW IS IT WE HAVE IT NOW, SIR?

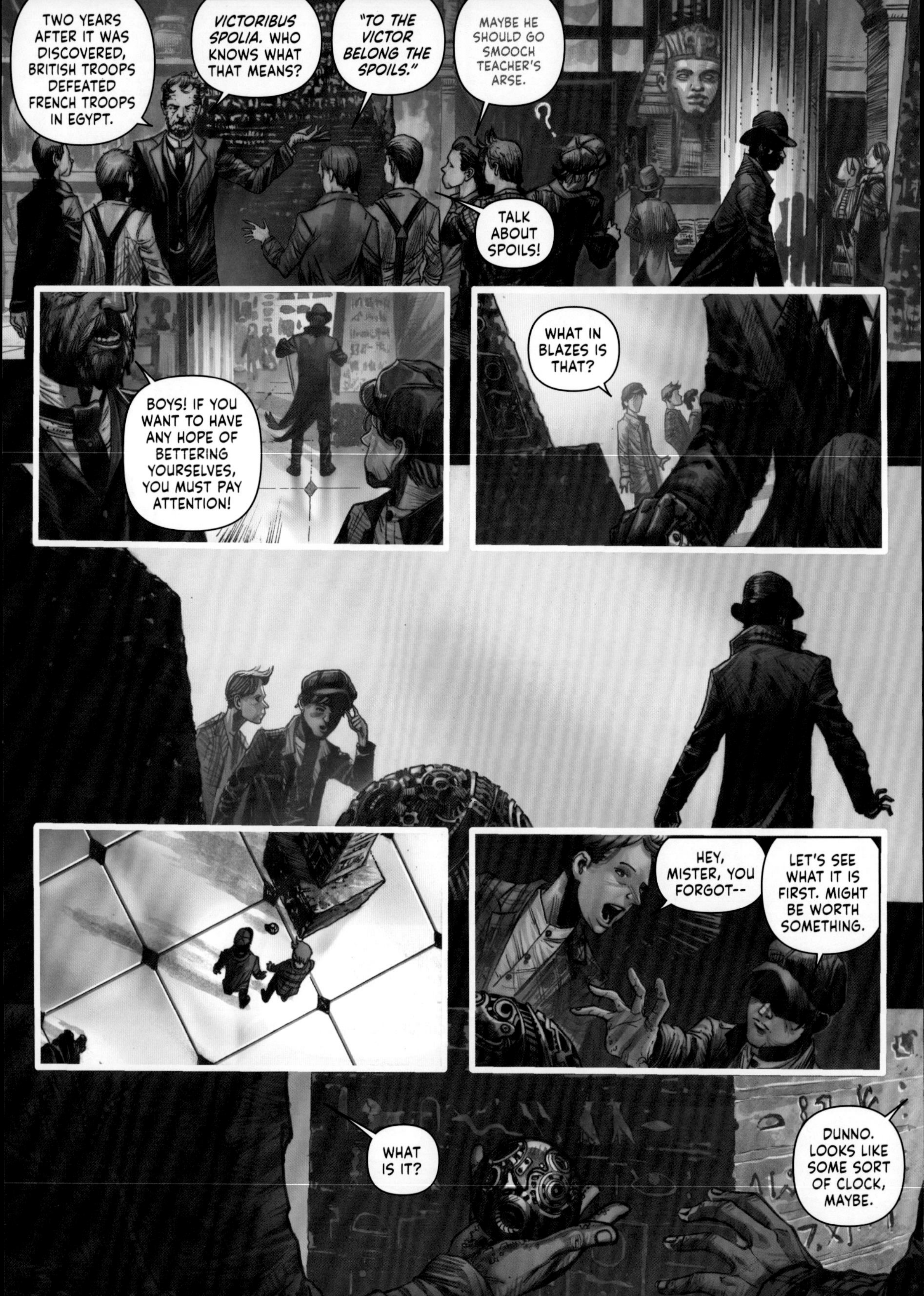
TWO YEARS AFTER IT WAS DISCOVERED, BRITISH TROOPS DEFEATED FRENCH TROOPS IN EGYPT.
VICTORIBUS SPOLIA. WHO KNOWS WHAT THAT MEANS?
"TO THE VICTOR BELONG THE SPOILS."
MAYBE HE SHOULD GO SMOOCH TEACHER'S ARSE.
?
TALK ABOUT SPOILS!
BOYS! IF YOU WANT TO HAVE ANY HOPE OF BETTERING YOURSELVES, YOU MUST PAY ATTENTION!
WHAT IN BLAZES IS THAT?
HEY, MISTER, YOU FORGOT--
LET'S SEE WHAT IT IS FIRST. MIGHT BE WORTH SOMETHING.
WHAT IS IT?
DUNNO. LOOKS LIKE SOME SORT OF CLOCK, MAYBE.

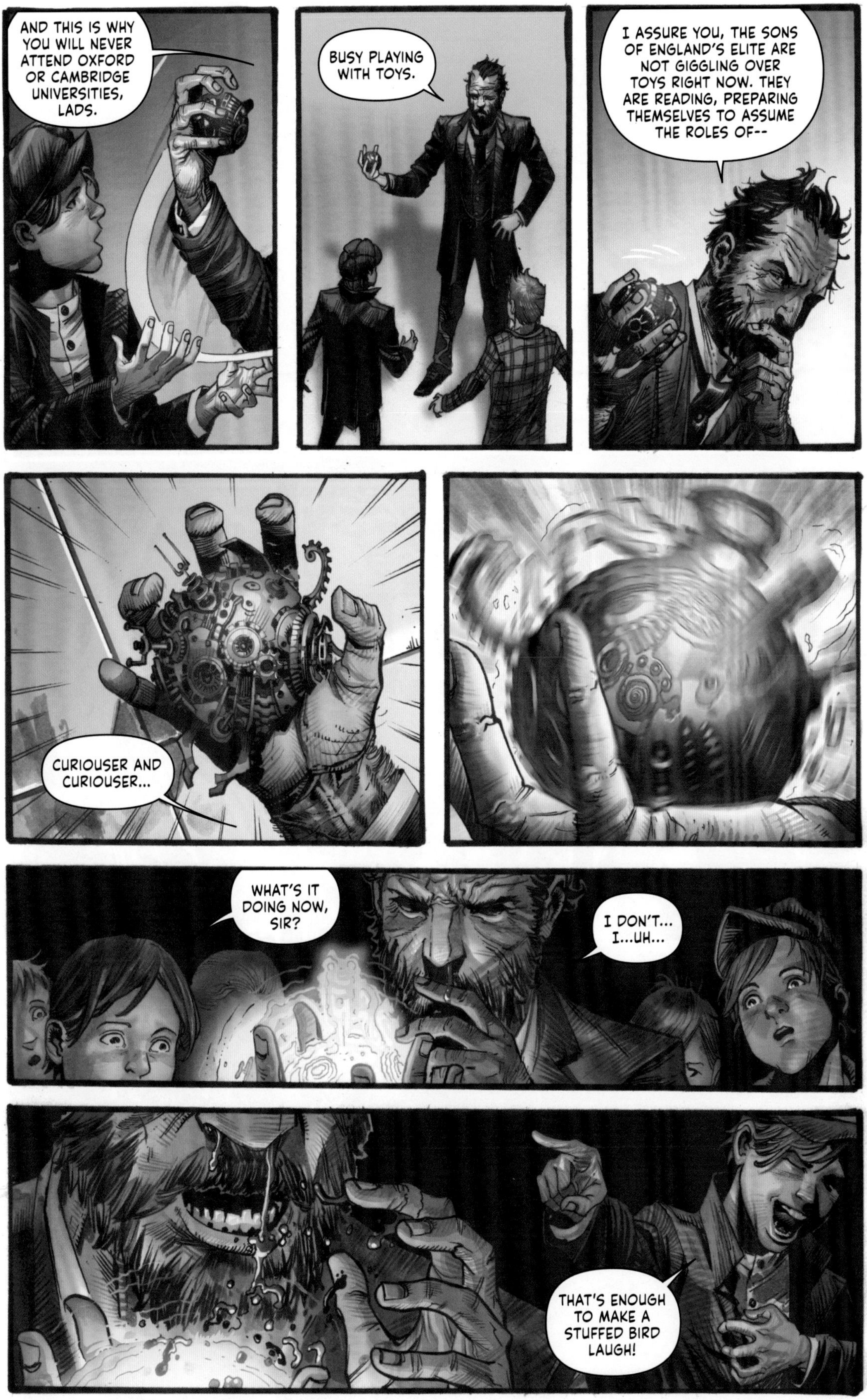
AND THIS IS WHY YOU WILL NEVER ATTEND OXFORD OR CAMBRIDGE UNIVERSITIES, LADS.
BUSY PLAYING WITH TOYS.
I ASSURE YOU, THE SONS OF ENGLAND'S ELITE ARE NOT GIGGLING OVER TOYS RIGHT NOW. THEY ARE READING, PREPARING THEMSELVES TO ASSUME THE ROLES OF--
CURIOUSER AND CURIOUSER...
WHAT'S IT DOING NOW, SIR?
I DON'T... I...UH...
THAT'S ENOUGH TO MAKE A STUFFED BIRD LAUGH!

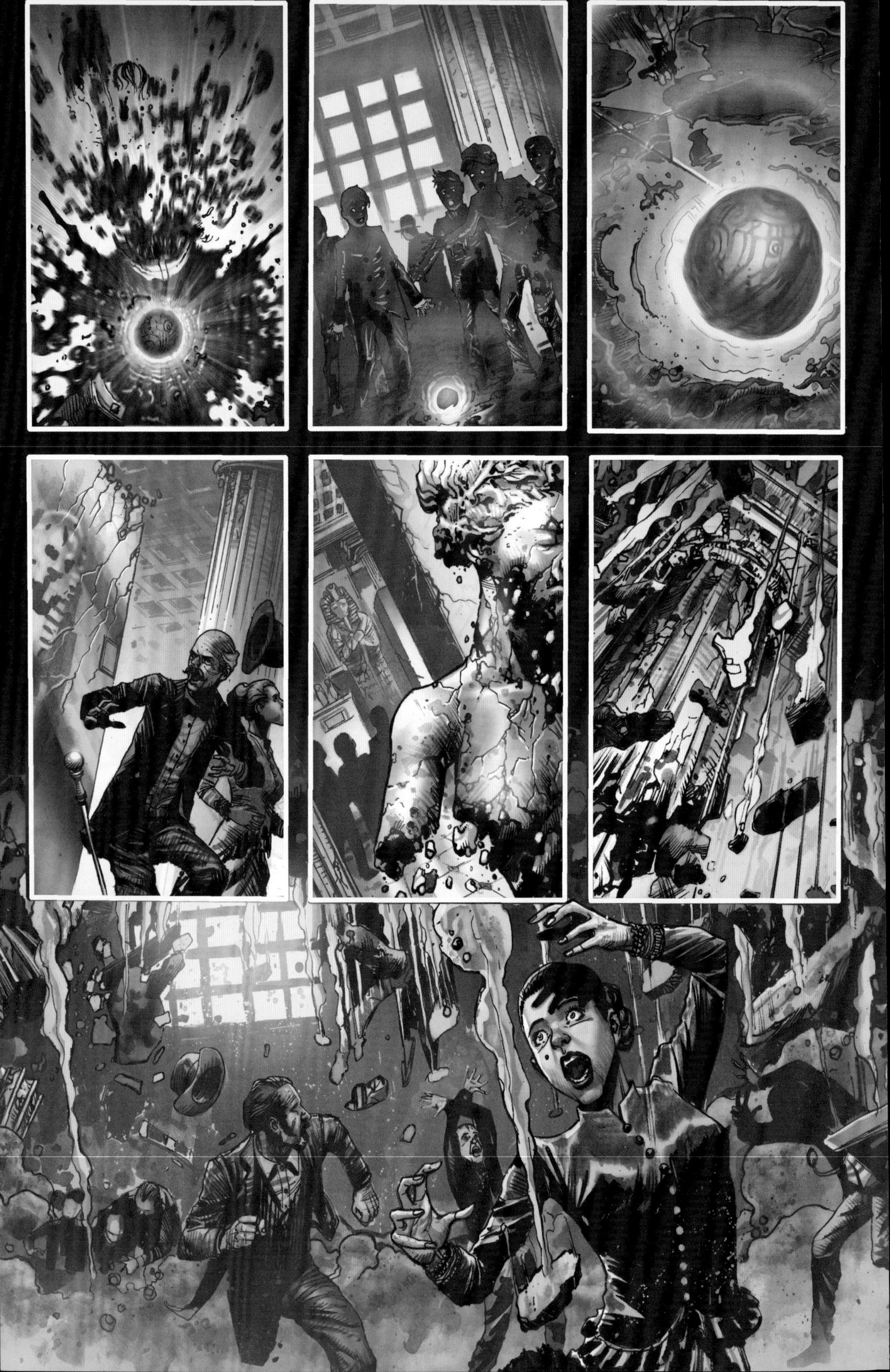

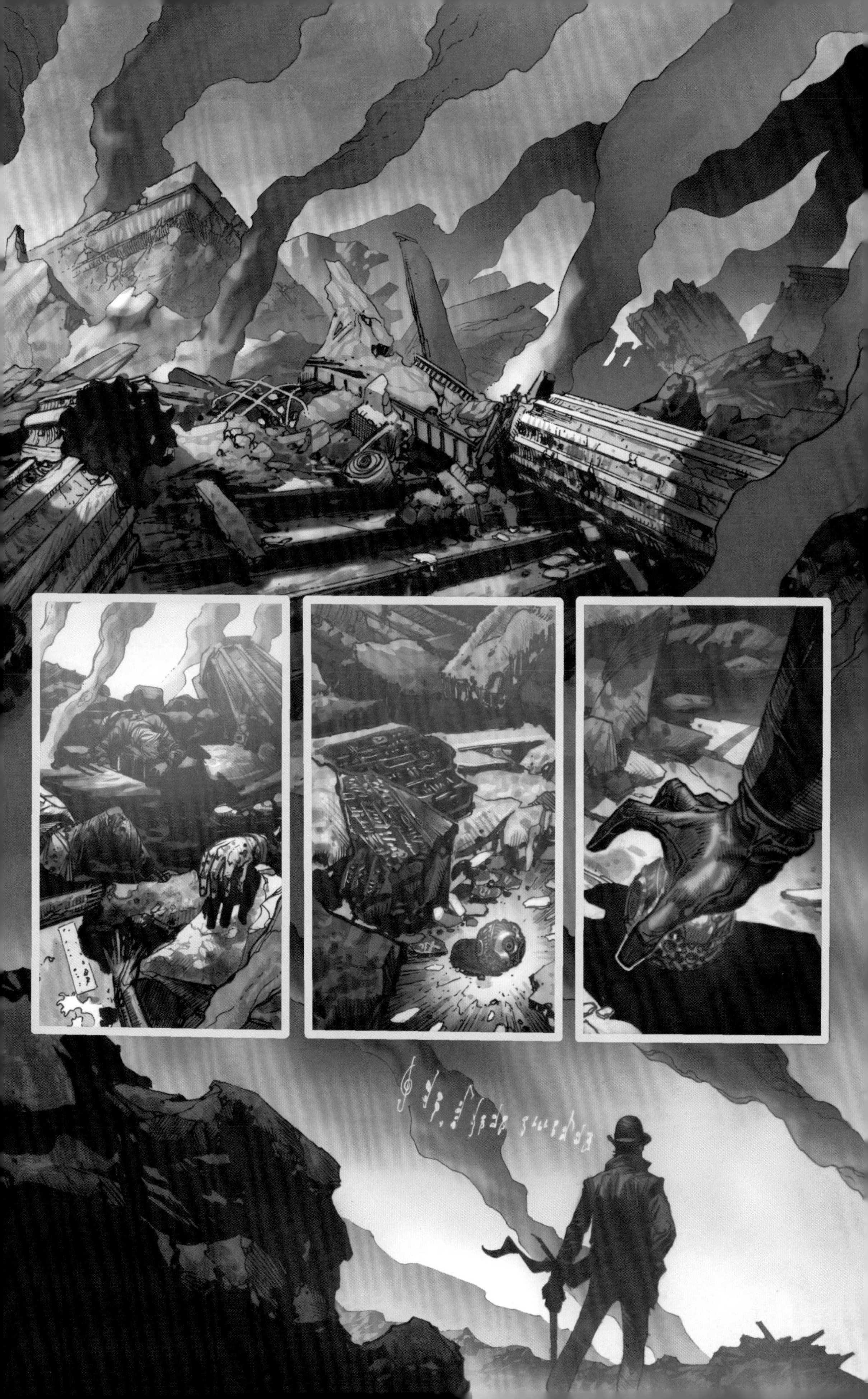

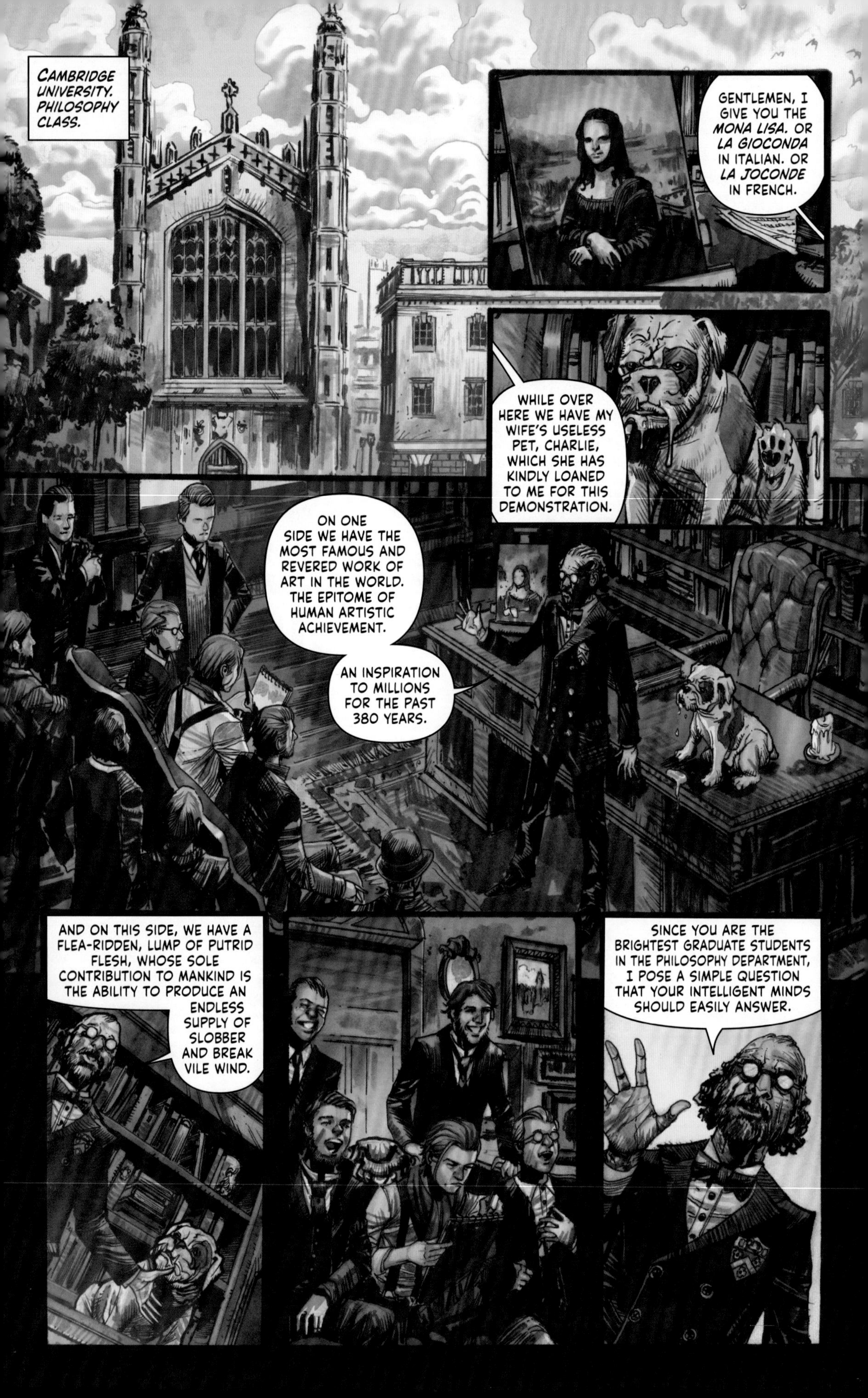
CAMBRIDGE UNIVERSITY. PHILOSOPHY CLASS.
GENTLEMEN, I GIVE YOU THE *MONA LISA.* OR *LA GIOCONDA* IN ITALIAN. OR *LA JOCONDE* IN FRENCH.
WHILE OVER HERE WE HAVE MY WIFE'S USELESS PET, CHARLIE, WHICH SHE HAS KINDLY LOANED TO ME FOR THIS DEMONSTRATION.
ON ONE SIDE WE HAVE THE MOST FAMOUS AND REVERED WORK OF ART IN THE WORLD. THE EPITOME OF HUMAN ARTISTIC ACHIEVEMENT.
AN INSPIRATION TO MILLIONS FOR THE PAST 380 YEARS.
AND ON THIS SIDE, WE HAVE A FLEA-RIDDEN, LUMP OF PUTRID FLESH, WHOSE SOLE CONTRIBUTION TO MANKIND IS THE ABILITY TO PRODUCE AN ENDLESS SUPPLY OF SLOBBER AND BREAK VILE WIND.
SINCE YOU ARE THE BRIGHTEST GRADUATE STUDENTS IN THE PHILOSOPHY DEPARTMENT, I POSE A SIMPLE QUESTION THAT YOUR INTELLIGENT MINDS SHOULD EASILY ANSWER.

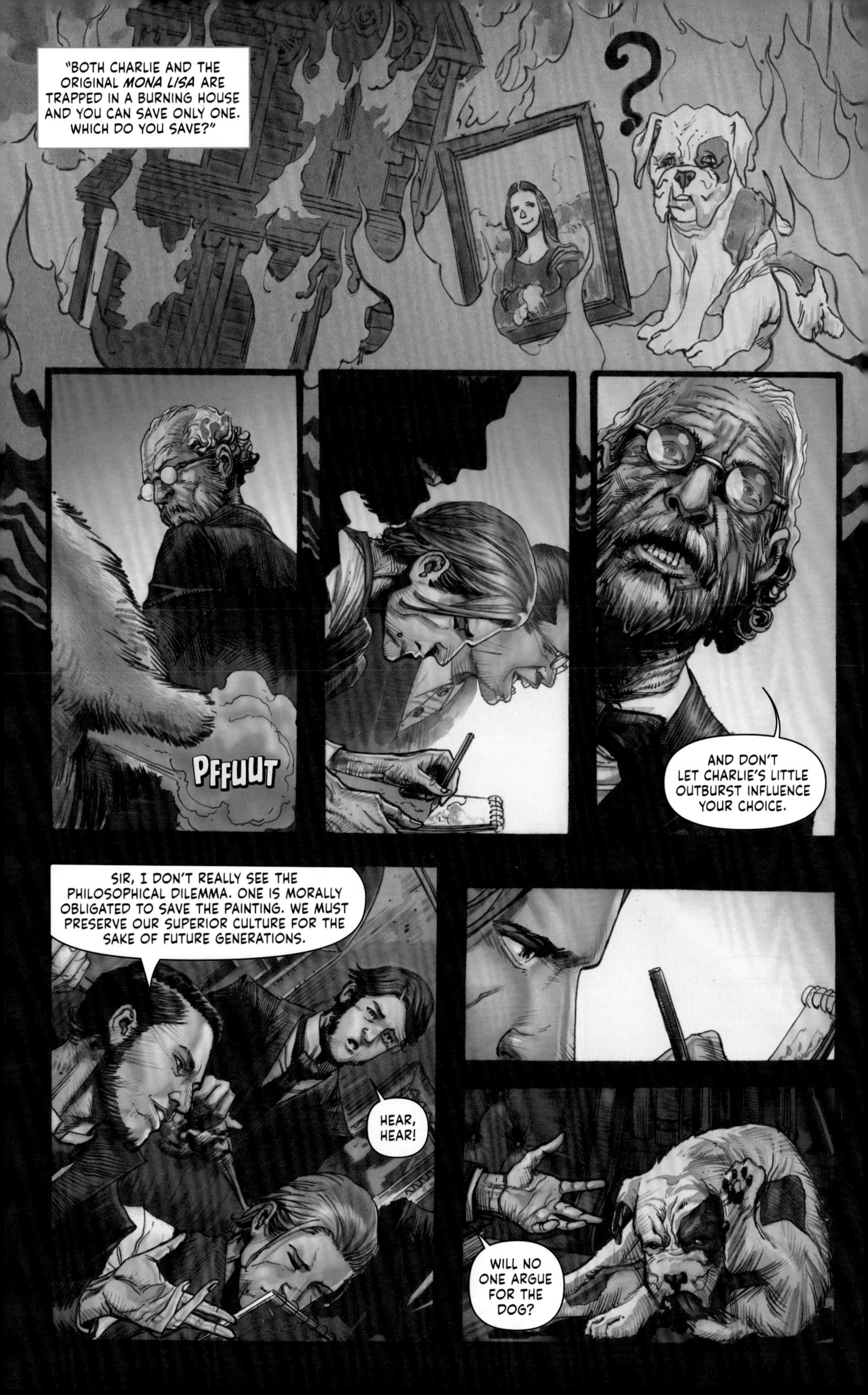
"BOTH CHARLIE AND THE ORIGINAL *MONA LISA* ARE TRAPPED IN A BURNING HOUSE AND YOU CAN SAVE ONLY ONE. WHICH DO YOU SAVE?"
?
PFFUUT
AND DON'T LET CHARLIE'S LITTLE OUTBURST INFLUENCE YOUR CHOICE.
SIR, I DON'T REALLY SEE THE PHILOSOPHICAL DILEMMA. ONE IS MORALLY OBLIGATED TO SAVE THE PAINTING. WE MUST PRESERVE OUR SUPERIOR CULTURE FOR THE SAKE OF FUTURE GENERATIONS.
HEAR, HEAR!
WILL NO ONE ARGUE FOR THE DOG?

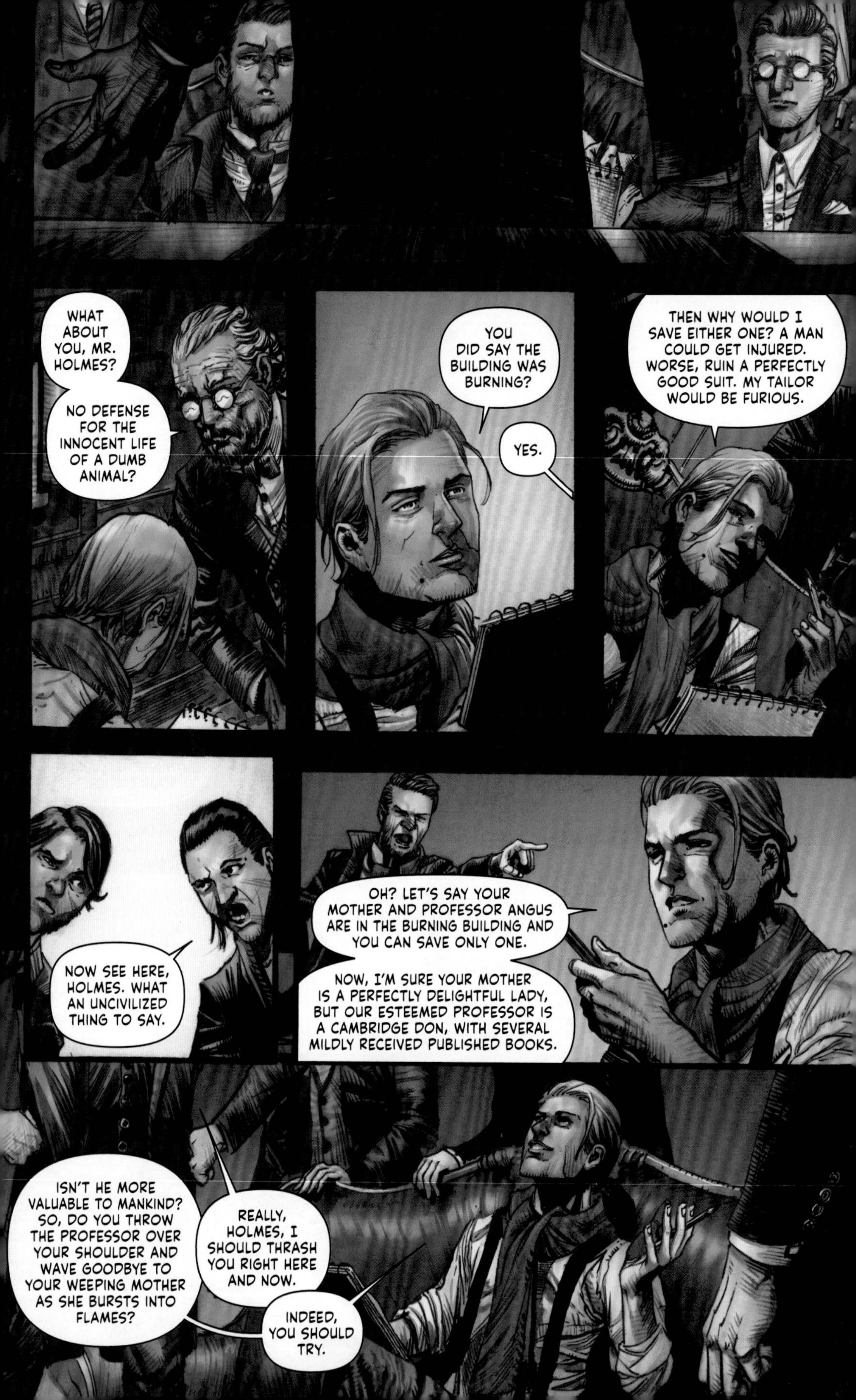
WHAT ABOUT YOU, MR. HOLMES?
NO DEFENSE FOR THE INNOCENT LIFE OF A DUMB ANIMAL?
YOU DID SAY THE BUILDING WAS BURNING?
YES.
THEN WHY WOULD I SAVE EITHER ONE? A MAN COULD GET INJURED. WORSE, RUIN A PERFECTLY GOOD SUIT. MY TAILOR WOULD BE FURIOUS.
NOW SEE HERE, HOLMES. WHAT AN UNCIVILIZED THING TO SAY.
OH? LET'S SAY YOUR MOTHER AND PROFESSOR ANGUS ARE IN THE BURNING BUILDING AND YOU CAN SAVE ONLY ONE.
NOW, I'M SURE YOUR MOTHER IS A PERFECTLY DELIGHTFUL LADY, BUT OUR ESTEEMED PROFESSOR IS A CAMBRIDGE DON, WITH SEVERAL MILDLY RECEIVED PUBLISHED BOOKS.
ISN'T HE MORE VALUABLE TO MANKIND? SO, DO YOU THROW THE PROFESSOR OVER YOUR SHOULDER AND WAVE GOODBYE TO YOUR WEEPING MOTHER AS SHE BURSTS INTO FLAMES?
REALLY, HOLMES, I SHOULD THRASH YOU RIGHT HERE AND NOW.
INDEED, YOU SHOULD TRY.

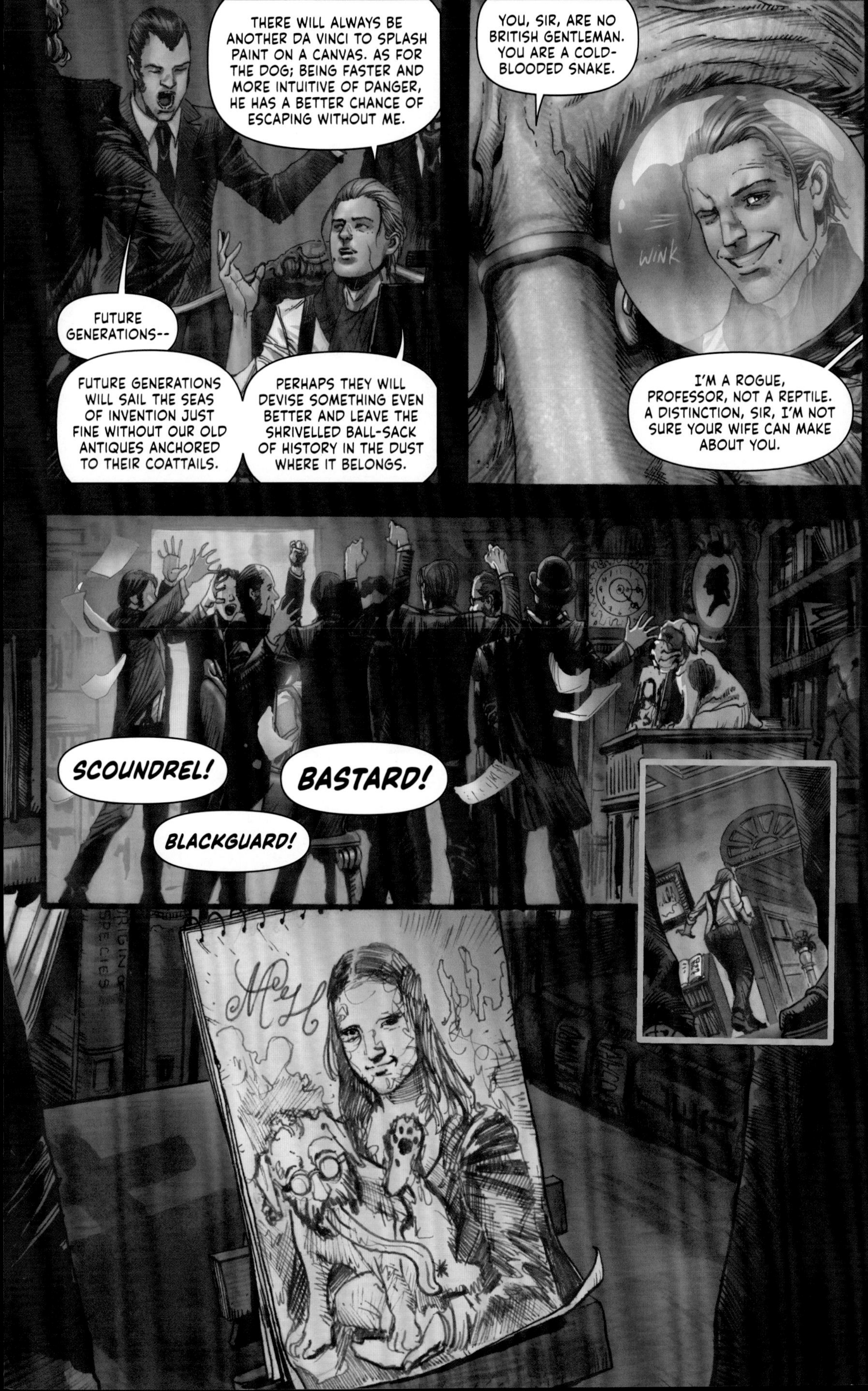
THERE WILL ALWAYS BE ANOTHER DA VINCI TO SPLASH PAINT ON A CANVAS. AS FOR THE DOG; BEING FASTER AND MORE INTUITIVE OF DANGER, HE HAS A BETTER CHANCE OF ESCAPING WITHOUT ME.
FUTURE GENERATIONS--
FUTURE GENERATIONS WILL SAIL THE SEAS OF INVENTION JUST FINE WITHOUT OUR OLD ANTIQUES ANCHORED TO THEIR COATTAILS.
PERHAPS THEY WILL DEVISE SOMETHING EVEN BETTER AND LEAVE THE SHRIVELLED BALL-SACK OF HISTORY IN THE DUST WHERE IT BELONGS.
YOU, SIR, ARE NO BRITISH GENTLEMAN. YOU ARE A COLD-BLOODED SNAKE.
WINK
I'M A ROGUE, PROFESSOR, NOT A REPTILE. A DISTINCTION, SIR, I'M NOT SURE YOUR WIFE CAN MAKE ABOUT YOU.
SCOUNDREL!
BASTARD!
BLACKGUARD!

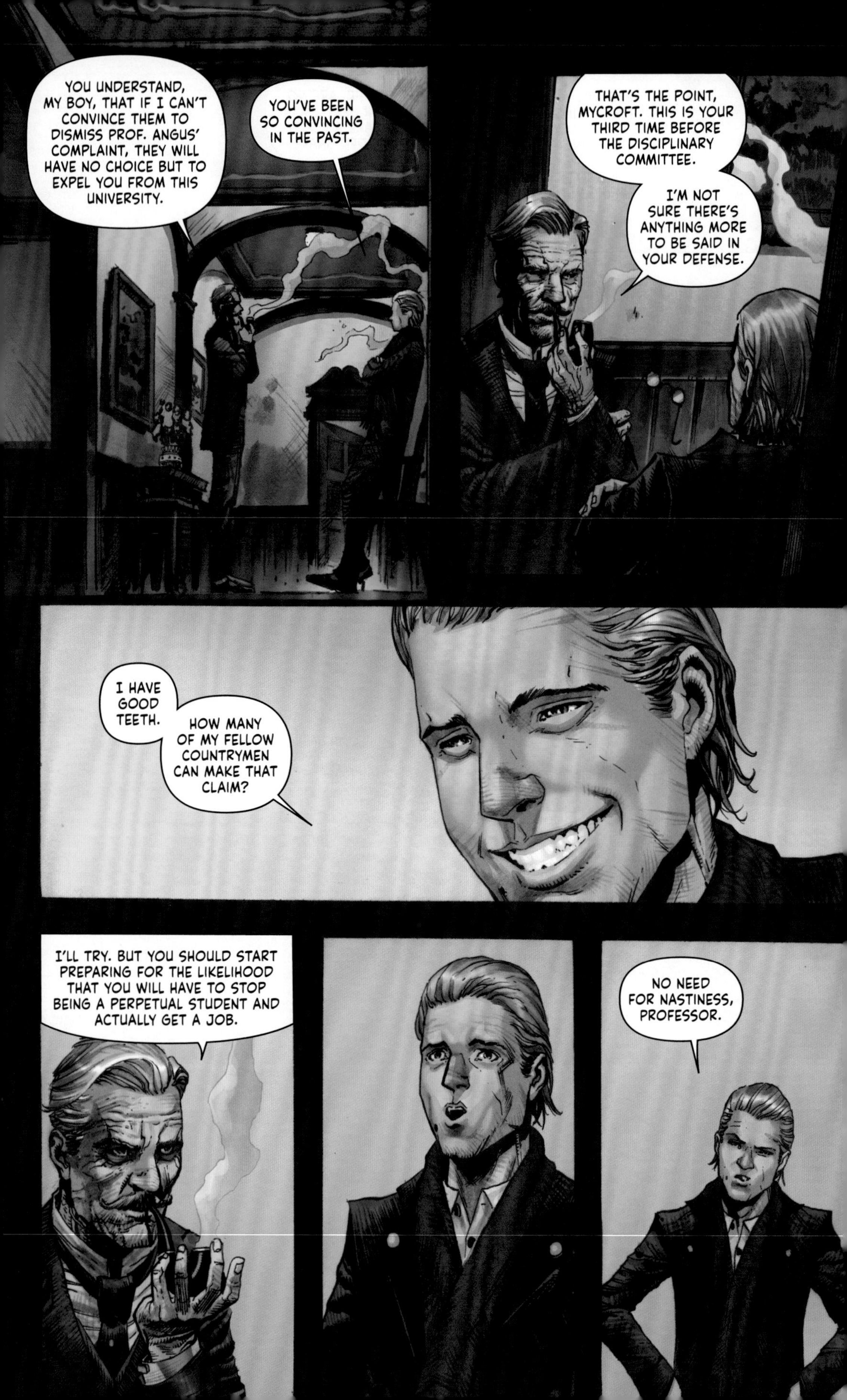
YOU UNDERSTAND, MY BOY, THAT IF I CAN'T CONVINCE THEM TO DISMISS PROF. ANGUS' COMPLAINT, THEY WILL HAVE NO CHOICE BUT TO EXPEL YOU FROM THIS UNIVERSITY.
YOU'VE BEEN SO CONVINCING IN THE PAST.
THAT'S THE POINT, MYCROFT. THIS IS YOUR THIRD TIME BEFORE THE DISCIPLINARY COMMITTEE.
I'M NOT SURE THERE'S ANYTHING MORE TO BE SAID IN YOUR DEFENSE.
I HAVE GOOD TEETH.
HOW MANY OF MY FELLOW COUNTRYMEN CAN MAKE THAT CLAIM?
I'LL TRY. BUT YOU SHOULD START PREPARING FOR THE LIKELIHOOD THAT YOU WILL HAVE TO STOP BEING A PERPETUAL STUDENT AND ACTUALLY GET A JOB.
NO NEED FOR NASTINESS, PROFESSOR.

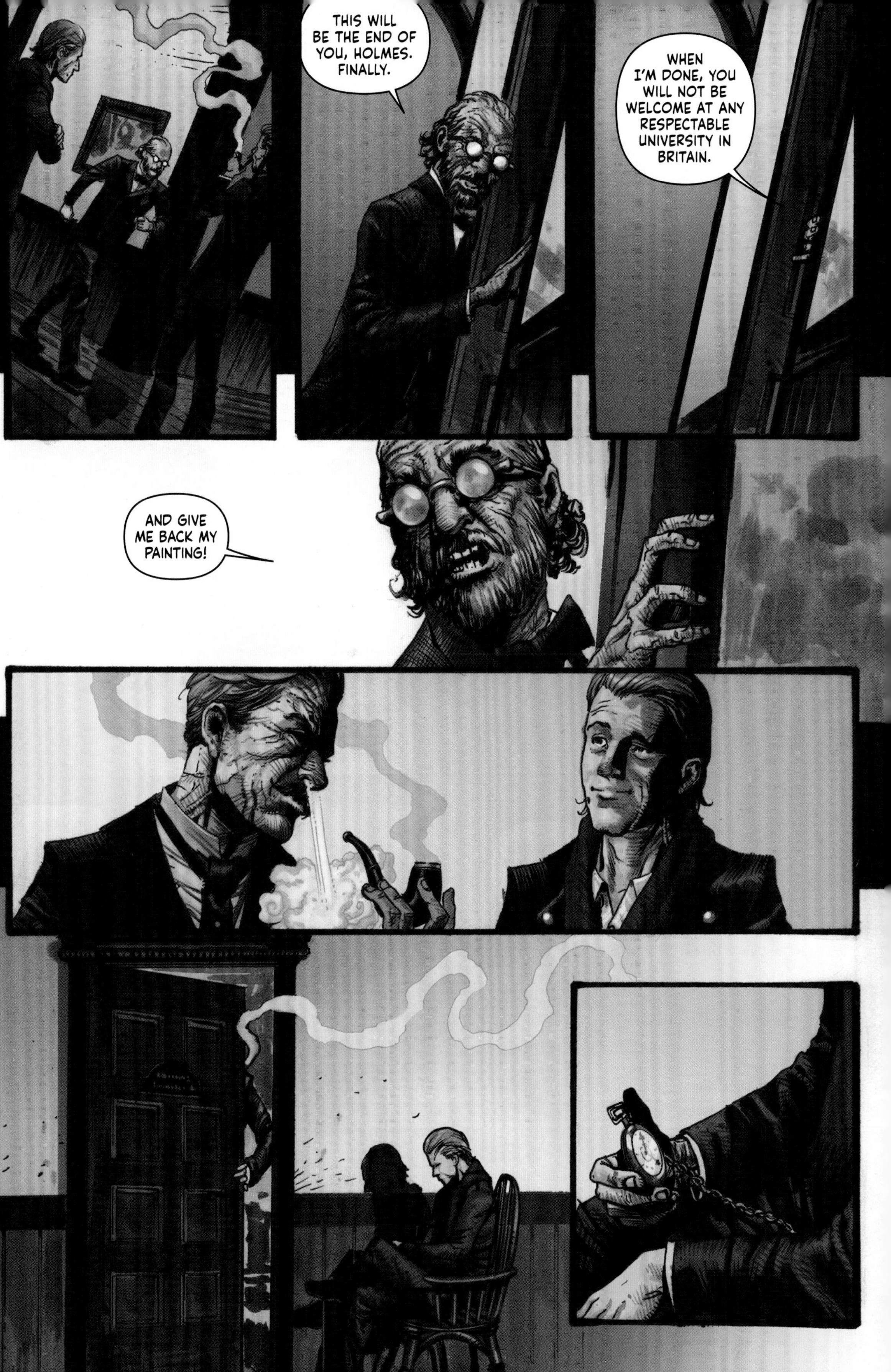
THIS WILL BE THE END OF YOU, HOLMES. FINALLY.
WHEN I'M DONE, YOU WILL NOT BE WELCOME AT ANY RESPECTABLE UNIVERSITY IN BRITAIN.
AND GIVE ME BACK MY PAINTING!

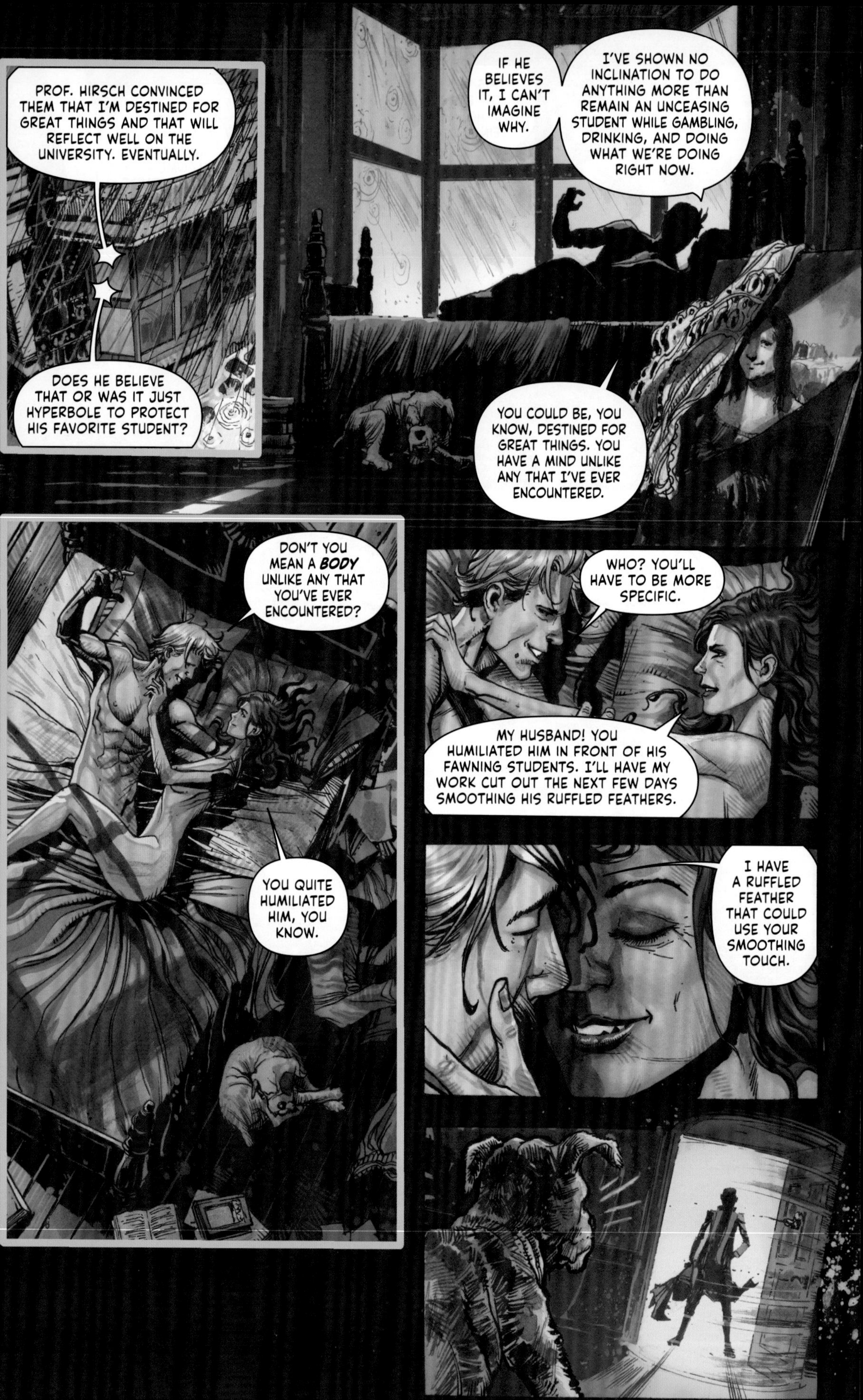
PROF. HIRSCH CONVINCED THEM THAT I'M DESTINED FOR GREAT THINGS AND THAT WILL REFLECT WELL ON THE UNIVERSITY. EVENTUALLY.
DOES HE BELIEVE THAT OR WAS IT JUST HYPERBOLE TO PROTECT HIS FAVORITE STUDENT?
IF HE BELIEVES IT, I CAN'T IMAGINE WHY.
I'VE SHOWN NO INCLINATION TO DO ANYTHING MORE THAN REMAIN AN UNCEASING STUDENT WHILE GAMBLING, DRINKING, AND DOING WHAT WE'RE DOING RIGHT NOW.
YOU COULD BE, YOU KNOW, DESTINED FOR GREAT THINGS. YOU HAVE A MIND UNLIKE ANY THAT I'VE EVER ENCOUNTERED.
DON'T YOU MEAN A ***BODY*** UNLIKE ANY THAT YOU'VE EVER ENCOUNTERED?
YOU QUITE HUMILIATED HIM, YOU KNOW.
WHO? YOU'LL HAVE TO BE MORE SPECIFIC.
MY HUSBAND! YOU HUMILIATED HIM IN FRONT OF HIS FAWNING STUDENTS. I'LL HAVE MY WORK CUT OUT THE NEXT FEW DAYS SMOOTHING HIS RUFFLED FEATHERS.
I HAVE A RUFFLED FEATHER THAT COULD USE YOUR SMOOTHING TOUCH.

AH. MY DEAR BROTHER SHITLICK.

MY DEAR BROTHER MYCROTCH.

DO COME IN, SHIRLEY.

I'VE TOLD YOU NOT TO CALL ME THAT.

JUST A NICKNAME, SHYLOCK.

...FOUR... FIVE...SIX...

...ONE... TWO... THREE...

SHAKE SHAKE SHAKE

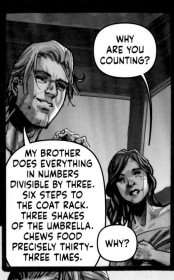

WHY ARE YOU COUNTING?

MY BROTHER DOES EVERYTHING IN NUMBERS DIVISIBLE BY THREE. SIX STEPS TO THE COAT RACK. THREE SHAKES OF THE UMBRELLA. CHEWS FOOD PRECISELY THIRTY-THREE TIMES.

WHY?

YES, SHIPWRECK, WHY? IS IT BECAUSE THE NUMBER THREE IS MENTIONED 476 TIMES IN THE BIBLE AND THEREFORE HAS RELIGIOUS SIGNIFICANCE?

NO, THAT CAN'T BE IT. WE HOLMES BROTHERS ARE NOT RELIGIOUS.

OR IS IT BECAUSE PLATO SAW THREE AS SYMBOLIC OF THE TRIANGLE, THE SIMPLEST SPATIAL SHAPE, AND BELIEVED THE WORLD WAS MADE UP OF TRIANGLES?

IT IS A MYSTERY I AM STILL WORKING TO UNRAVEL. NOT UNLIKE THE MYSTERY OF WHY MY BROTHER PREFERS THE COMPANY OF MARRIED WOMEN.

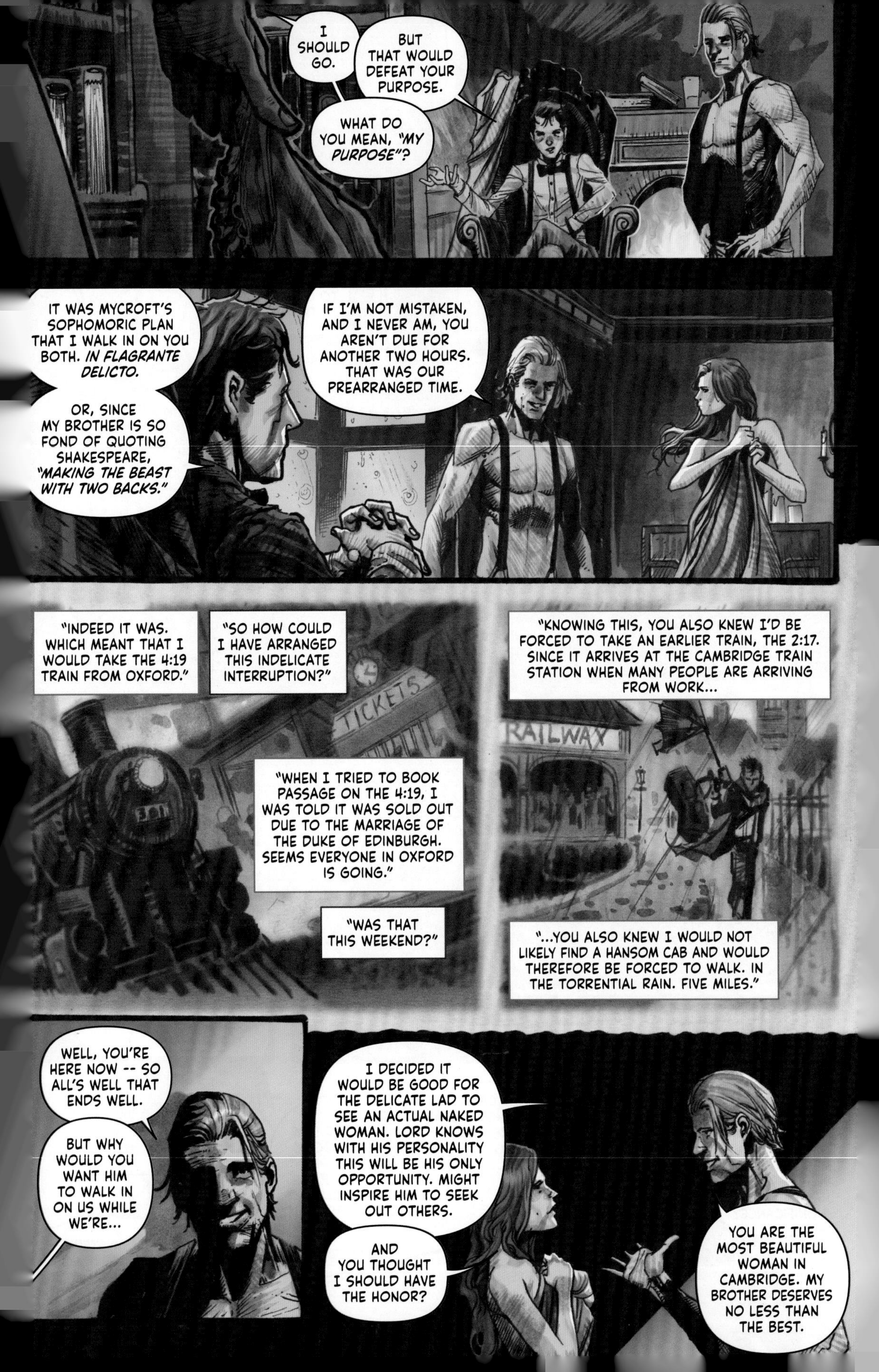
I SHOULD GO.
BUT THAT WOULD DEFEAT YOUR PURPOSE.
WHAT DO YOU MEAN, "MY PURPOSE"?
IT WAS MYCROFT'S SOPHOMORIC PLAN THAT I WALK IN ON YOU BOTH. IN FLAGRANTE DELICTO.
OR, SINCE MY BROTHER IS SO FOND OF QUOTING SHAKESPEARE, "MAKING THE BEAST WITH TWO BACKS."
IF I'M NOT MISTAKEN, AND I NEVER AM, YOU AREN'T DUE FOR ANOTHER TWO HOURS. THAT WAS OUR PREARRANGED TIME.
"INDEED IT WAS. WHICH MEANT THAT I WOULD TAKE THE 4:19 TRAIN FROM OXFORD."
"SO HOW COULD I HAVE ARRANGED THIS INDELICATE INTERRUPTION?"
TICKETS
"WHEN I TRIED TO BOOK PASSAGE ON THE 4:19, I WAS TOLD IT WAS SOLD OUT DUE TO THE MARRIAGE OF THE DUKE OF EDINBURGH. SEEMS EVERYONE IN OXFORD IS GOING."
"WAS THAT THIS WEEKEND?"
"KNOWING THIS, YOU ALSO KNEW I'D BE FORCED TO TAKE AN EARLIER TRAIN, THE 2:17. SINCE IT ARRIVES AT THE CAMBRIDGE TRAIN STATION WHEN MANY PEOPLE ARE ARRIVING FROM WORK...
RAILWAY
"...YOU ALSO KNEW I WOULD NOT LIKELY FIND A HANSOM CAB AND WOULD THEREFORE BE FORCED TO WALK. IN THE TORRENTIAL RAIN. FIVE MILES."
WELL, YOU'RE HERE NOW -- SO ALL'S WELL THAT ENDS WELL.
BUT WHY WOULD YOU WANT HIM TO WALK IN ON US WHILE WE'RE...
I DECIDED IT WOULD BE GOOD FOR THE DELICATE LAD TO SEE AN ACTUAL NAKED WOMAN. LORD KNOWS WITH HIS PERSONALITY THIS WILL BE HIS ONLY OPPORTUNITY. MIGHT INSPIRE HIM TO SEEK OUT OTHERS.
AND YOU THOUGHT I SHOULD HAVE THE HONOR?
YOU ARE THE MOST BEAUTIFUL WOMAN IN CAMBRIDGE. MY BROTHER DESERVES NO LESS THAN THE BEST.

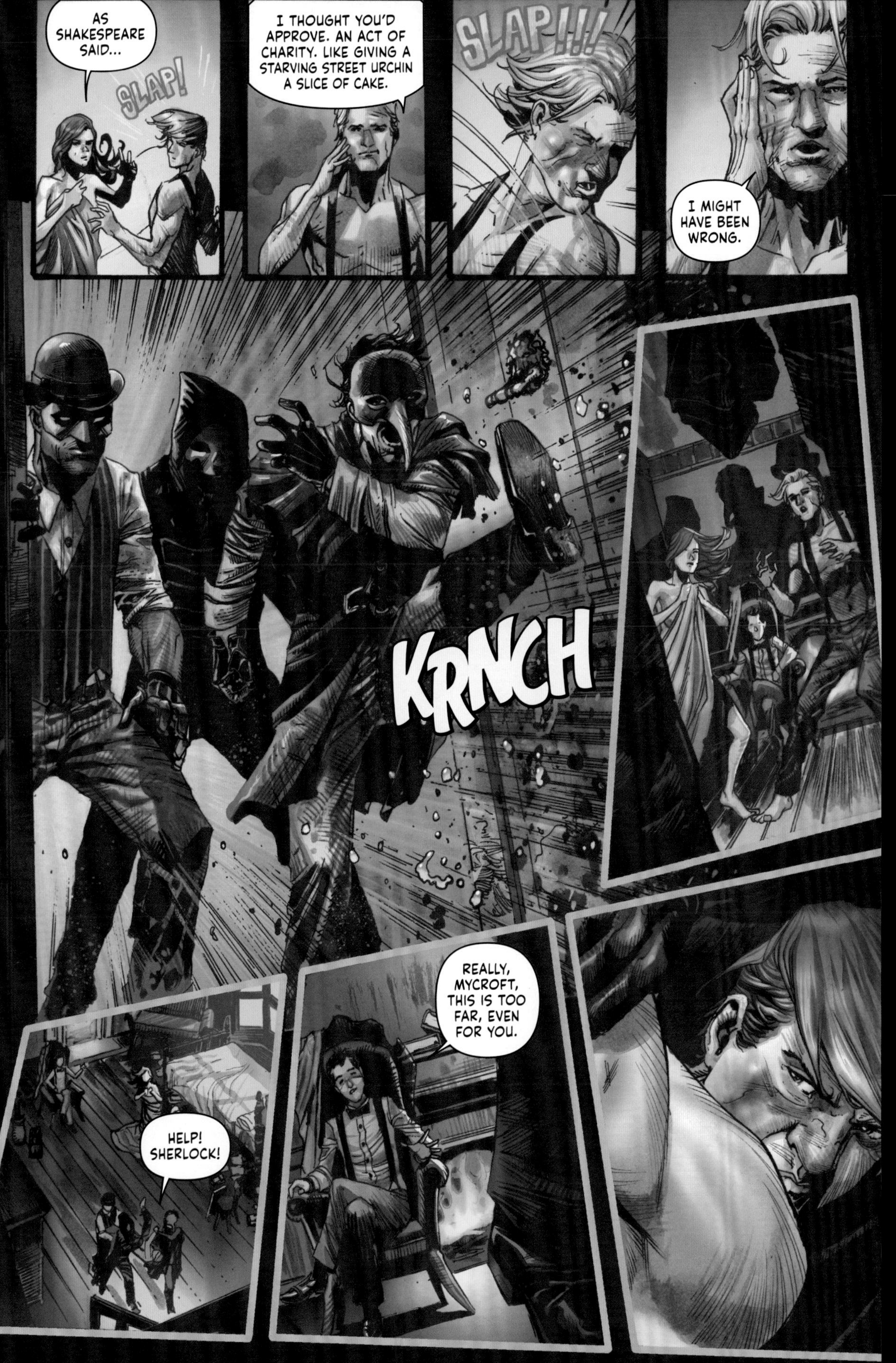
AS SHAKESPEARE SAID...
SLAP!
I THOUGHT YOU'D APPROVE. AN ACT OF CHARITY. LIKE GIVING A STARVING STREET URCHIN A SLICE OF CAKE.
SLAP!!!
I MIGHT HAVE BEEN WRONG.
KRNCH
HELP! SHERLOCK!
REALLY, MYCROFT, THIS IS TOO FAR, EVEN FOR YOU.

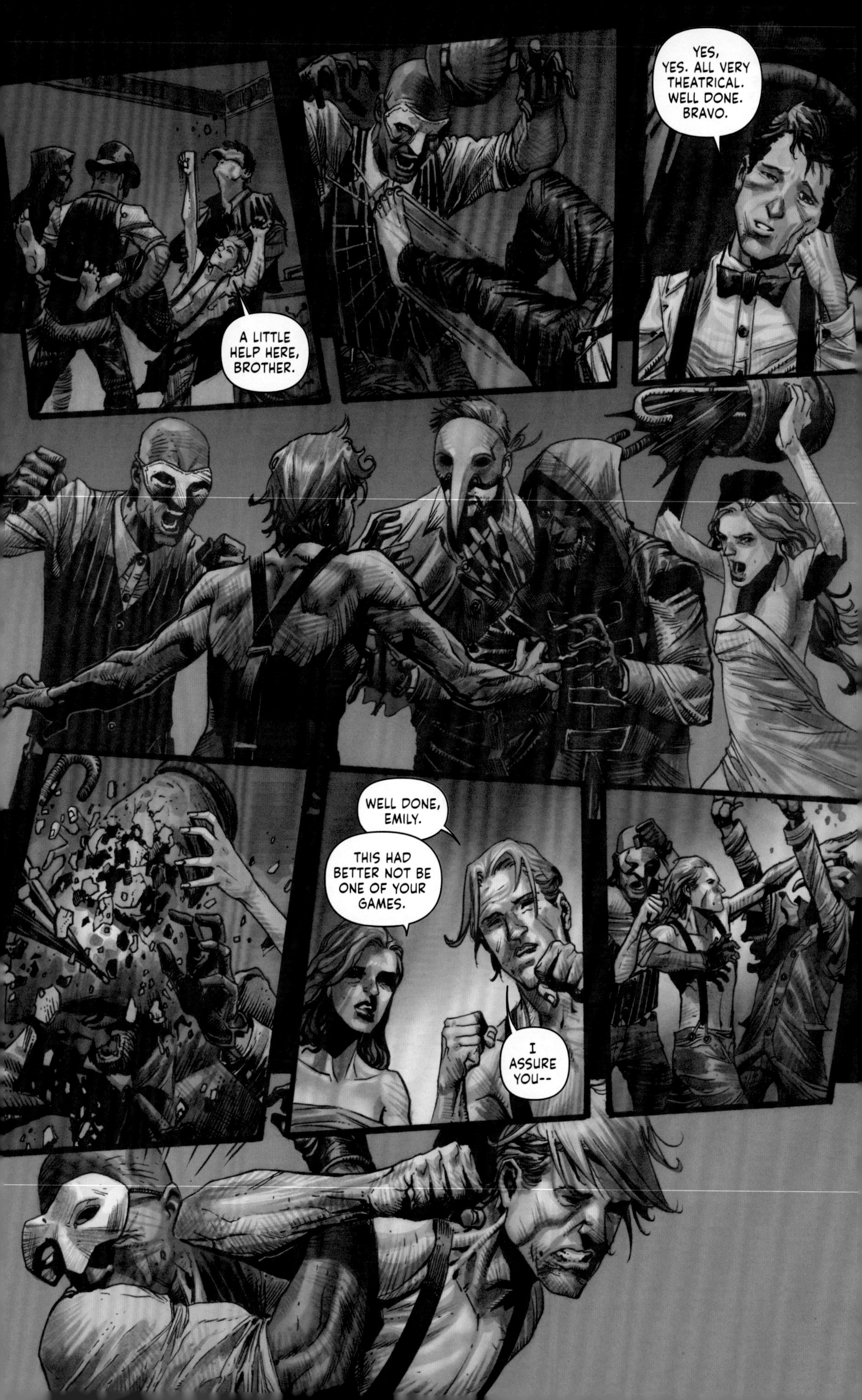
A LITTLE HELP HERE, BROTHER.
YES, YES. ALL VERY THEATRICAL. WELL DONE. BRAVO.
WELL DONE, EMILY.
THIS HAD BETTER NOT BE ONE OF YOUR GAMES.
I ASSURE YOU--

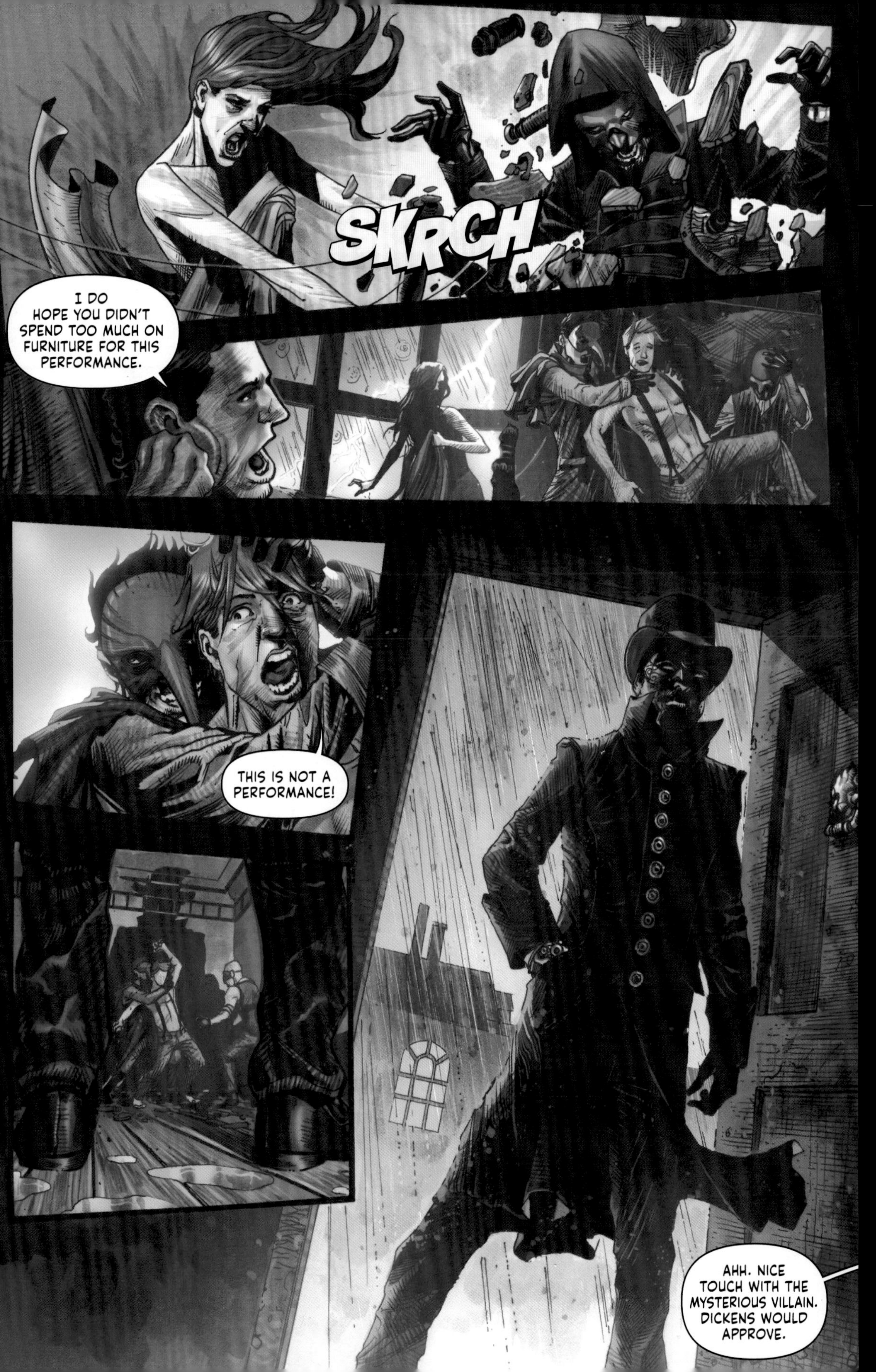
SKRCH
I DO HOPE YOU DIDN'T SPEND TOO MUCH ON FURNITURE FOR THIS PERFORMANCE.
THIS IS NOT A PERFORMANCE!
AHH. NICE TOUCH WITH THE MYSTERIOUS VILLAIN. DICKENS WOULD APPROVE.

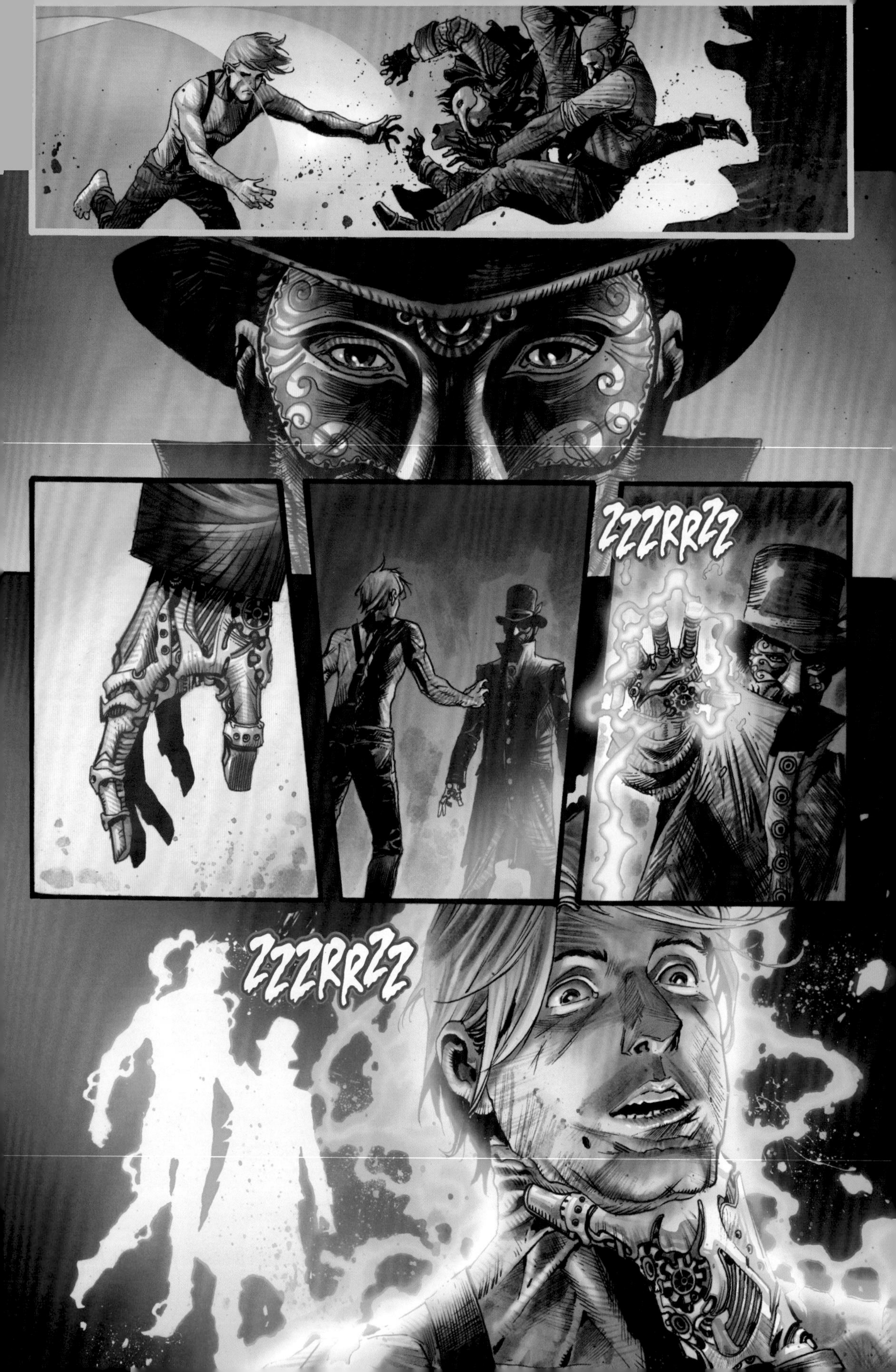
ZZZRRZZ
ZZZRRZZ

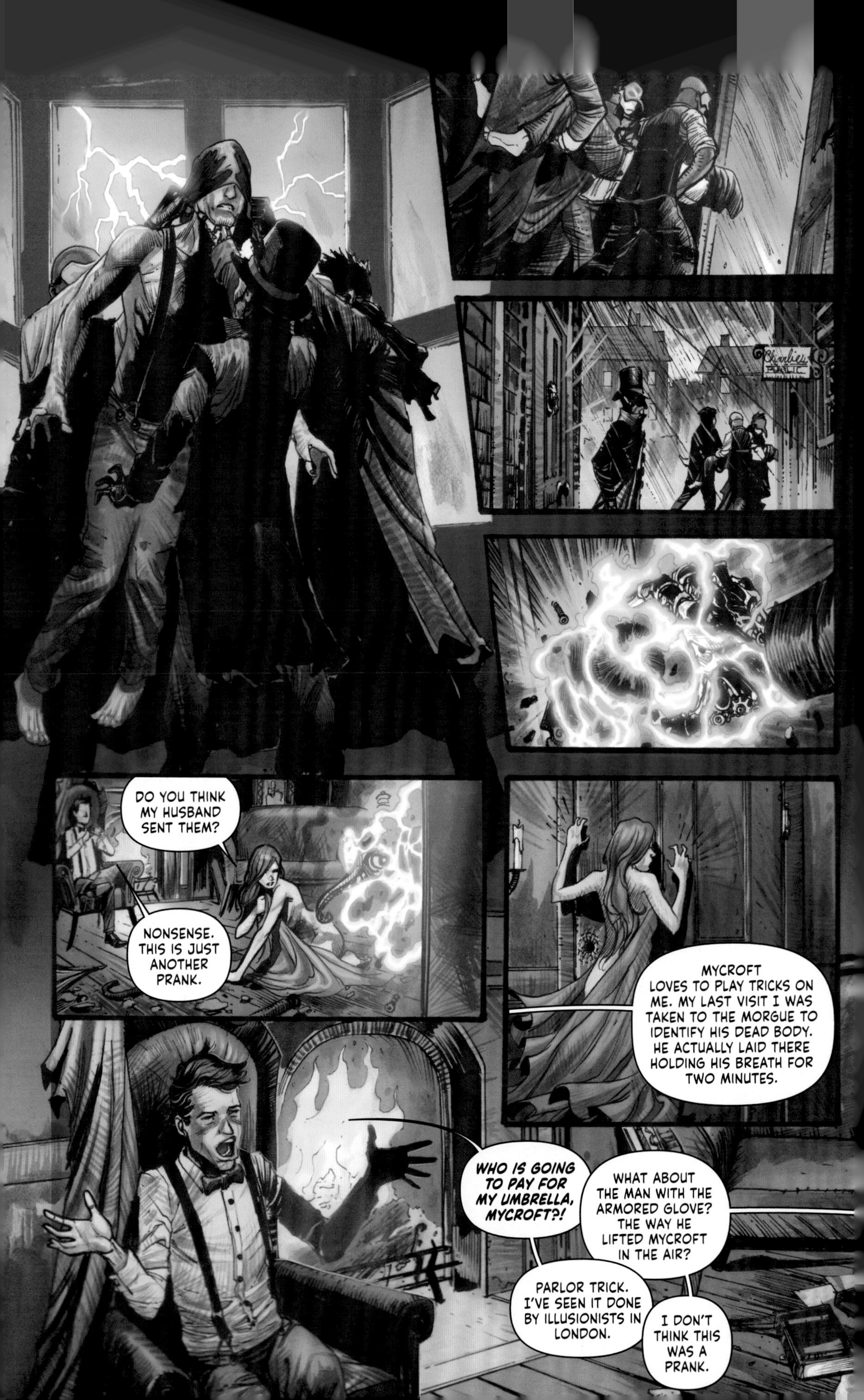
Charlie's
PUBLIC
DO YOU THINK MY HUSBAND SENT THEM?
NONSENSE. THIS IS JUST ANOTHER PRANK.
MYCROFT LOVES TO PLAY TRICKS ON ME. MY LAST VISIT I WAS TAKEN TO THE MORGUE TO IDENTIFY HIS DEAD BODY. HE ACTUALLY LAID THERE HOLDING HIS BREATH FOR TWO MINUTES.
WHO IS GOING TO PAY FOR MY UMBRELLA, MYCROFT?!
WHAT ABOUT THE MAN WITH THE ARMORED GLOVE? THE WAY HE LIFTED MYCROFT IN THE AIR?
PARLOR TRICK. I'VE SEEN IT DONE BY ILLUSIONISTS IN LONDON.
I DON'T THINK THIS WAS A PRANK.

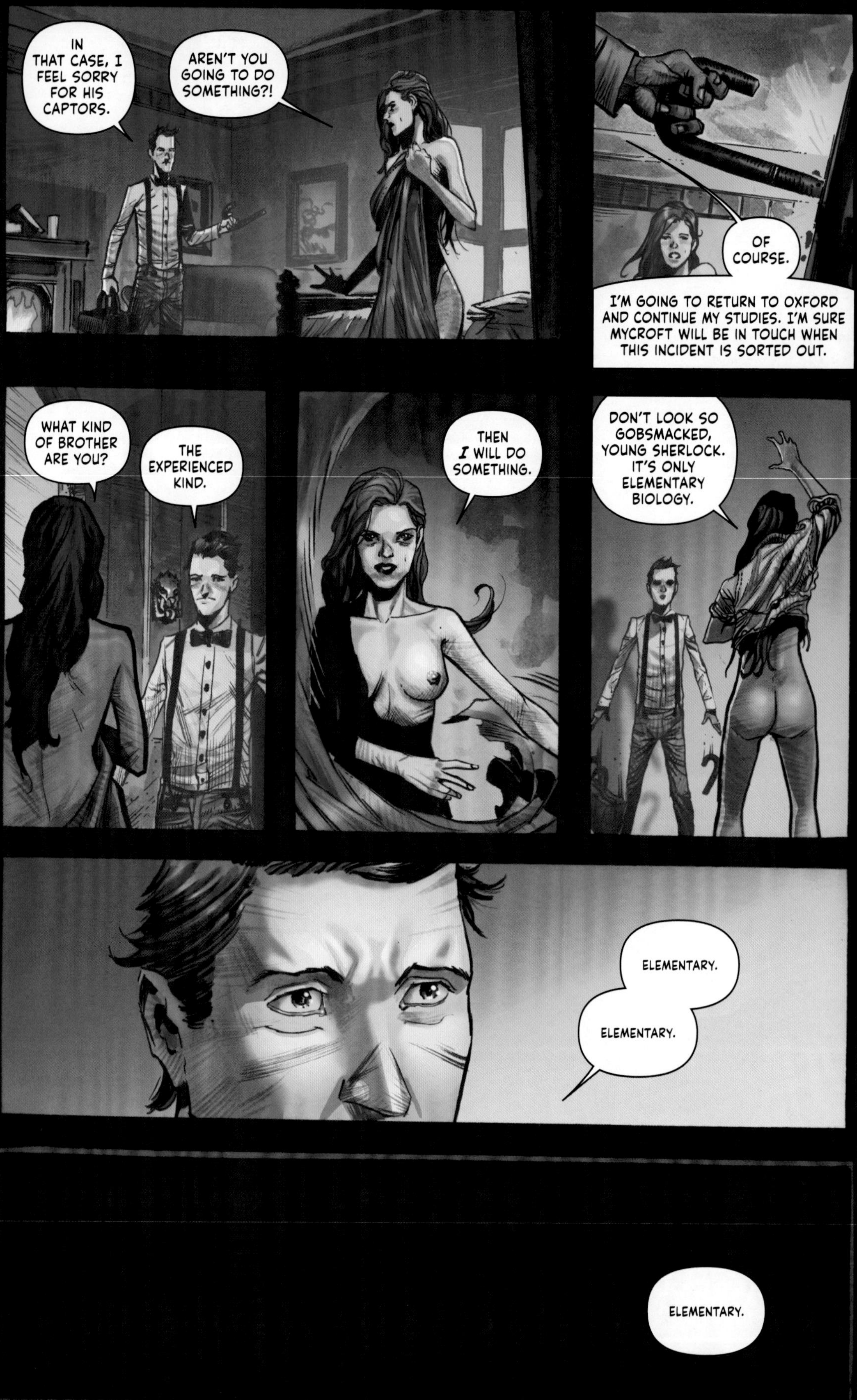
IN THAT CASE, I FEEL SORRY FOR HIS CAPTORS.
AREN'T YOU GOING TO DO SOMETHING?!
OF COURSE.
I'M GOING TO RETURN TO OXFORD AND CONTINUE MY STUDIES. I'M SURE MYCROFT WILL BE IN TOUCH WHEN THIS INCIDENT IS SORTED OUT.
WHAT KIND OF BROTHER ARE YOU?
THE EXPERIENCED KIND.
THEN *I* WILL DO SOMETHING.
DON'T LOOK SO GOBSMACKED, YOUNG SHERLOCK. IT'S ONLY ELEMENTARY BIOLOGY.
ELEMENTARY.
ELEMENTARY.
ELEMENTARY.

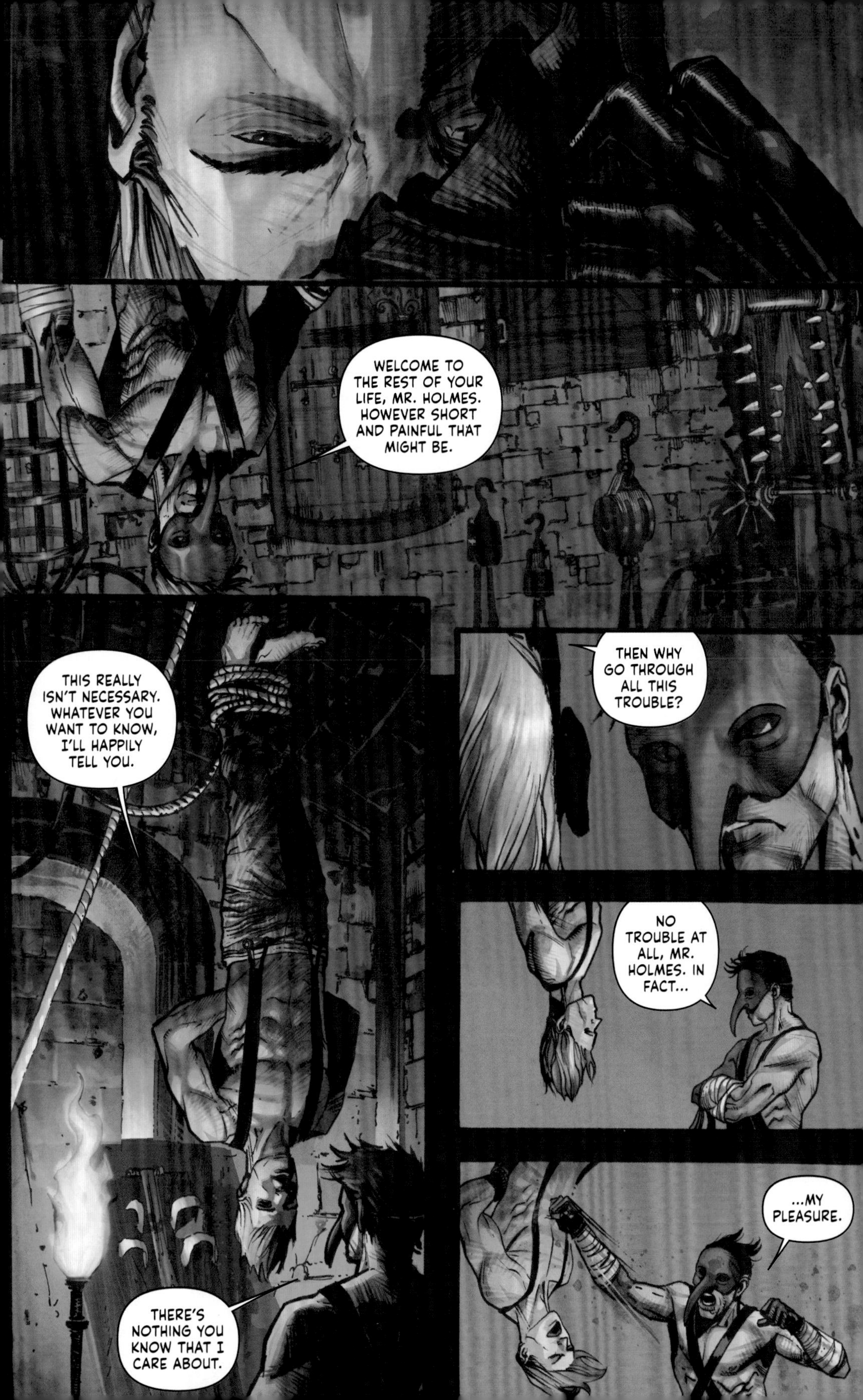
WELCOME TO THE REST OF YOUR LIFE, MR. HOLMES. HOWEVER SHORT AND PAINFUL THAT MIGHT BE.
THIS REALLY ISN'T NECESSARY. WHATEVER YOU WANT TO KNOW, I'LL HAPPILY TELL YOU.
THERE'S NOTHING YOU KNOW THAT I CARE ABOUT.
THEN WHY GO THROUGH ALL THIS TROUBLE?
NO TROUBLE AT ALL, MR. HOLMES. IN FACT...
...MY PLEASURE.

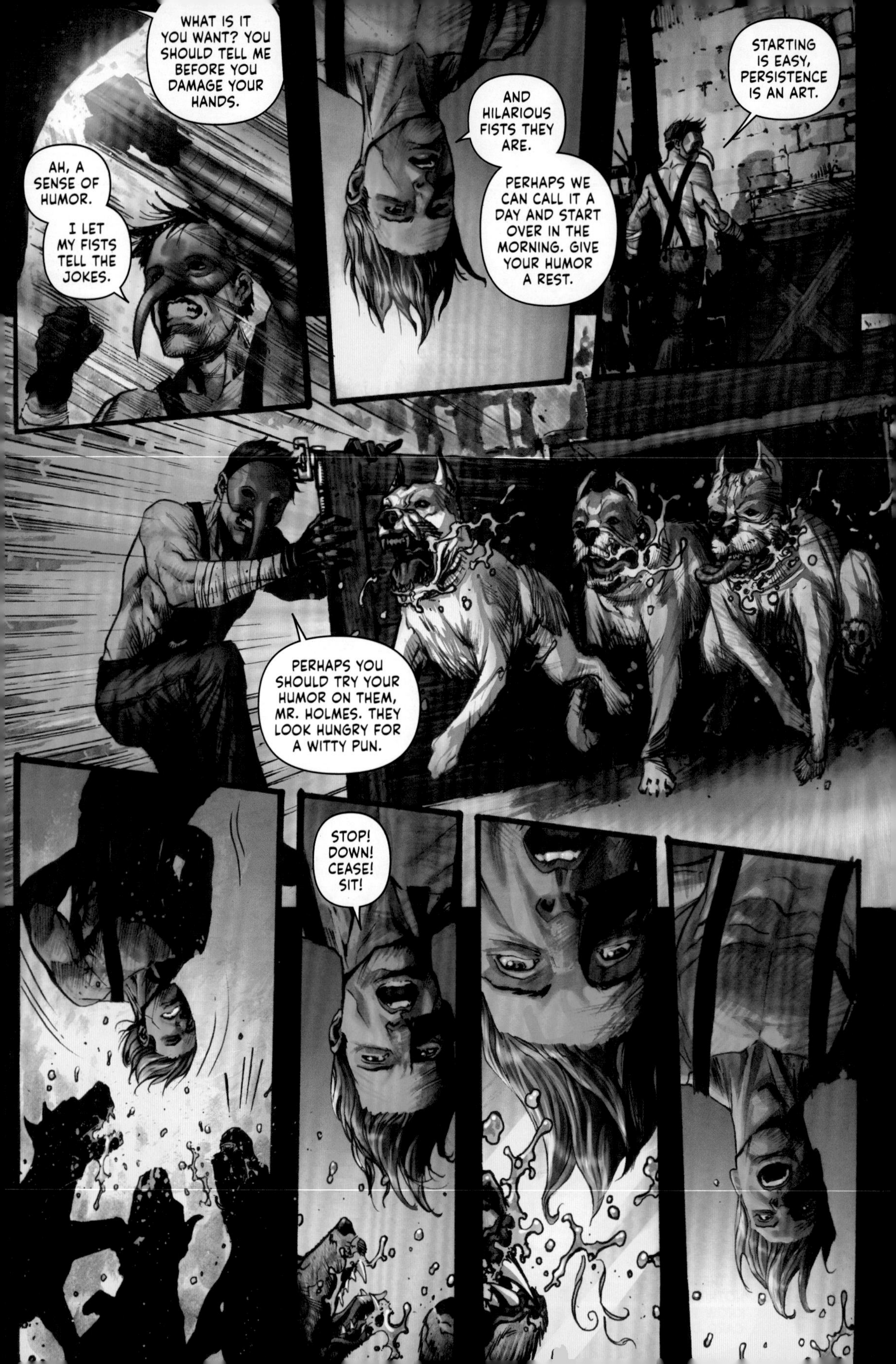
WHAT IS IT YOU WANT? YOU SHOULD TELL ME BEFORE YOU DAMAGE YOUR HANDS.
AH, A SENSE OF HUMOR.
I LET MY FISTS TELL THE JOKES.
AND HILARIOUS FISTS THEY ARE.
PERHAPS WE CAN CALL IT A DAY AND START OVER IN THE MORNING. GIVE YOUR HUMOR A REST.
STARTING IS EASY, PERSISTENCE IS AN ART.
PERHAPS YOU SHOULD TRY YOUR HUMOR ON THEM, MR. HOLMES. THEY LOOK HUNGRY FOR A WITTY PUN.
STOP! DOWN! CEASE! SIT!

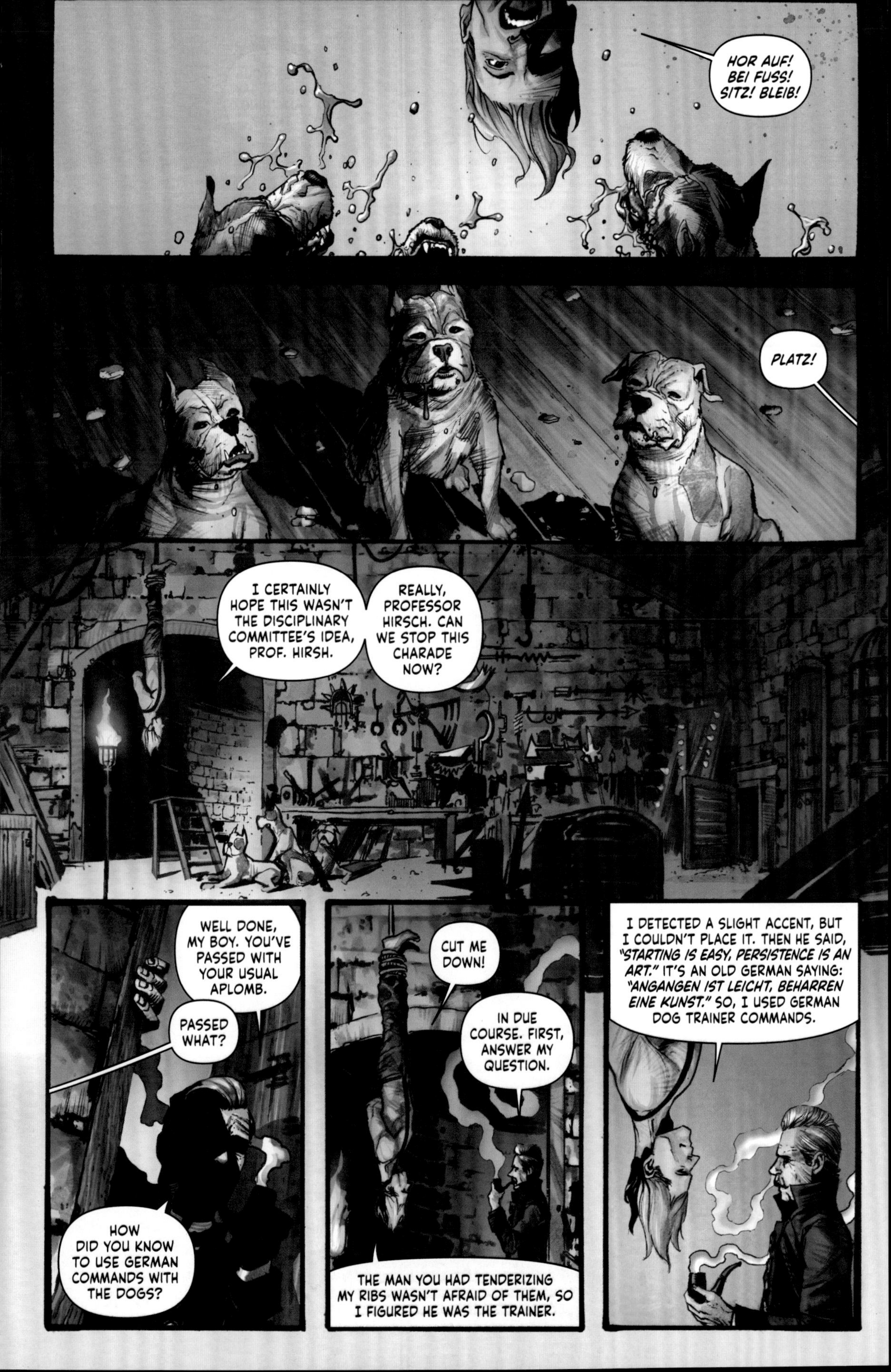
HOR AUF! BEI FUSS! SITZ! BLEIB!
PLATZ!
I CERTAINLY HOPE THIS WASN'T THE DISCIPLINARY COMMITTEE'S IDEA, PROF. HIRSH.
REALLY, PROFESSOR HIRSCH. CAN WE STOP THIS CHARADE NOW?
WELL DONE, MY BOY. YOU'VE PASSED WITH YOUR USUAL APLOMB.
PASSED WHAT?
HOW DID YOU KNOW TO USE GERMAN COMMANDS WITH THE DOGS?
CUT ME DOWN!
IN DUE COURSE. FIRST, ANSWER MY QUESTION.
THE MAN YOU HAD TENDERIZING MY RIBS WASN'T AFRAID OF THEM, SO I FIGURED HE WAS THE TRAINER.
I DETECTED A SLIGHT ACCENT, BUT I COULDN'T PLACE IT. THEN HE SAID, *"STARTING IS EASY, PERSISTENCE IS AN ART."* IT'S AN OLD GERMAN SAYING: *"ANGANGEN IST LEICHT, BEHARREN EINE KUNST."* SO, I USED GERMAN DOG TRAINER COMMANDS.

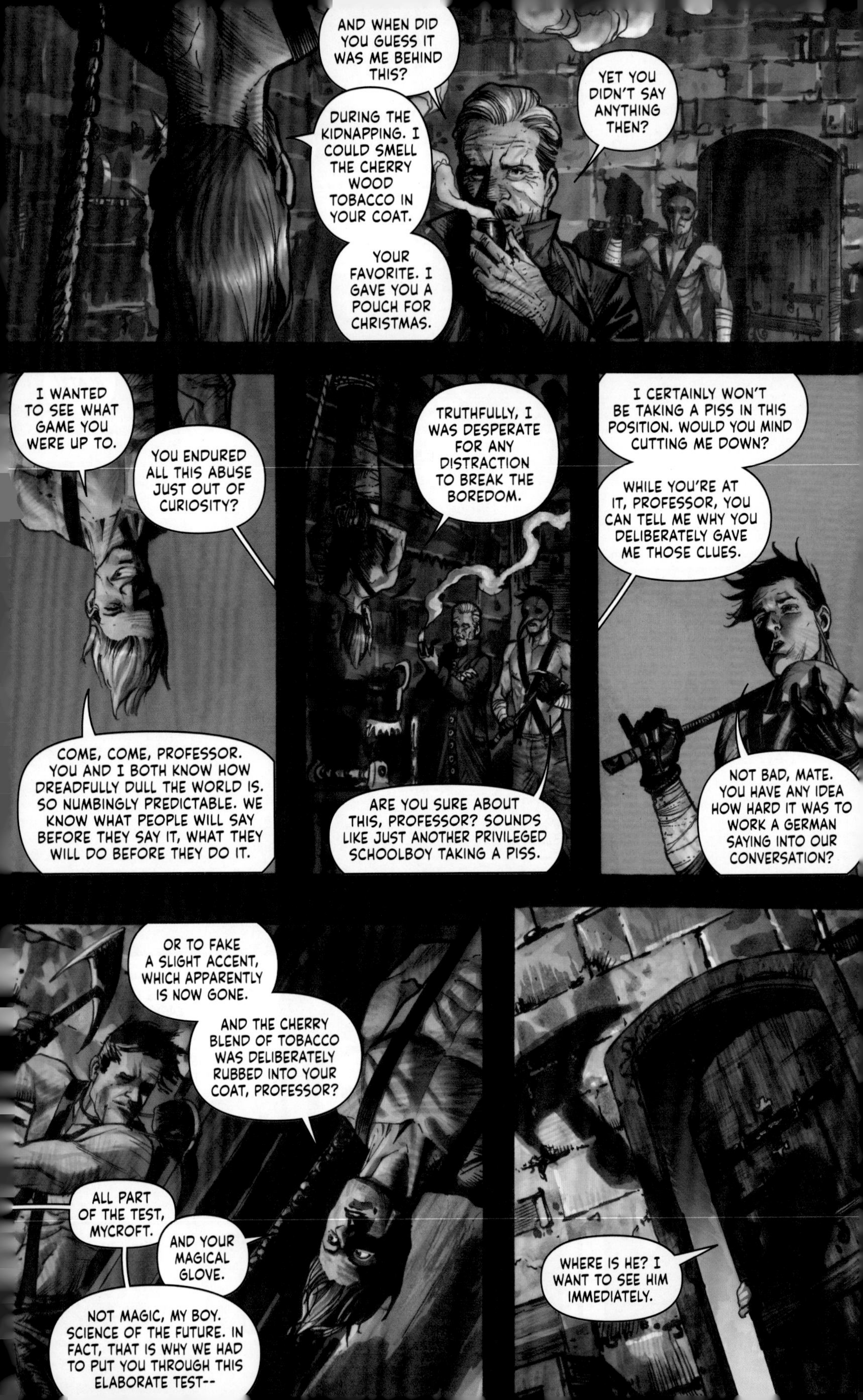
AND WHEN DID YOU GUESS IT WAS ME BEHIND THIS?
DURING THE KIDNAPPING. I COULD SMELL THE CHERRY WOOD TOBACCO IN YOUR COAT.
YOUR FAVORITE. I GAVE YOU A POUCH FOR CHRISTMAS.
YET YOU DIDN'T SAY ANYTHING THEN?
I WANTED TO SEE WHAT GAME YOU WERE UP TO.
YOU ENDURED ALL THIS ABUSE JUST OUT OF CURIOSITY?
COME, COME, PROFESSOR. YOU AND I BOTH KNOW HOW DREADFULLY DULL THE WORLD IS. SO NUMBINGLY PREDICTABLE. WE KNOW WHAT PEOPLE WILL SAY BEFORE THEY SAY IT, WHAT THEY WILL DO BEFORE THEY DO IT.
TRUTHFULLY, I WAS DESPERATE FOR ANY DISTRACTION TO BREAK THE BOREDOM.
ARE YOU SURE ABOUT THIS, PROFESSOR? SOUNDS LIKE JUST ANOTHER PRIVILEGED SCHOOLBOY TAKING A PISS.
I CERTAINLY WON'T BE TAKING A PISS IN THIS POSITION. WOULD YOU MIND CUTTING ME DOWN?
WHILE YOU'RE AT IT, PROFESSOR, YOU CAN TELL ME WHY YOU DELIBERATELY GAVE ME THOSE CLUES.
NOT BAD, MATE. YOU HAVE ANY IDEA HOW HARD IT WAS TO WORK A GERMAN SAYING INTO OUR CONVERSATION?
OR TO FAKE A SLIGHT ACCENT, WHICH APPARENTLY IS NOW GONE.
AND THE CHERRY BLEND OF TOBACCO WAS DELIBERATELY RUBBED INTO YOUR COAT, PROFESSOR?
ALL PART OF THE TEST, MYCROFT.
AND YOUR MAGICAL GLOVE.
NOT MAGIC, MY BOY. SCIENCE OF THE FUTURE. IN FACT, THAT IS WHY WE HAD TO PUT YOU THROUGH THIS ELABORATE TEST--
WHERE IS HE? I WANT TO SEE HIM IMMEDIATELY.

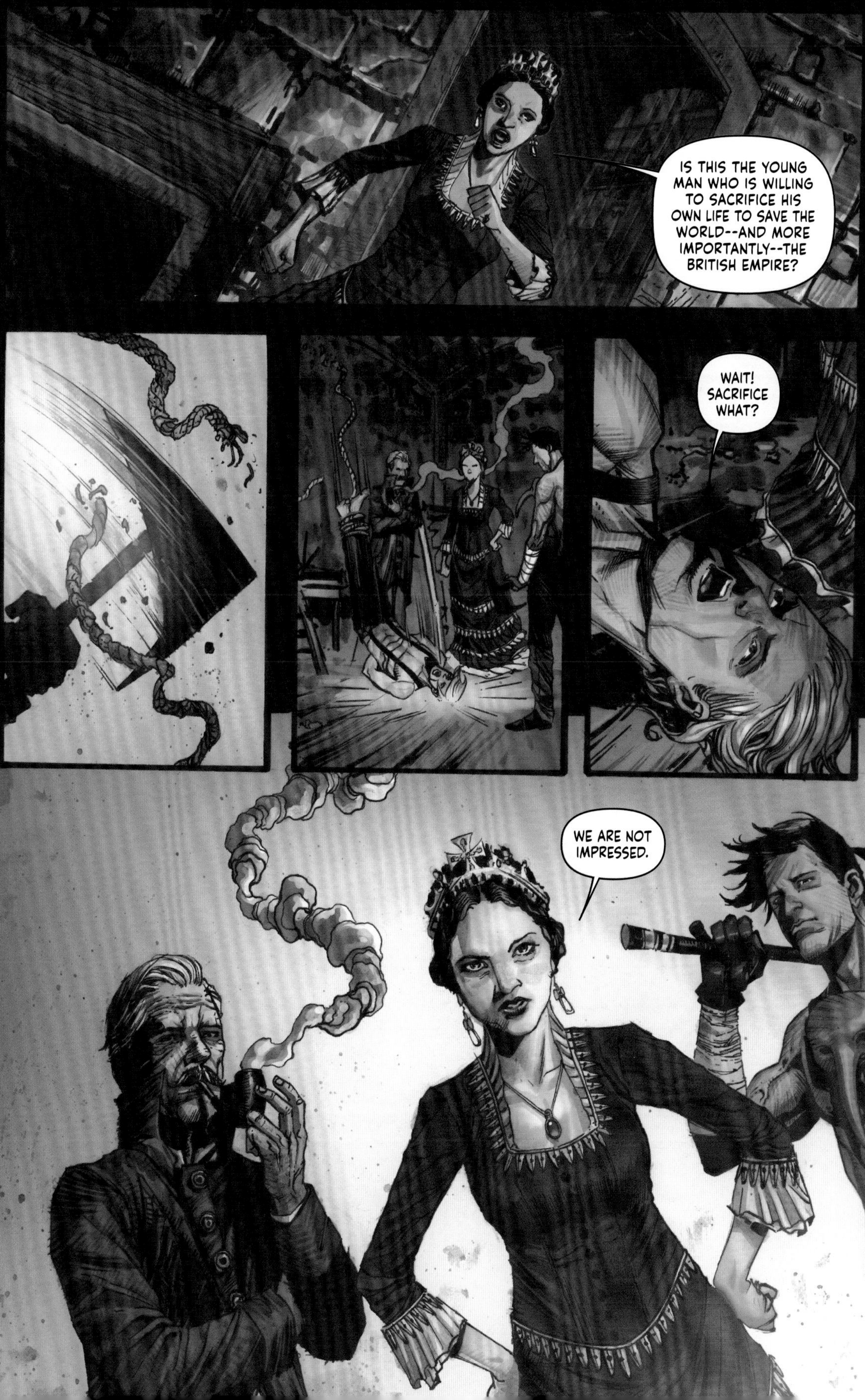
IS THIS THE YOUNG MAN WHO IS WILLING TO SACRIFICE HIS OWN LIFE TO SAVE THE WORLD--AND MORE IMPORTANTLY--THE BRITISH EMPIRE?
WAIT! SACRIFICE WHAT?
WE ARE NOT IMPRESSED.

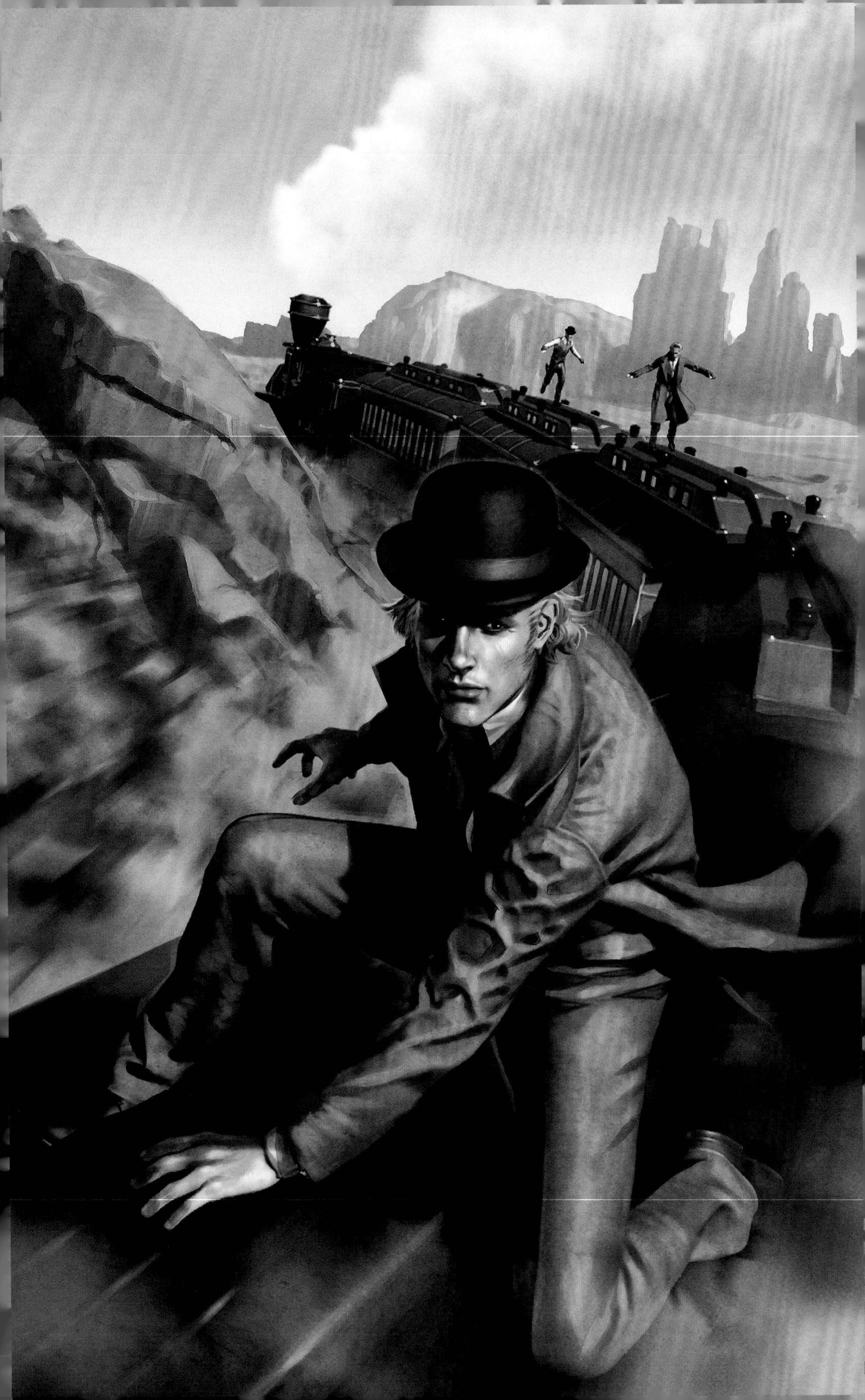

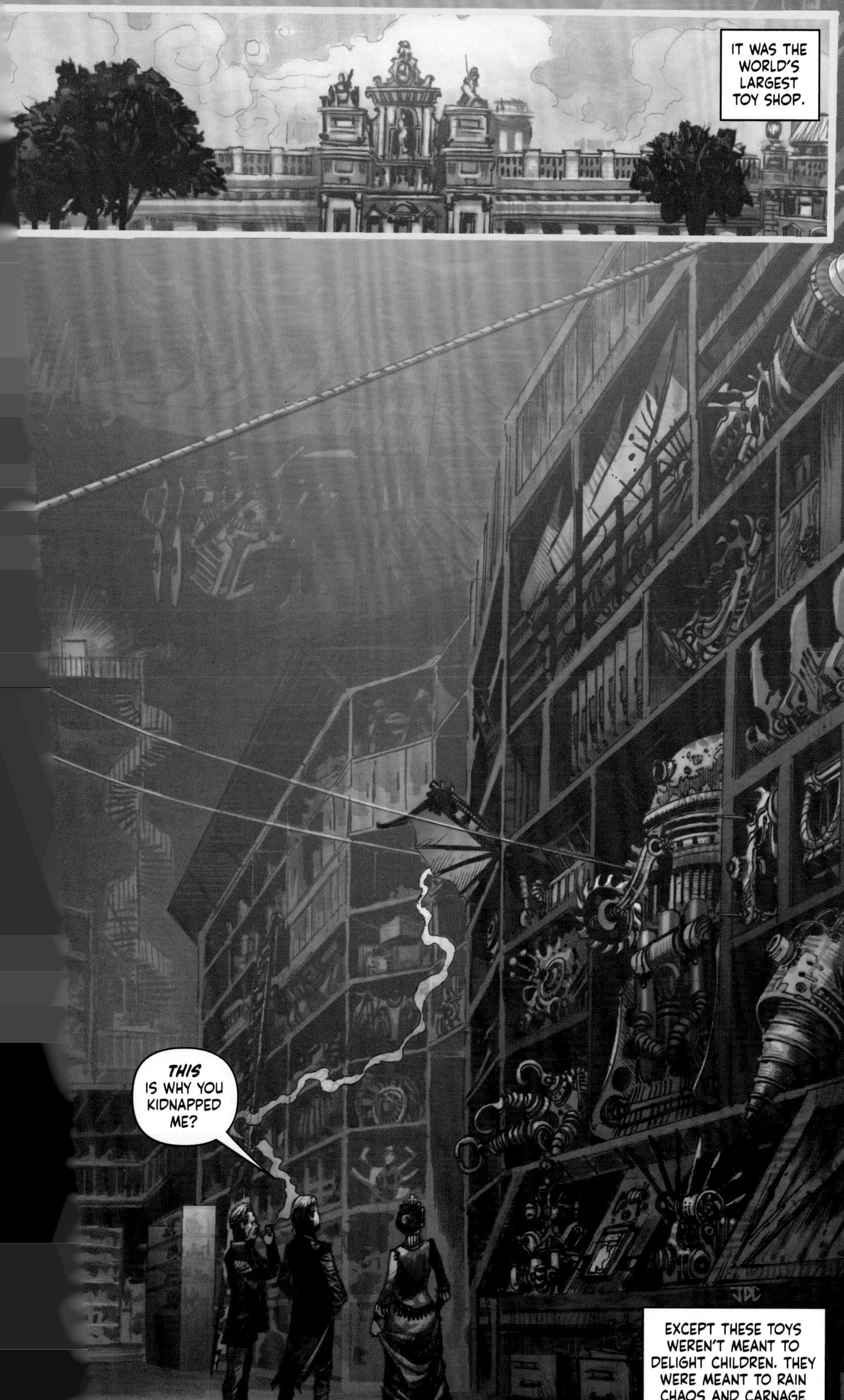
IT WAS THE WORLD'S LARGEST TOY SHOP.
THIS IS WHY YOU KIDNAPPED ME?
EXCEPT THESE TOYS WEREN'T MEANT TO DELIGHT CHILDREN. THEY WERE MEANT TO RAIN CHAOS AND CARNAGE ON THE WORLD.

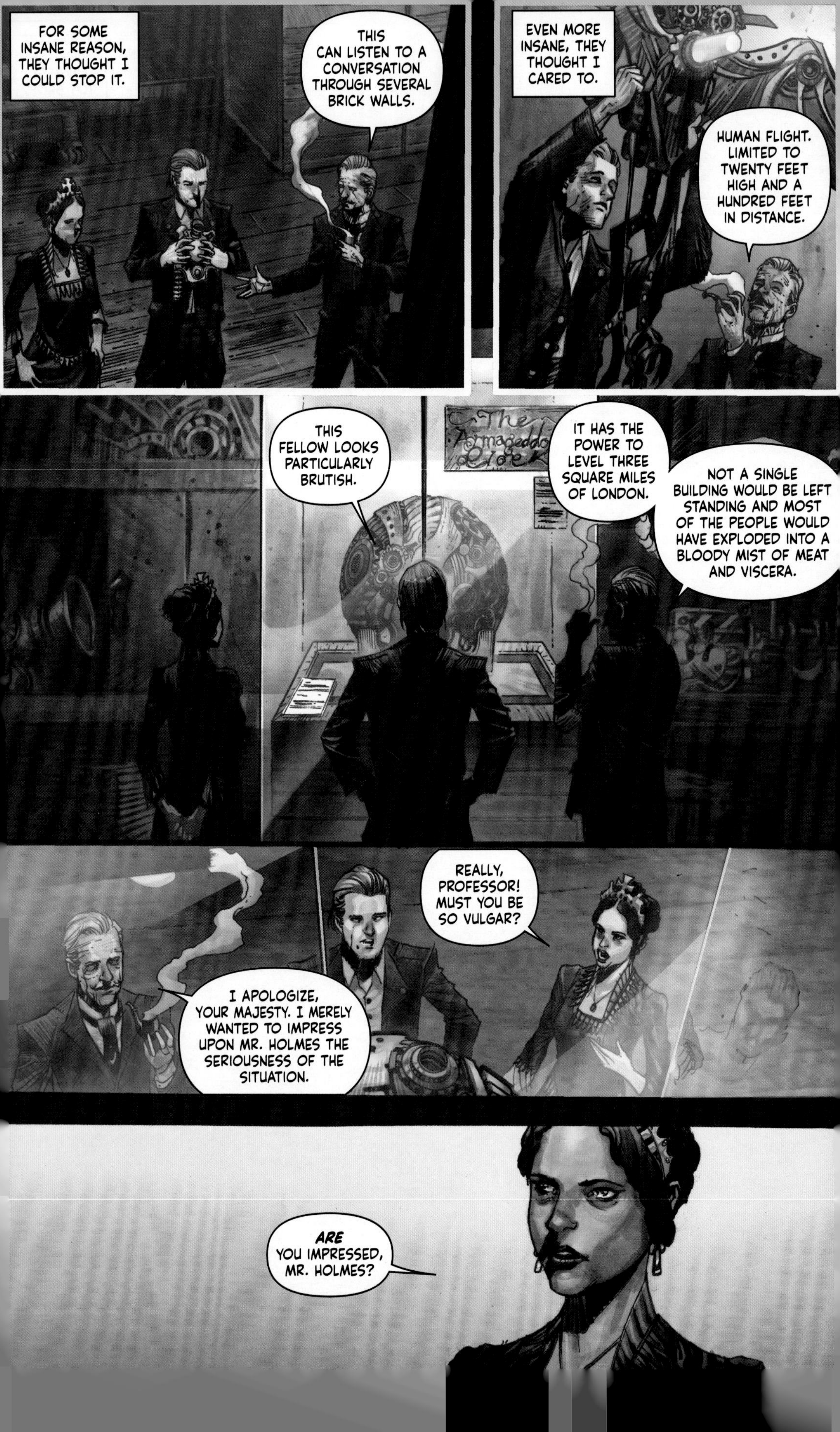
FOR SOME INSANE REASON, THEY THOUGHT I COULD STOP IT.
THIS CAN LISTEN TO A CONVERSATION THROUGH SEVERAL BRICK WALLS.
EVEN MORE INSANE, THEY THOUGHT I CARED TO.
HUMAN FLIGHT. LIMITED TO TWENTY FEET HIGH AND A HUNDRED FEET IN DISTANCE.
THIS FELLOW LOOKS PARTICULARLY BRUTISH.
IT HAS THE POWER TO LEVEL THREE SQUARE MILES OF LONDON.
NOT A SINGLE BUILDING WOULD BE LEFT STANDING AND MOST OF THE PEOPLE WOULD HAVE EXPLODED INTO A BLOODY MIST OF MEAT AND VISCERA.
REALLY, PROFESSOR! MUST YOU BE SO VULGAR?
I APOLOGIZE, YOUR MAJESTY. I MERELY WANTED TO IMPRESS UPON MR. HOLMES THE SERIOUSNESS OF THE SITUATION.
ARE YOU IMPRESSED, MR. HOLMES?

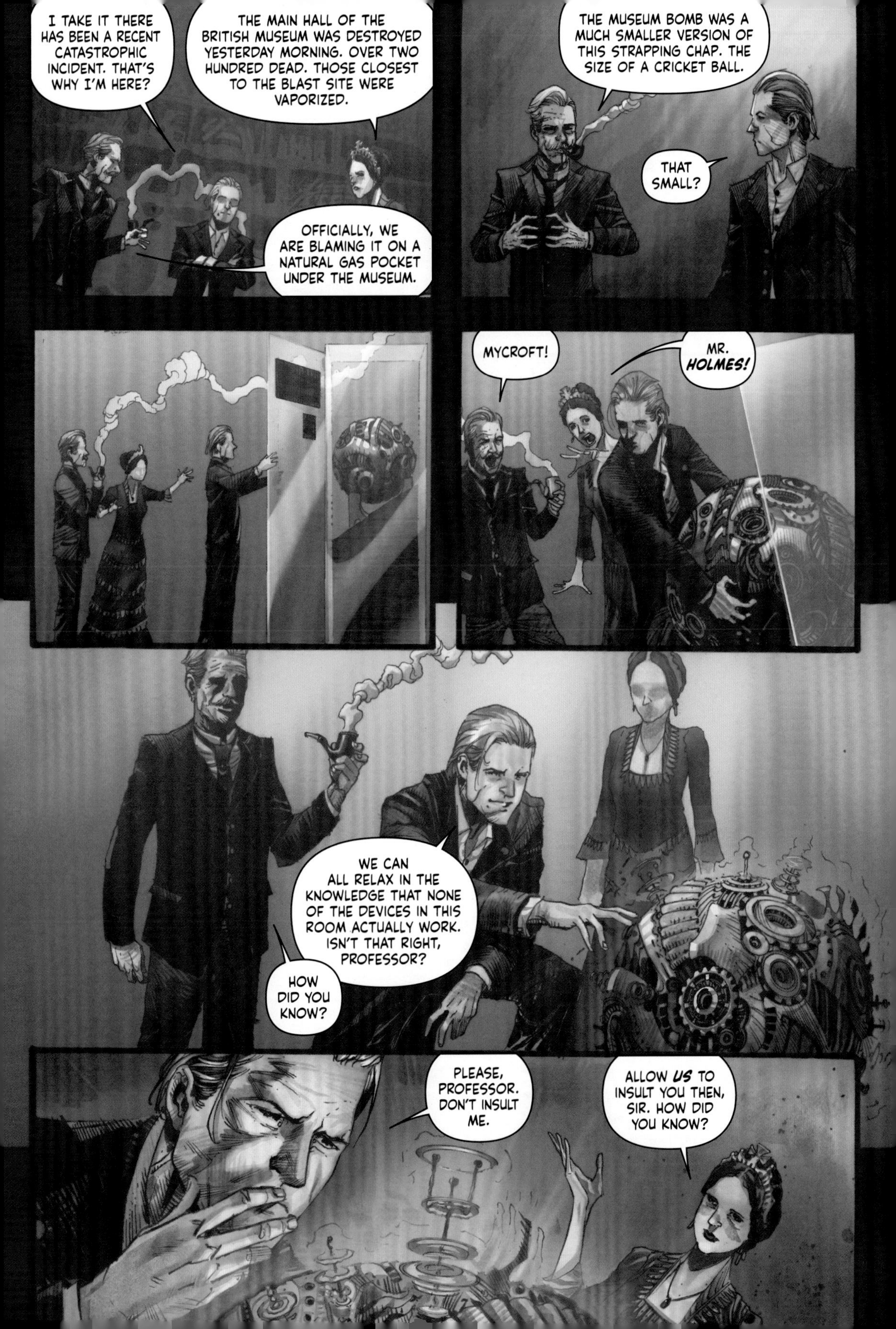
I TAKE IT THERE HAS BEEN A RECENT CATASTROPHIC INCIDENT. THAT'S WHY I'M HERE?
THE MAIN HALL OF THE BRITISH MUSEUM WAS DESTROYED YESTERDAY MORNING. OVER TWO HUNDRED DEAD. THOSE CLOSEST TO THE BLAST SITE WERE VAPORIZED.
OFFICIALLY, WE ARE BLAMING IT ON A NATURAL GAS POCKET UNDER THE MUSEUM.
THE MUSEUM BOMB WAS A MUCH SMALLER VERSION OF THIS STRAPPING CHAP. THE SIZE OF A CRICKET BALL.
THAT SMALL?
MYCROFT!
MR. ***HOLMES!***
WE CAN ALL RELAX IN THE KNOWLEDGE THAT NONE OF THE DEVICES IN THIS ROOM ACTUALLY WORK. ISN'T THAT RIGHT, PROFESSOR?
HOW DID YOU KNOW?
PLEASE, PROFESSOR. DON'T INSULT ME.
ALLOW ***US*** TO INSULT YOU THEN, SIR. HOW DID YOU KNOW?

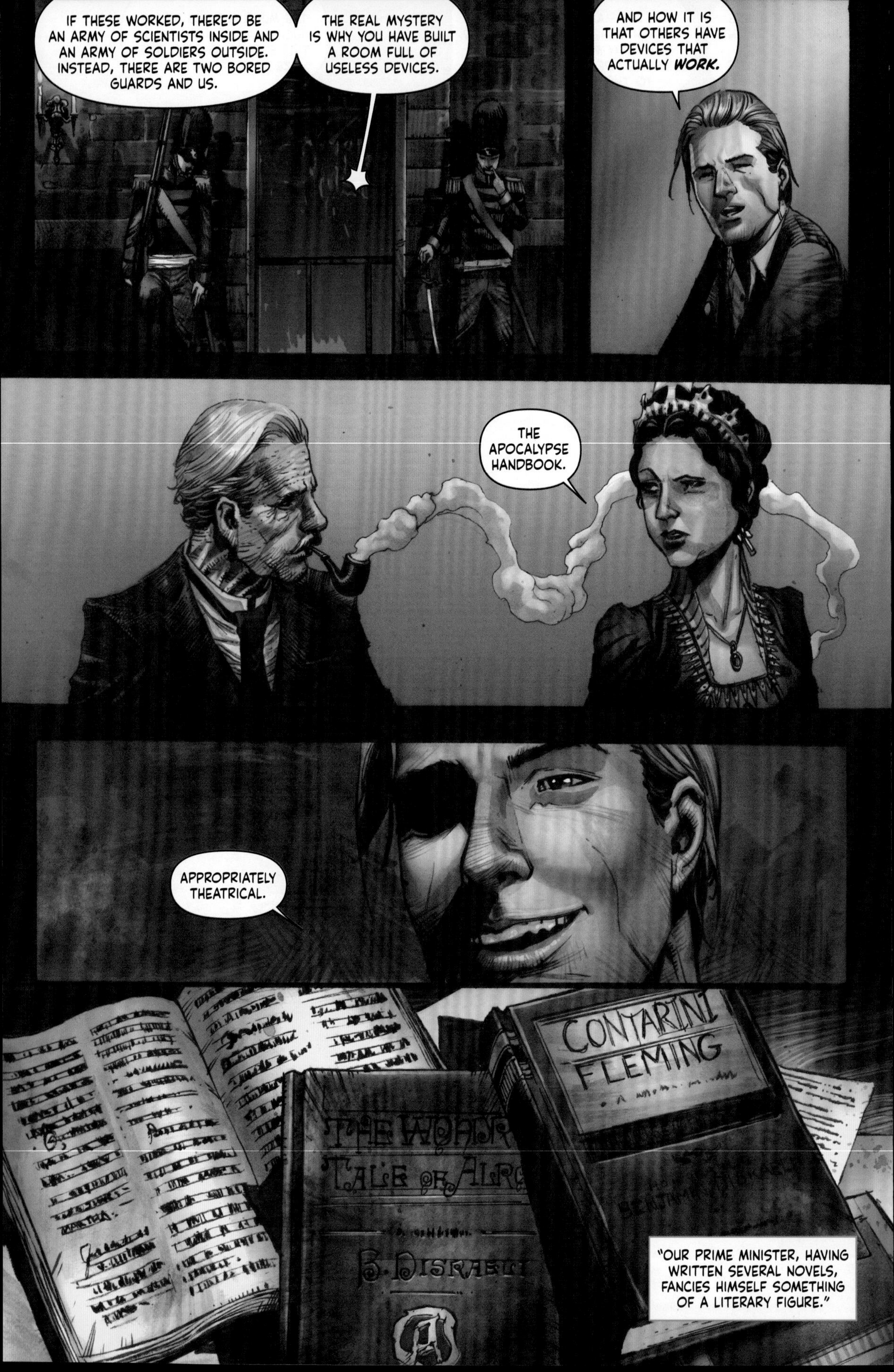
IF THESE WORKED, THERE'D BE AN ARMY OF SCIENTISTS INSIDE AND AN ARMY OF SOLDIERS OUTSIDE. INSTEAD, THERE ARE TWO BORED GUARDS AND US.
THE REAL MYSTERY IS WHY YOU HAVE BUILT A ROOM FULL OF USELESS DEVICES.
AND HOW IT IS THAT OTHERS HAVE DEVICES THAT ACTUALLY ***WORK.***
THE APOCALYPSE HANDBOOK.
APPROPRIATELY THEATRICAL.
CONTARINI FLEMING
B. DISRAELI
"OUR PRIME MINISTER, HAVING WRITTEN SEVERAL NOVELS, FANCIES HIMSELF SOMETHING OF A LITERARY FIGURE."

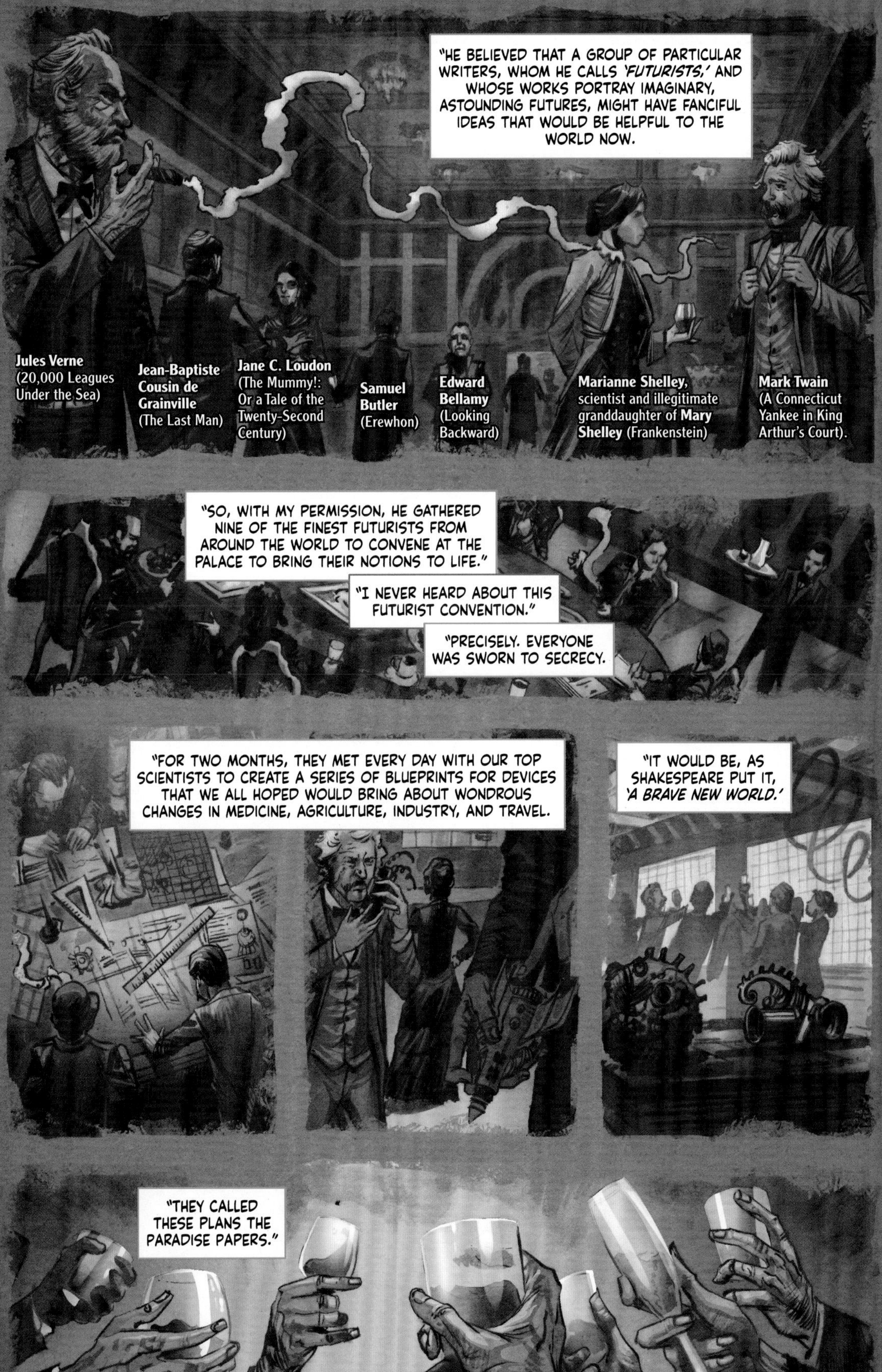
"HE BELIEVED THAT A GROUP OF PARTICULAR WRITERS, WHOM HE CALLS 'FUTURISTS,' AND WHOSE WORKS PORTRAY IMAGINARY, ASTOUNDING FUTURES, MIGHT HAVE FANCIFUL IDEAS THAT WOULD BE HELPFUL TO THE WORLD NOW.
Jules Verne (20,000 Leagues Under the Sea)
Jean-Baptiste Cousin de Grainville (The Last Man)
Jane C. Loudon (The Mummy!: Or a Tale of the Twenty-Second Century)
Samuel Butler (Erewhon)
Edward Bellamy (Looking Backward)
Marianne Shelley, scientist and illegitimate granddaughter of Mary Shelley (Frankenstein)
Mark Twain (A Connecticut Yankee in King Arthur's Court).
"SO, WITH MY PERMISSION, HE GATHERED NINE OF THE FINEST FUTURISTS FROM AROUND THE WORLD TO CONVENE AT THE PALACE TO BRING THEIR NOTIONS TO LIFE."
"I NEVER HEARD ABOUT THIS FUTURIST CONVENTION."
"PRECISELY. EVERYONE WAS SWORN TO SECRECY.
"FOR TWO MONTHS, THEY MET EVERY DAY WITH OUR TOP SCIENTISTS TO CREATE A SERIES OF BLUEPRINTS FOR DEVICES THAT WE ALL HOPED WOULD BRING ABOUT WONDROUS CHANGES IN MEDICINE, AGRICULTURE, INDUSTRY, AND TRAVEL.
"IT WOULD BE, AS SHAKESPEARE PUT IT, 'A BRAVE NEW WORLD.'
"THEY CALLED THESE PLANS THE PARADISE PAPERS."

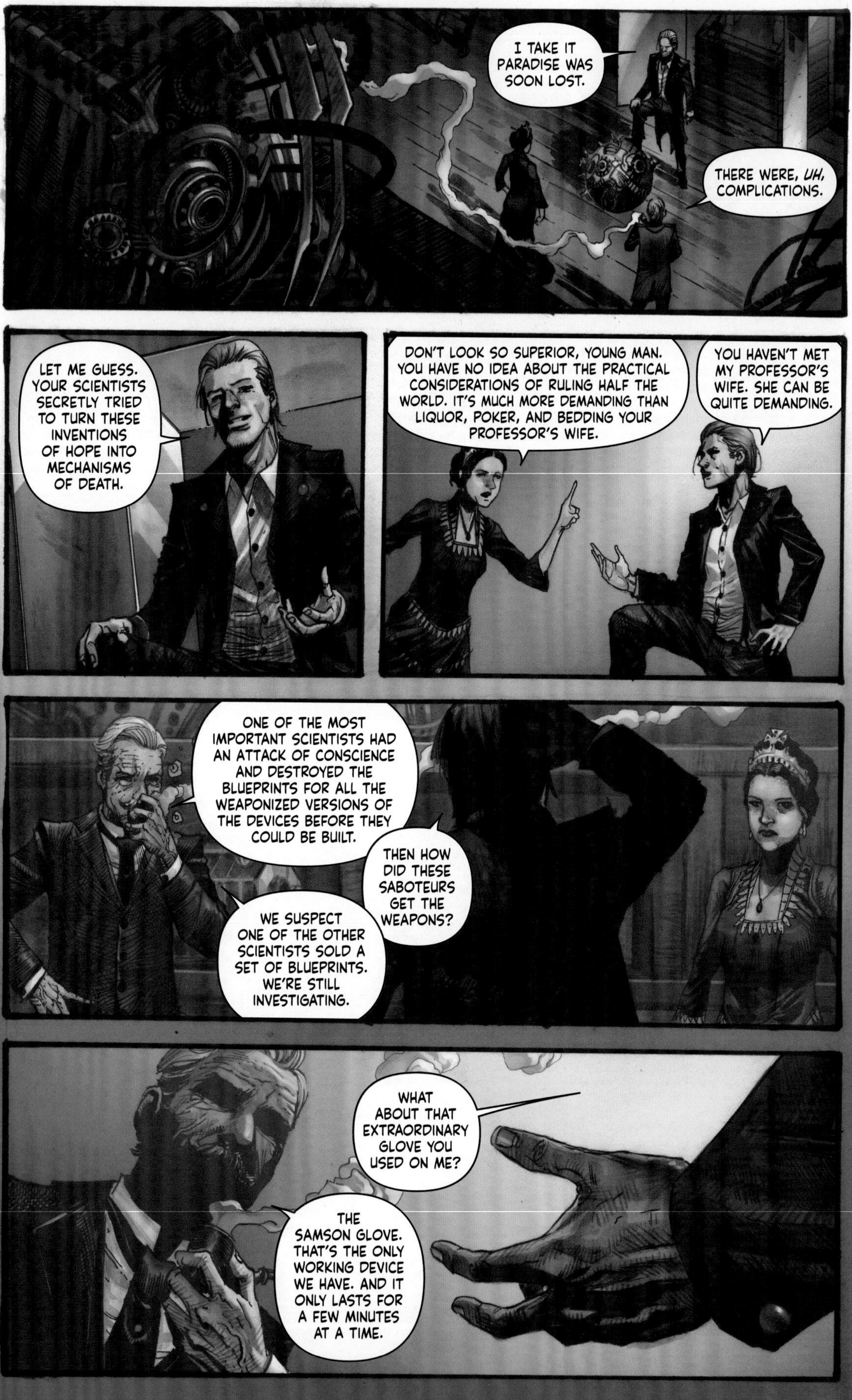
I TAKE IT PARADISE WAS SOON LOST.
THERE WERE, *UH*, COMPLICATIONS.
LET ME GUESS. YOUR SCIENTISTS SECRETLY TRIED TO TURN THESE INVENTIONS OF HOPE INTO MECHANISMS OF DEATH.
DON'T LOOK SO SUPERIOR, YOUNG MAN. YOU HAVE NO IDEA ABOUT THE PRACTICAL CONSIDERATIONS OF RULING HALF THE WORLD. IT'S MUCH MORE DEMANDING THAN LIQUOR, POKER, AND BEDDING YOUR PROFESSOR'S WIFE.
YOU HAVEN'T MET MY PROFESSOR'S WIFE. SHE CAN BE QUITE DEMANDING.
ONE OF THE MOST IMPORTANT SCIENTISTS HAD AN ATTACK OF CONSCIENCE AND DESTROYED THE BLUEPRINTS FOR ALL THE WEAPONIZED VERSIONS OF THE DEVICES BEFORE THEY COULD BE BUILT.
THEN HOW DID THESE SABOTEURS GET THE WEAPONS?
WE SUSPECT ONE OF THE OTHER SCIENTISTS SOLD A SET OF BLUEPRINTS. WE'RE STILL INVESTIGATING.
WHAT ABOUT THAT EXTRAORDINARY GLOVE YOU USED ON ME?
THE SAMSON GLOVE. THAT'S THE ONLY WORKING DEVICE WE HAVE. AND IT ONLY LASTS FOR A FEW MINUTES AT A TIME.

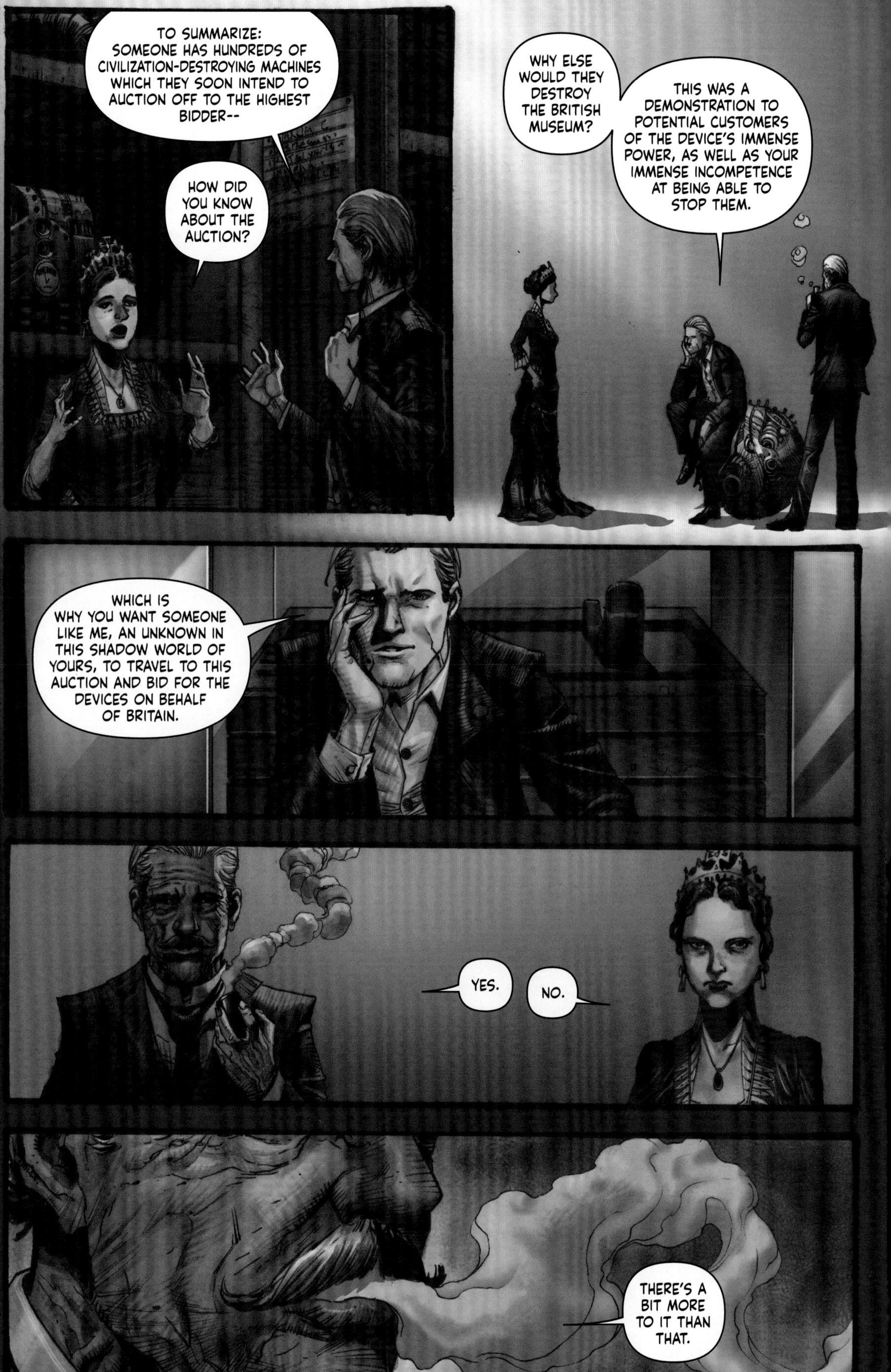
TO SUMMARIZE: SOMEONE HAS HUNDREDS OF CIVILIZATION-DESTROYING MACHINES WHICH THEY SOON INTEND TO AUCTION OFF TO THE HIGHEST BIDDER--
HOW DID YOU KNOW ABOUT THE AUCTION?
WHY ELSE WOULD THEY DESTROY THE BRITISH MUSEUM?
THIS WAS A DEMONSTRATION TO POTENTIAL CUSTOMERS OF THE DEVICE'S IMMENSE POWER, AS WELL AS YOUR IMMENSE INCOMPETENCE AT BEING ABLE TO STOP THEM.
WHICH IS WHY YOU WANT SOMEONE LIKE ME, AN UNKNOWN IN THIS SHADOW WORLD OF YOURS, TO TRAVEL TO THIS AUCTION AND BID FOR THE DEVICES ON BEHALF OF BRITAIN.
YES.
NO.
THERE'S A BIT MORE TO IT THAN THAT.

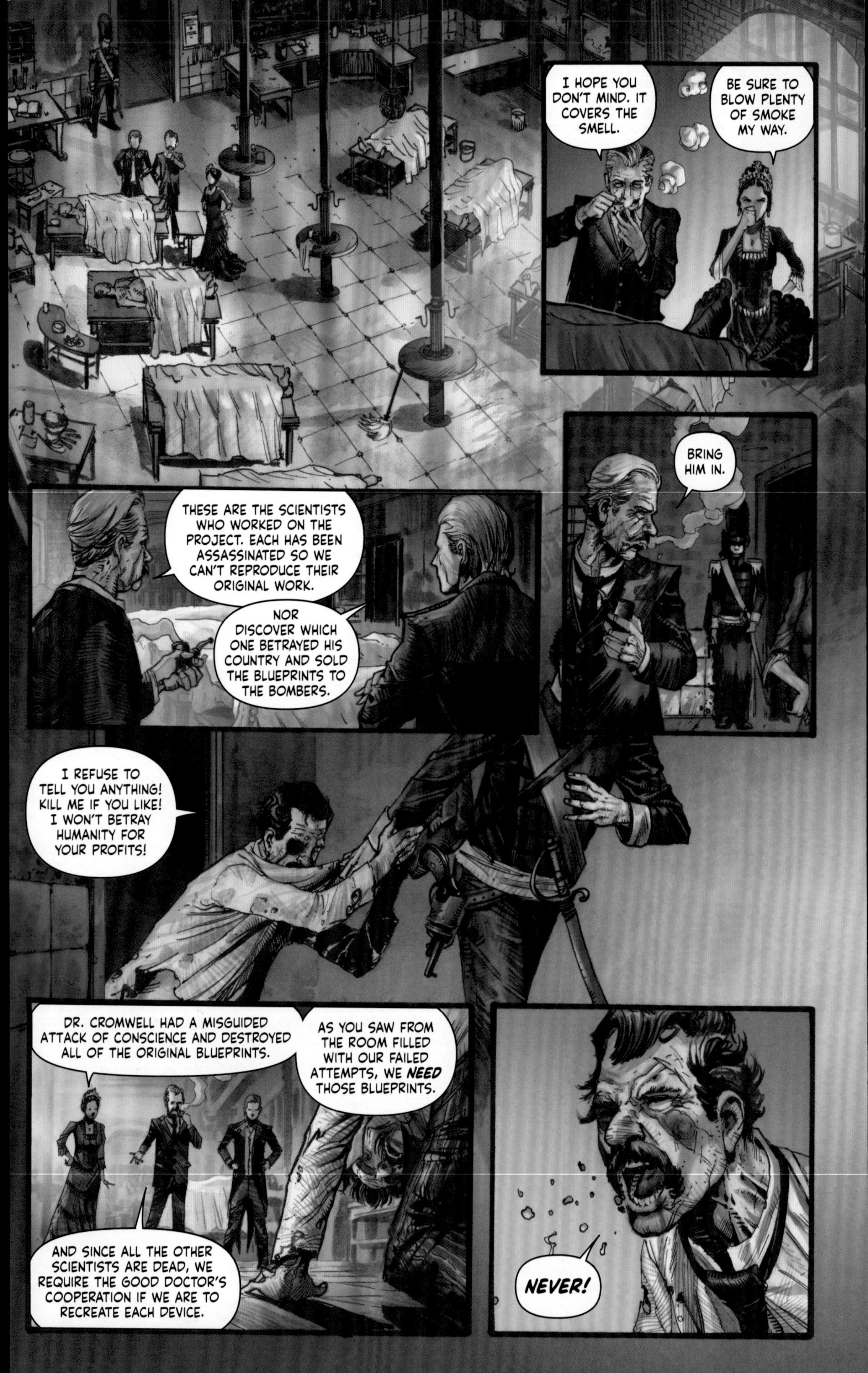
I HOPE YOU DON'T MIND. IT COVERS THE SMELL.
BE SURE TO BLOW PLENTY OF SMOKE MY WAY.
THESE ARE THE SCIENTISTS WHO WORKED ON THE PROJECT. EACH HAS BEEN ASSASSINATED SO WE CAN'T REPRODUCE THEIR ORIGINAL WORK.
NOR DISCOVER WHICH ONE BETRAYED HIS COUNTRY AND SOLD THE BLUEPRINTS TO THE BOMBERS.
BRING HIM IN.
I REFUSE TO TELL YOU ANYTHING! KILL ME IF YOU LIKE! I WON'T BETRAY HUMANITY FOR YOUR PROFITS!
DR. CROMWELL HAD A MISGUIDED ATTACK OF CONSCIENCE AND DESTROYED ALL OF THE ORIGINAL BLUEPRINTS.
AS YOU SAW FROM THE ROOM FILLED WITH OUR FAILED ATTEMPTS, WE *NEED* THOSE BLUEPRINTS.
AND SINCE ALL THE OTHER SCIENTISTS ARE DEAD, WE REQUIRE THE GOOD DOCTOR'S COOPERATION IF WE ARE TO RECREATE EACH DEVICE.
NEVER!

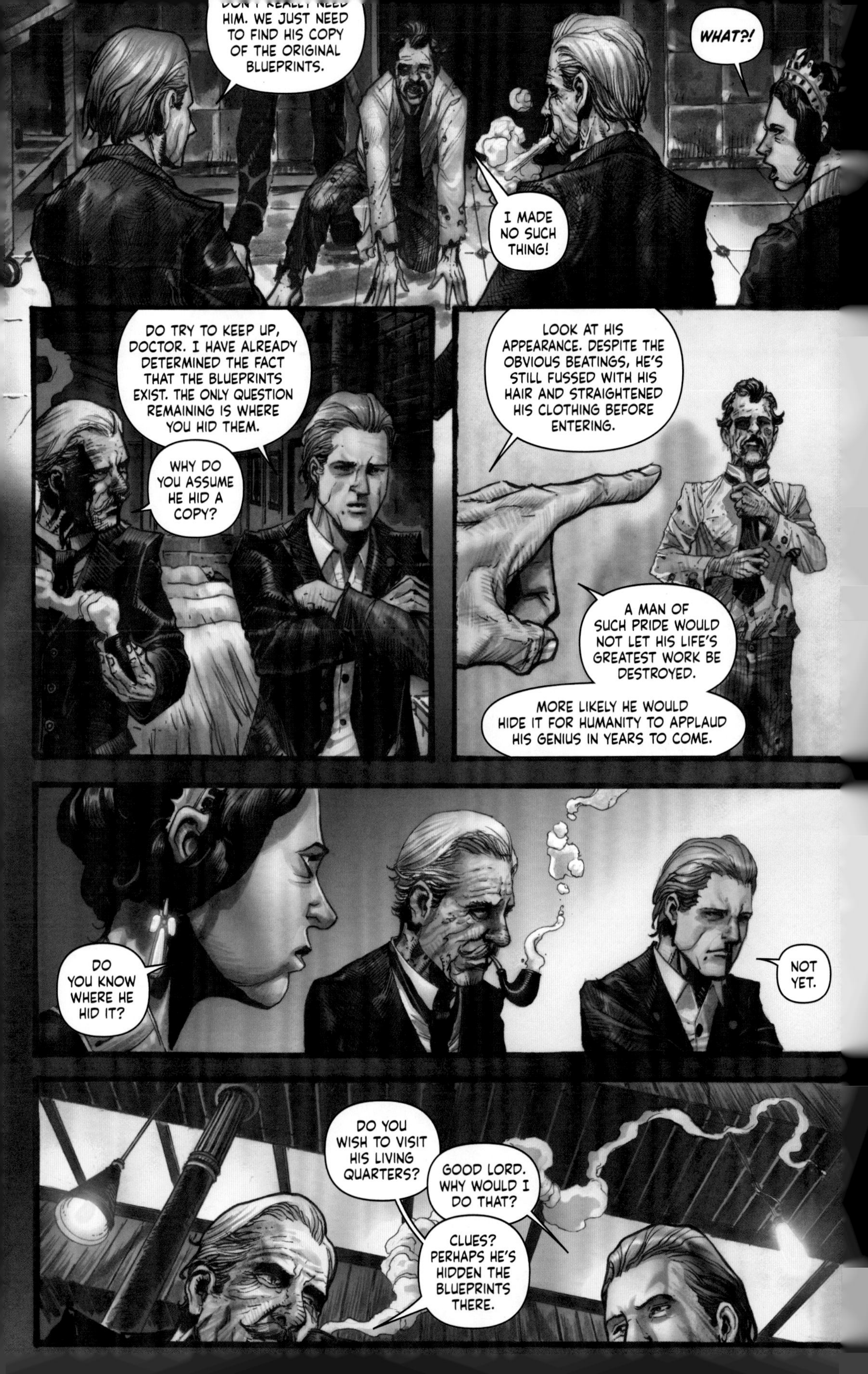
HIM. WE JUST NEED TO FIND HIS COPY OF THE ORIGINAL BLUEPRINTS.
WHAT?!
I MADE NO SUCH THING!
DO TRY TO KEEP UP, DOCTOR. I HAVE ALREADY DETERMINED THE FACT THAT THE BLUEPRINTS EXIST. THE ONLY QUESTION REMAINING IS WHERE YOU HID THEM.
WHY DO YOU ASSUME HE HID A COPY?
LOOK AT HIS APPEARANCE. DESPITE THE OBVIOUS BEATINGS, HE'S STILL FUSSED WITH HIS HAIR AND STRAIGHTENED HIS CLOTHING BEFORE ENTERING.
A MAN OF SUCH PRIDE WOULD NOT LET HIS LIFE'S GREATEST WORK BE DESTROYED.
MORE LIKELY HE WOULD HIDE IT FOR HUMANITY TO APPLAUD HIS GENIUS IN YEARS TO COME.
DO YOU KNOW WHERE HE HID IT?
NOT YET.
DO YOU WISH TO VISIT HIS LIVING QUARTERS?
GOOD LORD. WHY WOULD I DO THAT?
CLUES? PERHAPS HE'S HIDDEN THE BLUEPRINTS THERE.

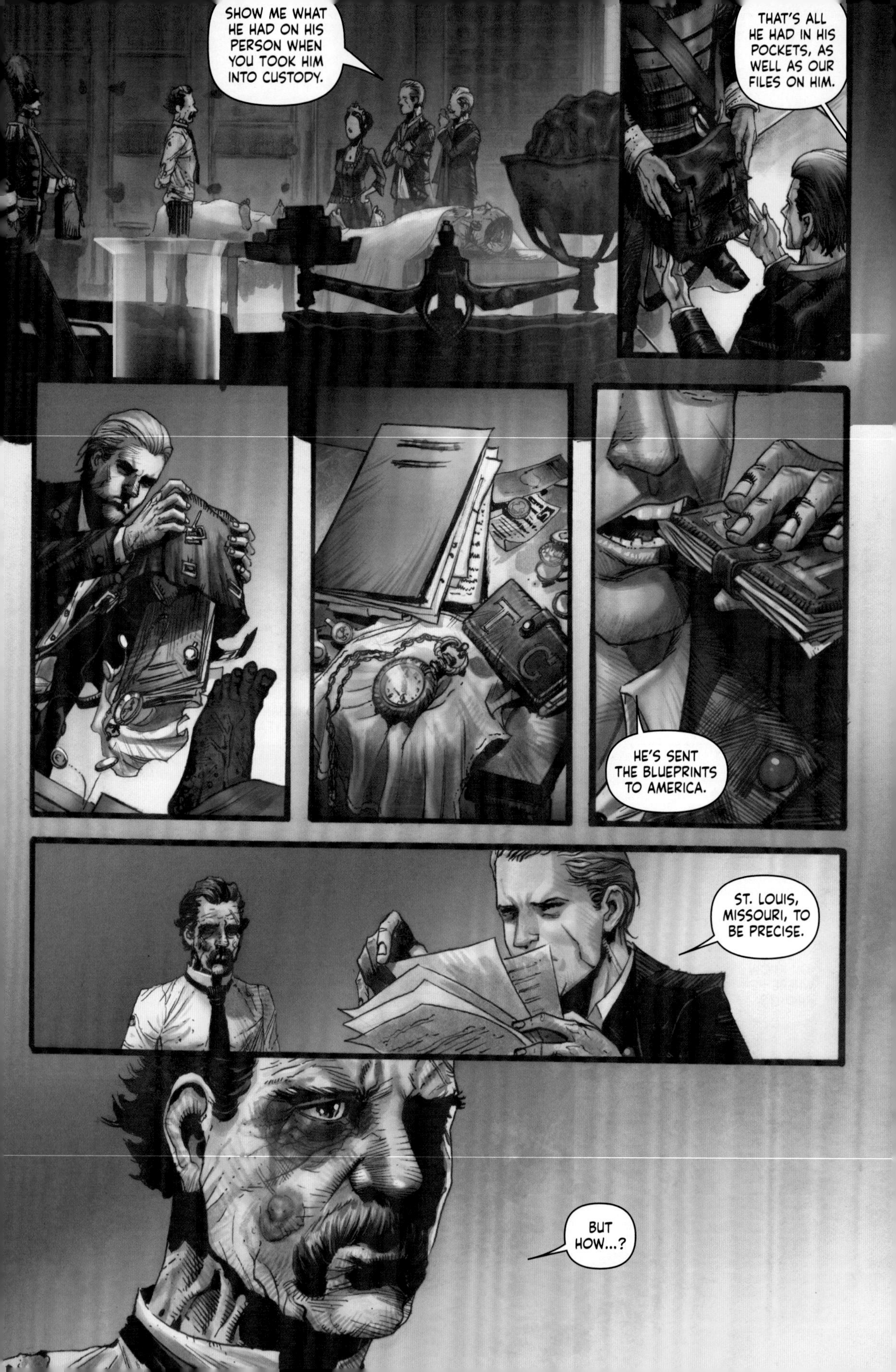
SHOW ME WHAT HE HAD ON HIS PERSON WHEN YOU TOOK HIM INTO CUSTODY.
THAT'S ALL HE HAD IN HIS POCKETS, AS WELL AS OUR FILES ON HIM.
HE'S SENT THE BLUEPRINTS TO AMERICA.
ST. LOUIS, MISSOURI, TO BE PRECISE.
BUT HOW...?

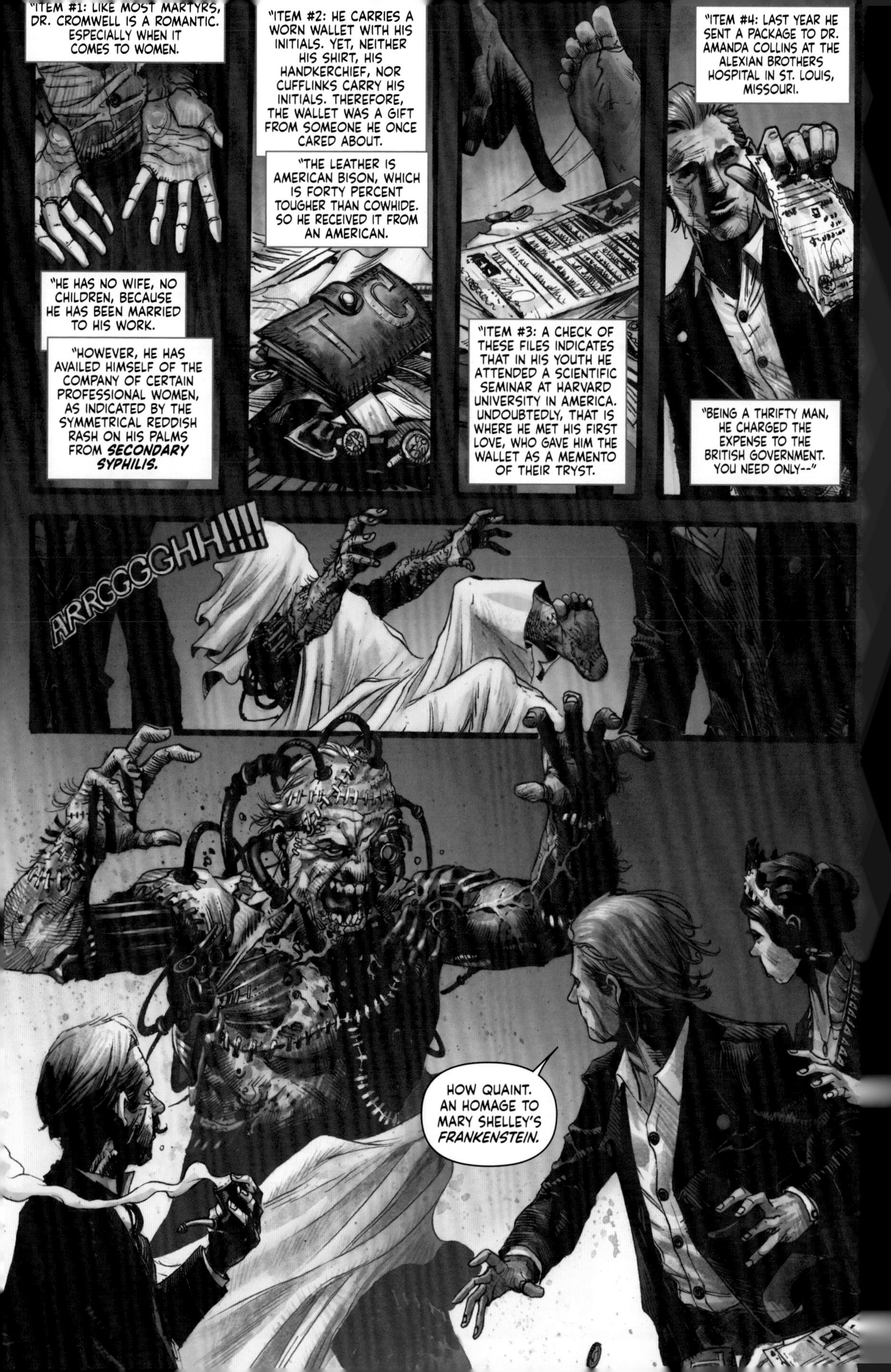
"ITEM #1: LIKE MOST MARTYRS, DR. CROMWELL IS A ROMANTIC. ESPECIALLY WHEN IT COMES TO WOMEN.
"HE HAS NO WIFE, NO CHILDREN, BECAUSE HE HAS BEEN MARRIED TO HIS WORK.
"HOWEVER, HE HAS AVAILED HIMSELF OF THE COMPANY OF CERTAIN PROFESSIONAL WOMEN, AS INDICATED BY THE SYMMETRICAL REDDISH RASH ON HIS PALMS FROM SECONDARY SYPHILIS.
"ITEM #2: HE CARRIES A WORN WALLET WITH HIS INITIALS. YET, NEITHER HIS SHIRT, HIS HANDKERCHIEF, NOR CUFFLINKS CARRY HIS INITIALS. THEREFORE, THE WALLET WAS A GIFT FROM SOMEONE HE ONCE CARED ABOUT.
"THE LEATHER IS AMERICAN BISON, WHICH IS FORTY PERCENT TOUGHER THAN COWHIDE. SO HE RECEIVED IT FROM AN AMERICAN.
"ITEM #3: A CHECK OF THESE FILES INDICATES THAT IN HIS YOUTH HE ATTENDED A SCIENTIFIC SEMINAR AT HARVARD UNIVERSITY IN AMERICA. UNDOUBTEDLY, THAT IS WHERE HE MET HIS FIRST LOVE, WHO GAVE HIM THE WALLET AS A MEMENTO OF THEIR TRYST.
"ITEM #4: LAST YEAR HE SENT A PACKAGE TO DR. AMANDA COLLINS AT THE ALEXIAN BROTHERS HOSPITAL IN ST. LOUIS, MISSOURI.
"BEING A THRIFTY MAN, HE CHARGED THE EXPENSE TO THE BRITISH GOVERNMENT. YOU NEED ONLY--"
ARRGGGGHH!!!!
HOW QUAINT. AN HOMAGE TO MARY SHELLEY'S FRANKENSTEIN.

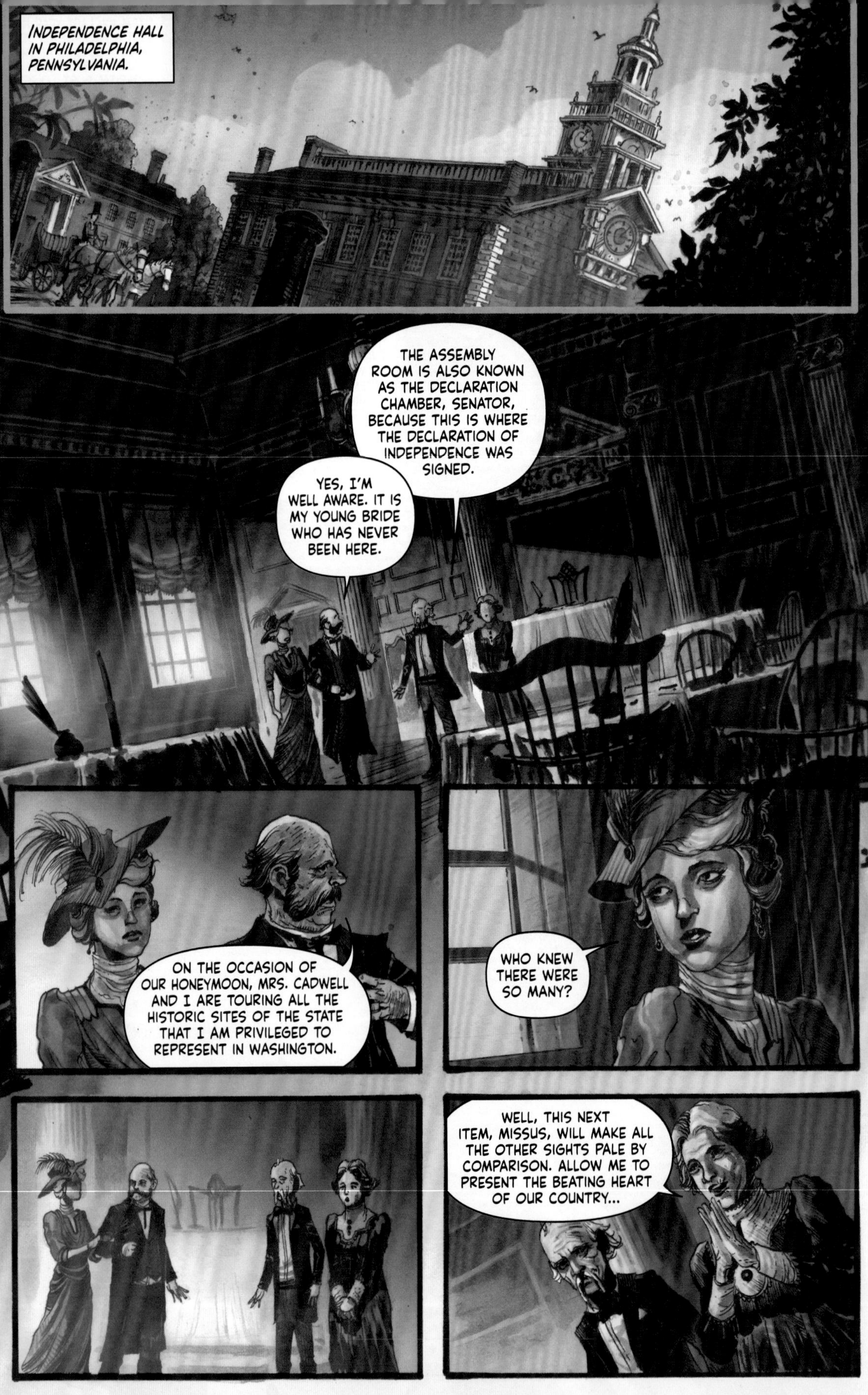
INDEPENDENCE HALL IN PHILADELPHIA, PENNSYLVANIA.
THE ASSEMBLY ROOM IS ALSO KNOWN AS THE DECLARATION CHAMBER, SENATOR, BECAUSE THIS IS WHERE THE DECLARATION OF INDEPENDENCE WAS SIGNED.
YES, I'M WELL AWARE. IT IS MY YOUNG BRIDE WHO HAS NEVER BEEN HERE.
ON THE OCCASION OF OUR HONEYMOON, MRS. CADWELL AND I ARE TOURING ALL THE HISTORIC SITES OF THE STATE THAT I AM PRIVILEGED TO REPRESENT IN WASHINGTON.
WHO KNEW THERE WERE SO MANY?
WELL, THIS NEXT ITEM, MISSUS, WILL MAKE ALL THE OTHER SIGHTS PALE BY COMPARISON. ALLOW ME TO PRESENT THE BEATING HEART OF OUR COUNTRY...

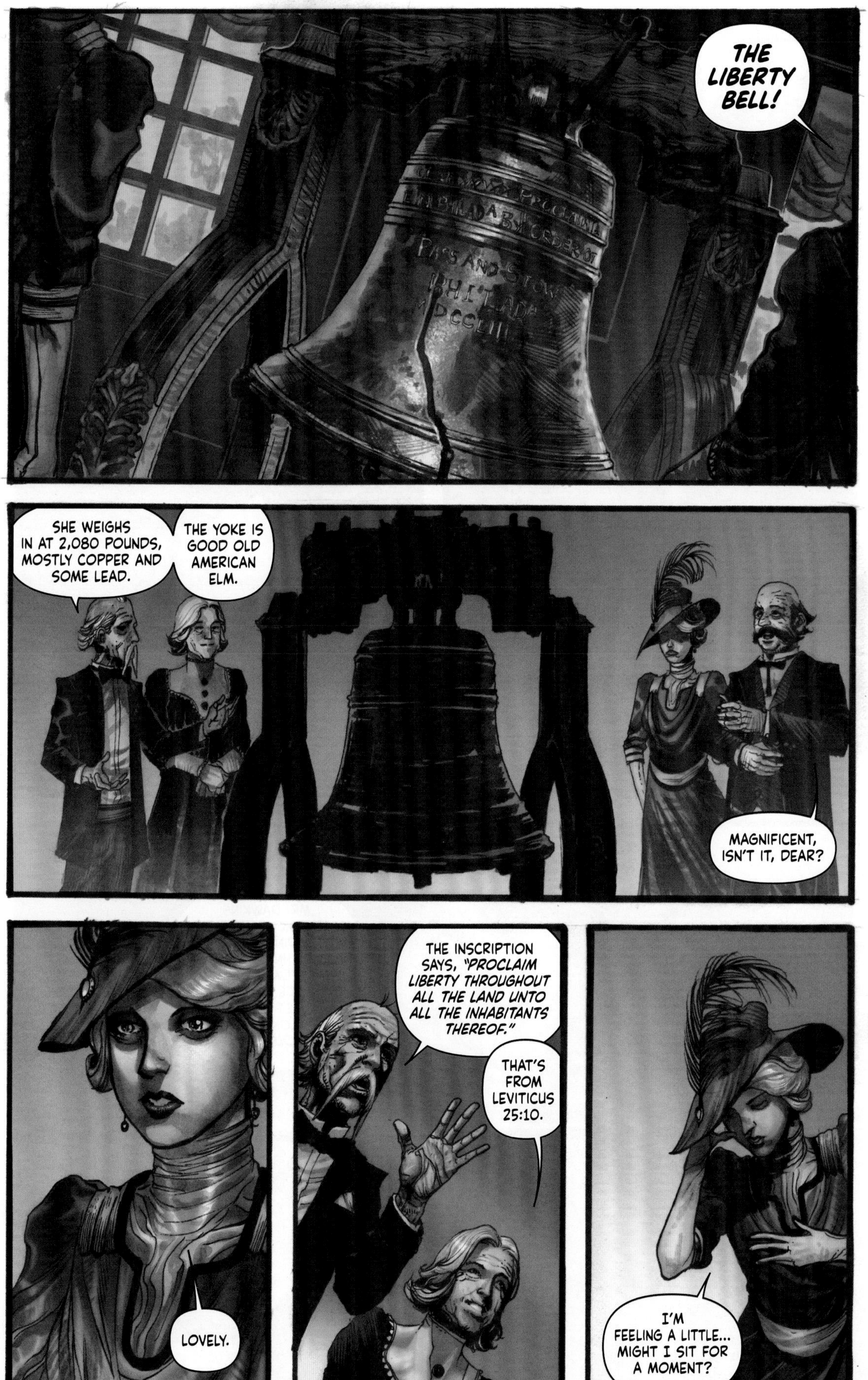
THE LIBERTY BELL!
SHE WEIGHS IN AT 2,080 POUNDS, MOSTLY COPPER AND SOME LEAD.
THE YOKE IS GOOD OLD AMERICAN ELM.
MAGNIFICENT, ISN'T IT, DEAR?
LOVELY.
THE INSCRIPTION SAYS, *"PROCLAIM LIBERTY THROUGHOUT ALL THE LAND UNTO ALL THE INHABITANTS THEREOF."*
THAT'S FROM LEVITICUS 25:10.
I'M FEELING A LITTLE... MIGHT I SIT FOR A MOMENT?

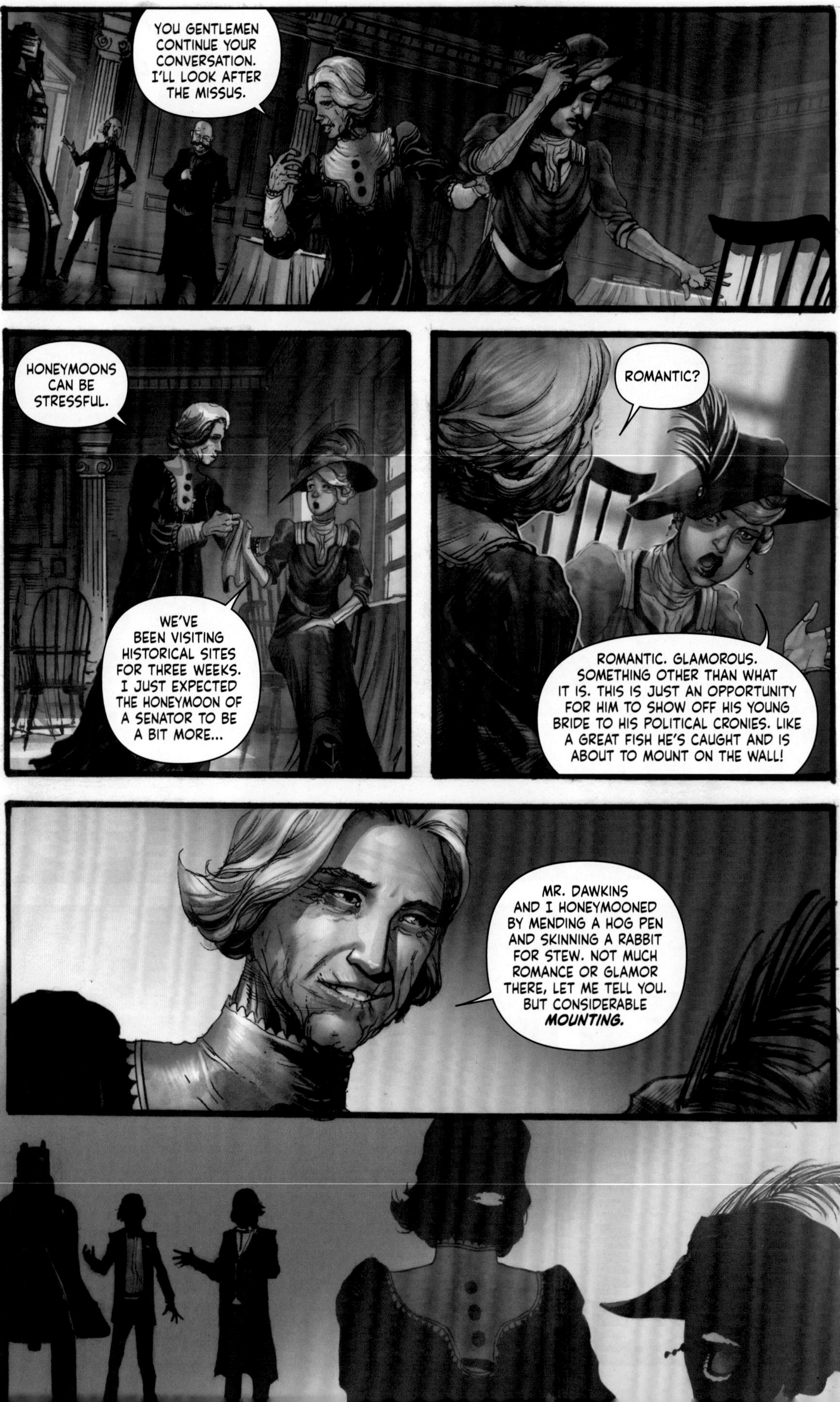
YOU GENTLEMEN CONTINUE YOUR CONVERSATION. I'LL LOOK AFTER THE MISSUS.
HONEYMOONS CAN BE STRESSFUL.
WE'VE BEEN VISITING HISTORICAL SITES FOR THREE WEEKS. I JUST EXPECTED THE HONEYMOON OF A SENATOR TO BE A BIT MORE...
ROMANTIC?
ROMANTIC. GLAMOROUS. SOMETHING OTHER THAN WHAT IT IS. THIS IS JUST AN OPPORTUNITY FOR HIM TO SHOW OFF HIS YOUNG BRIDE TO HIS POLITICAL CRONIES. LIKE A GREAT FISH HE'S CAUGHT AND IS ABOUT TO MOUNT ON THE WALL!
MR. DAWKINS AND I HONEYMOONED BY MENDING A HOG PEN AND SKINNING A RABBIT FOR STEW. NOT MUCH ROMANCE OR GLAMOR THERE, LET ME TELL YOU. BUT CONSIDERABLE *MOUNTING.*

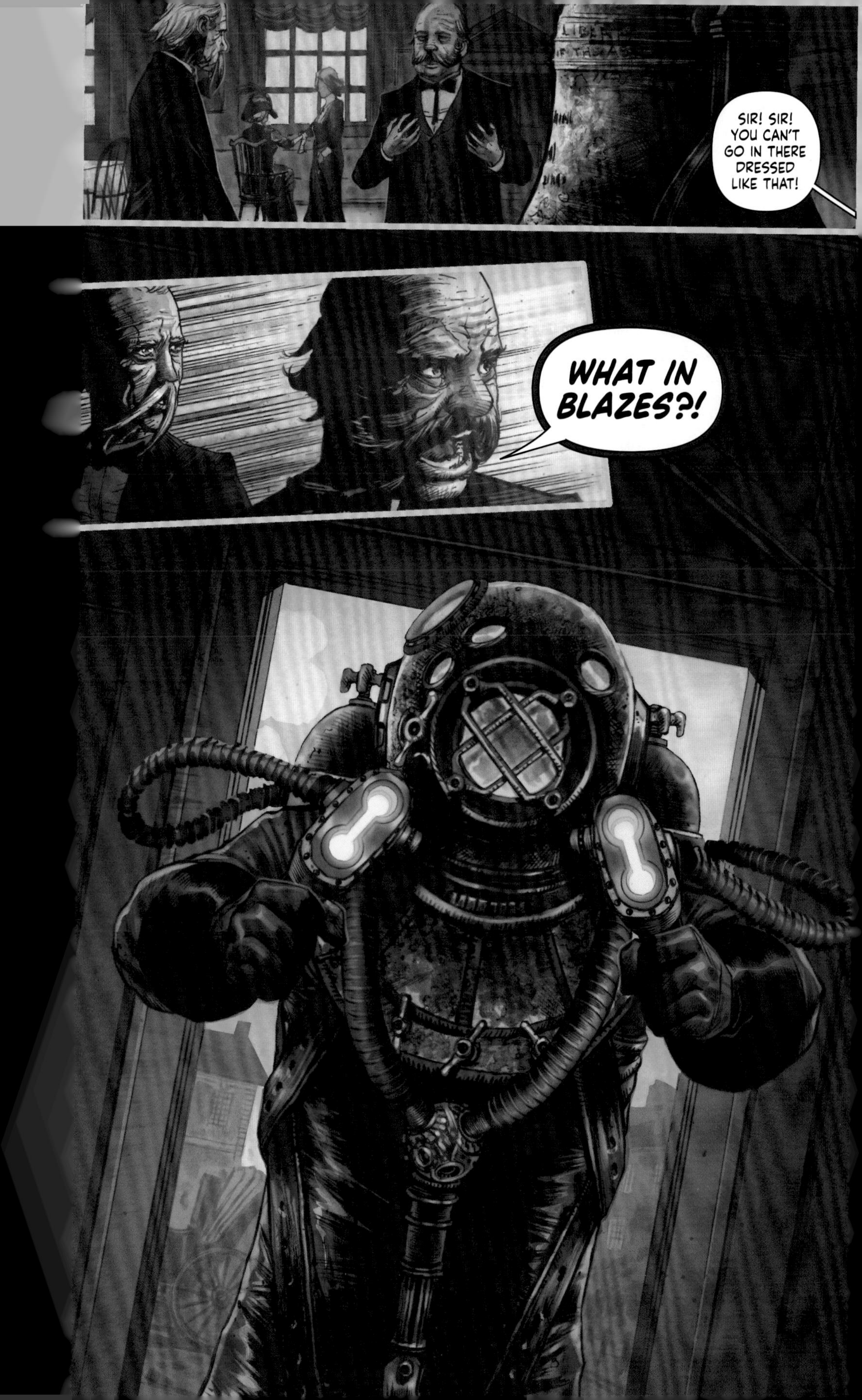
SIR! SIR! YOU CAN'T GO IN THERE DRESSED LIKE THAT!
WHAT IN BLAZES?!

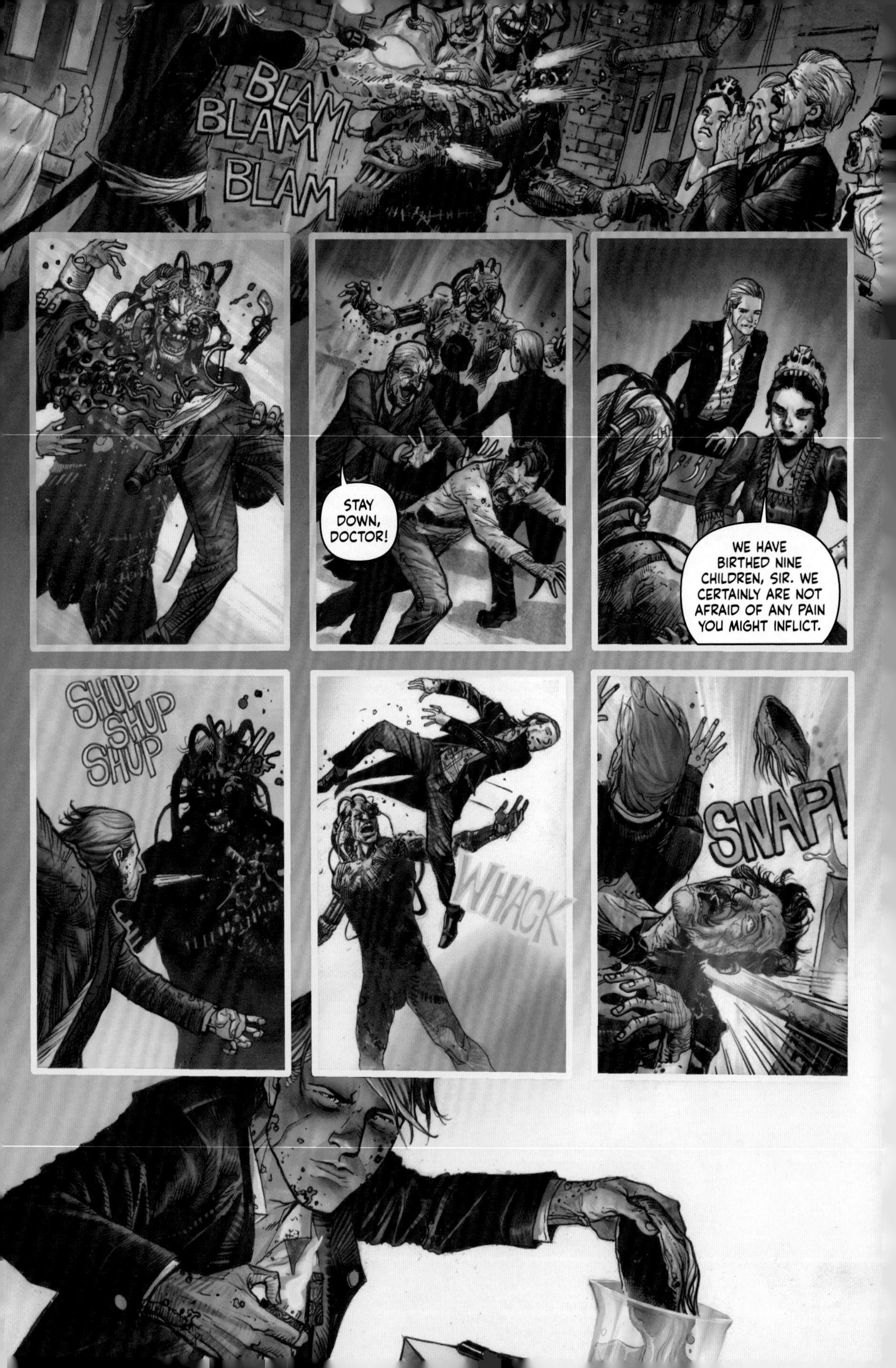
BLAM
BLAM
BLAM
STAY DOWN, DOCTOR!
WE HAVE BIRTHED NINE CHILDREN, SIR. WE CERTAINLY ARE NOT AFRAID OF ANY PAIN YOU MIGHT INFLICT.
SHUP
SHUP
SHUP
WHACK
SNAP!

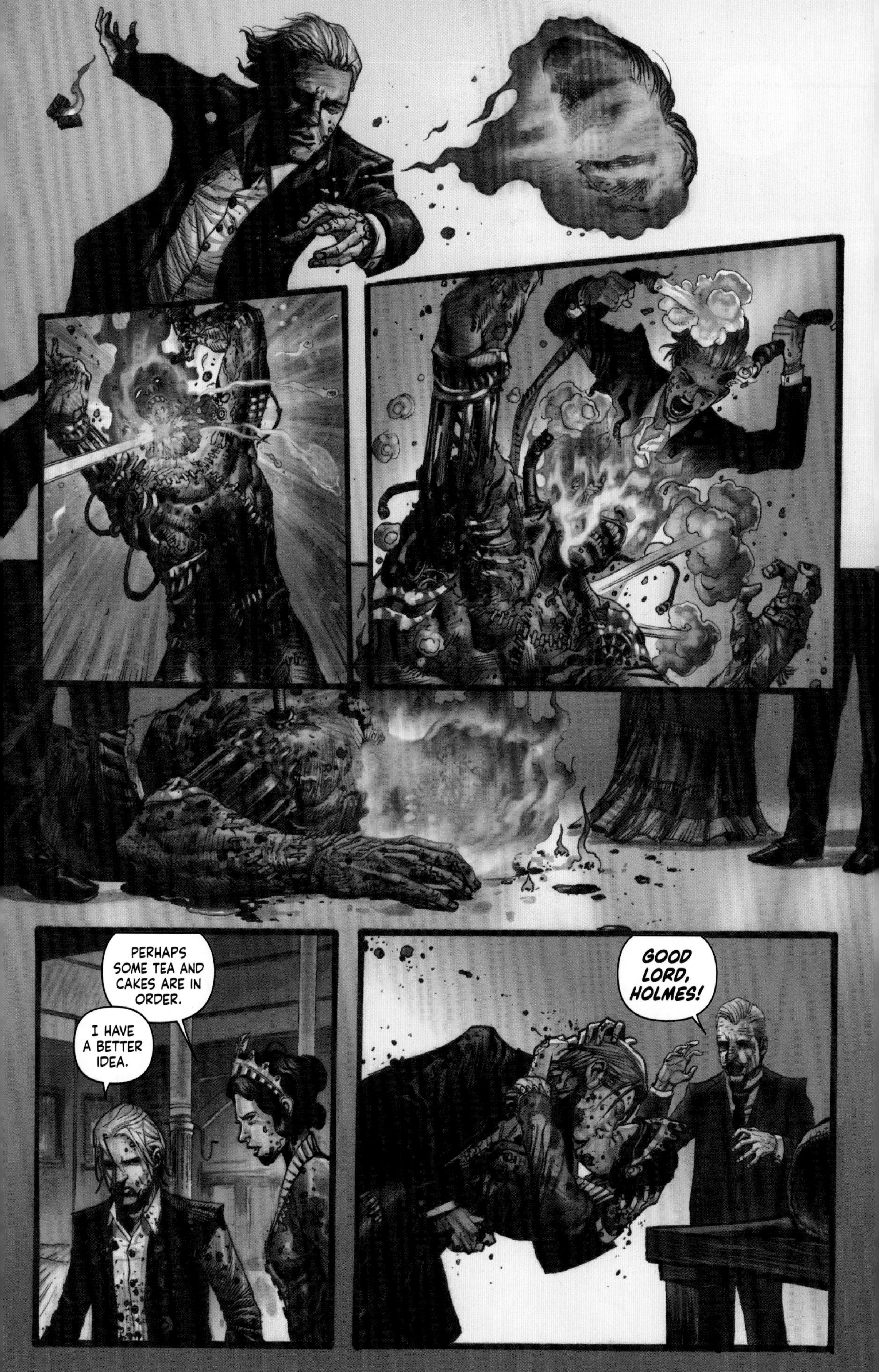
PERHAPS SOME TEA AND CAKES ARE IN ORDER.
I HAVE A BETTER IDEA.
GOOD LORD, HOLMES!

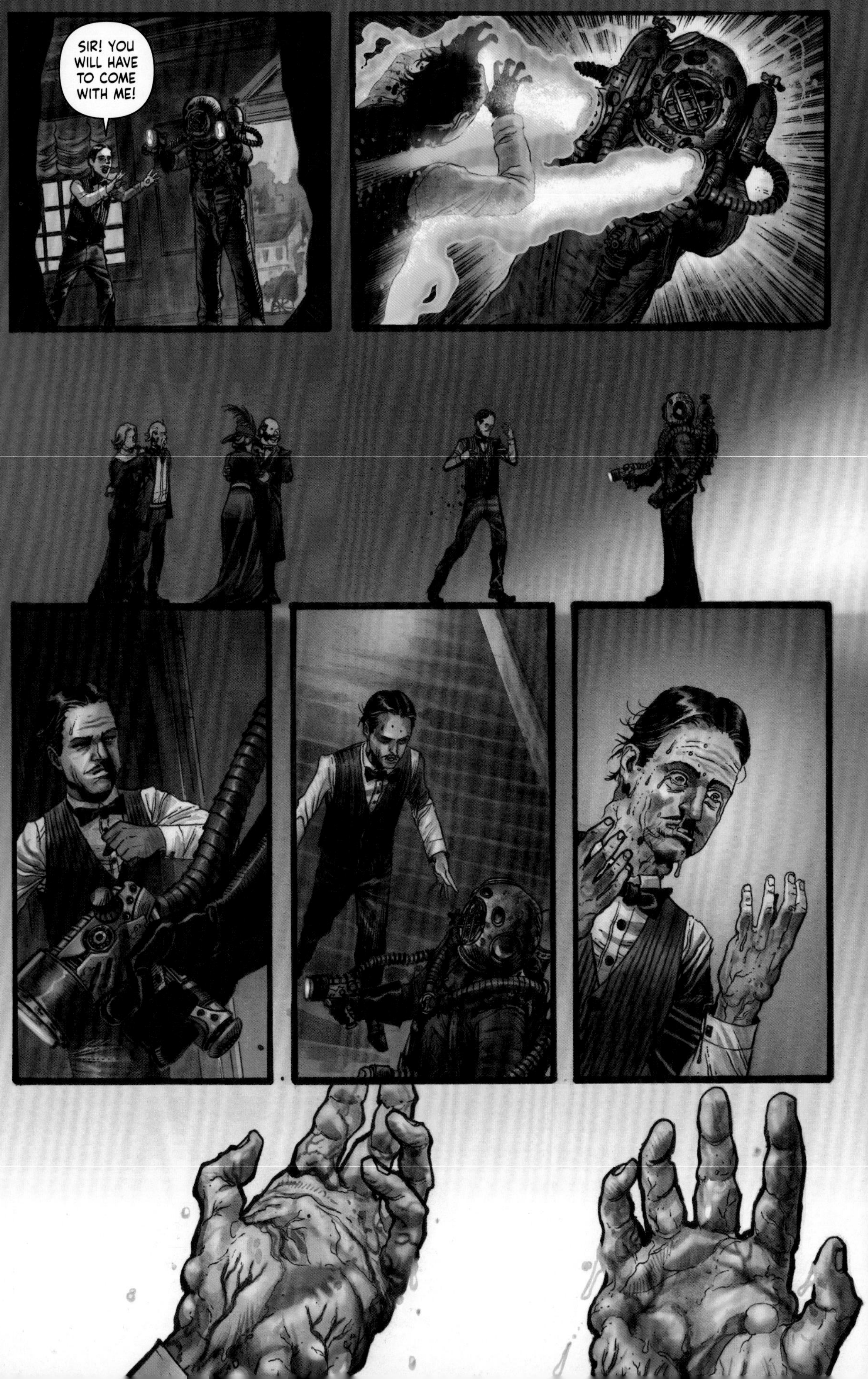
SIR! YOU WILL HAVE TO COME WITH ME!

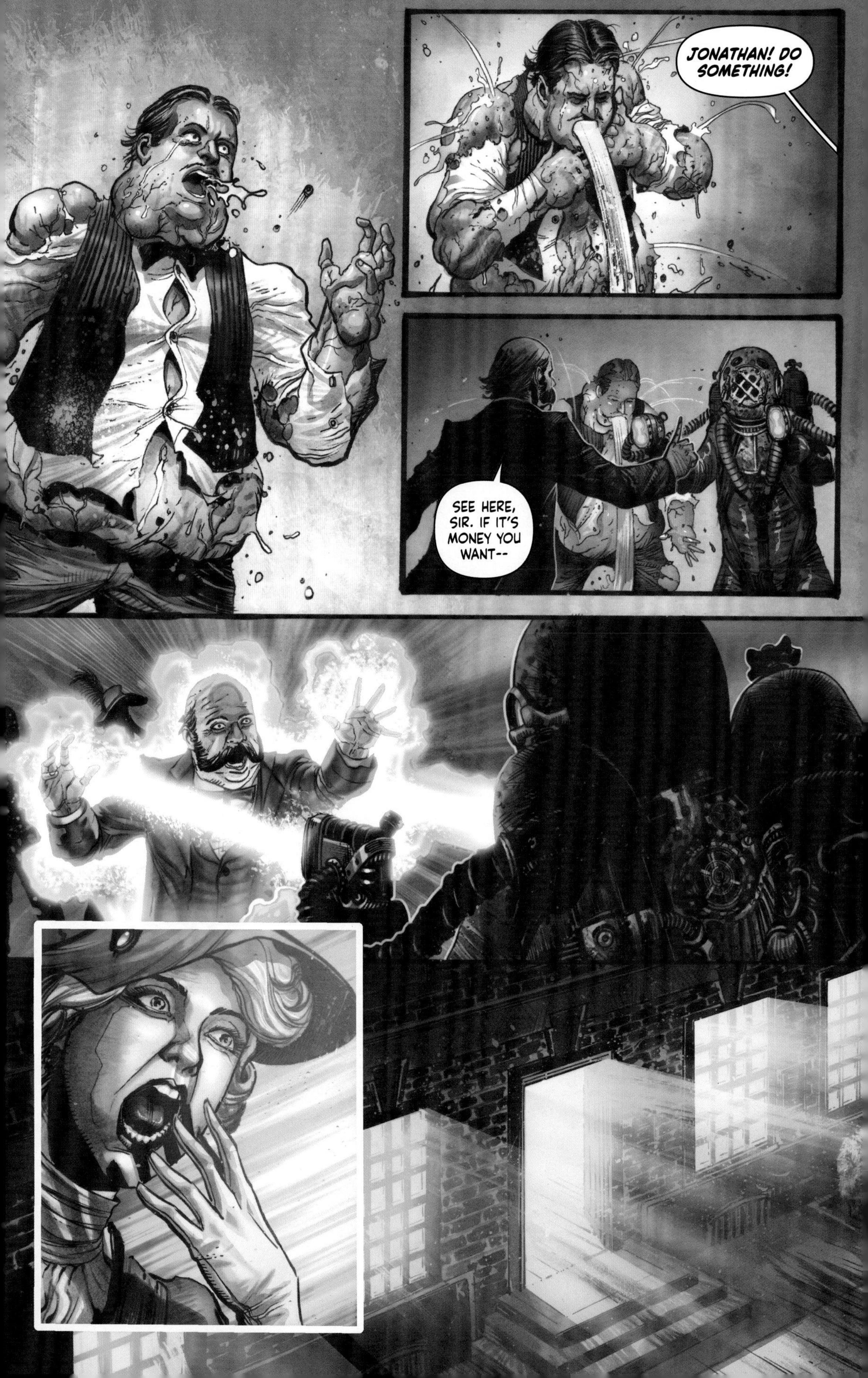
JONATHAN! DO SOMETHING!
SEE HERE, SIR. IF IT'S MONEY YOU WANT--

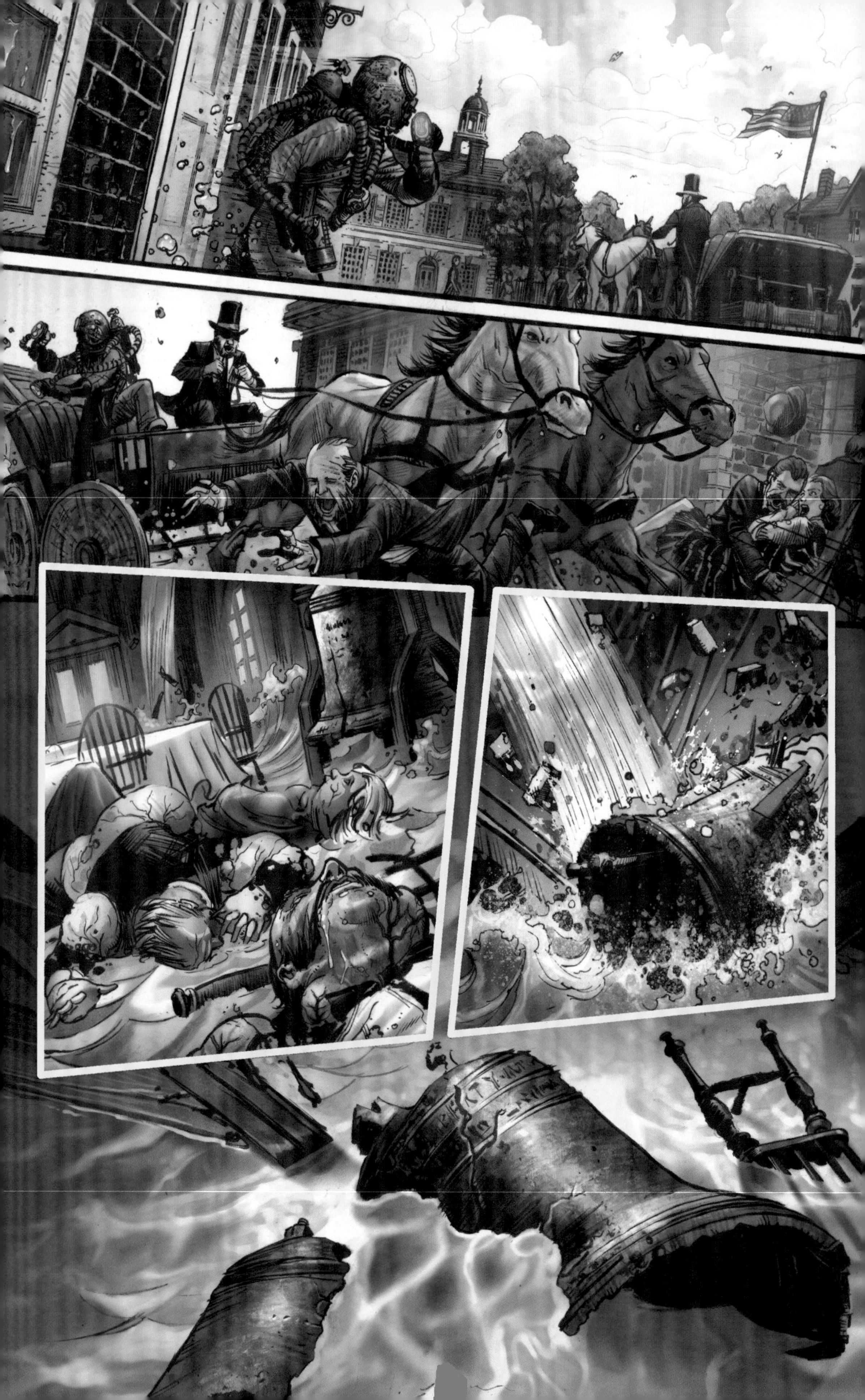

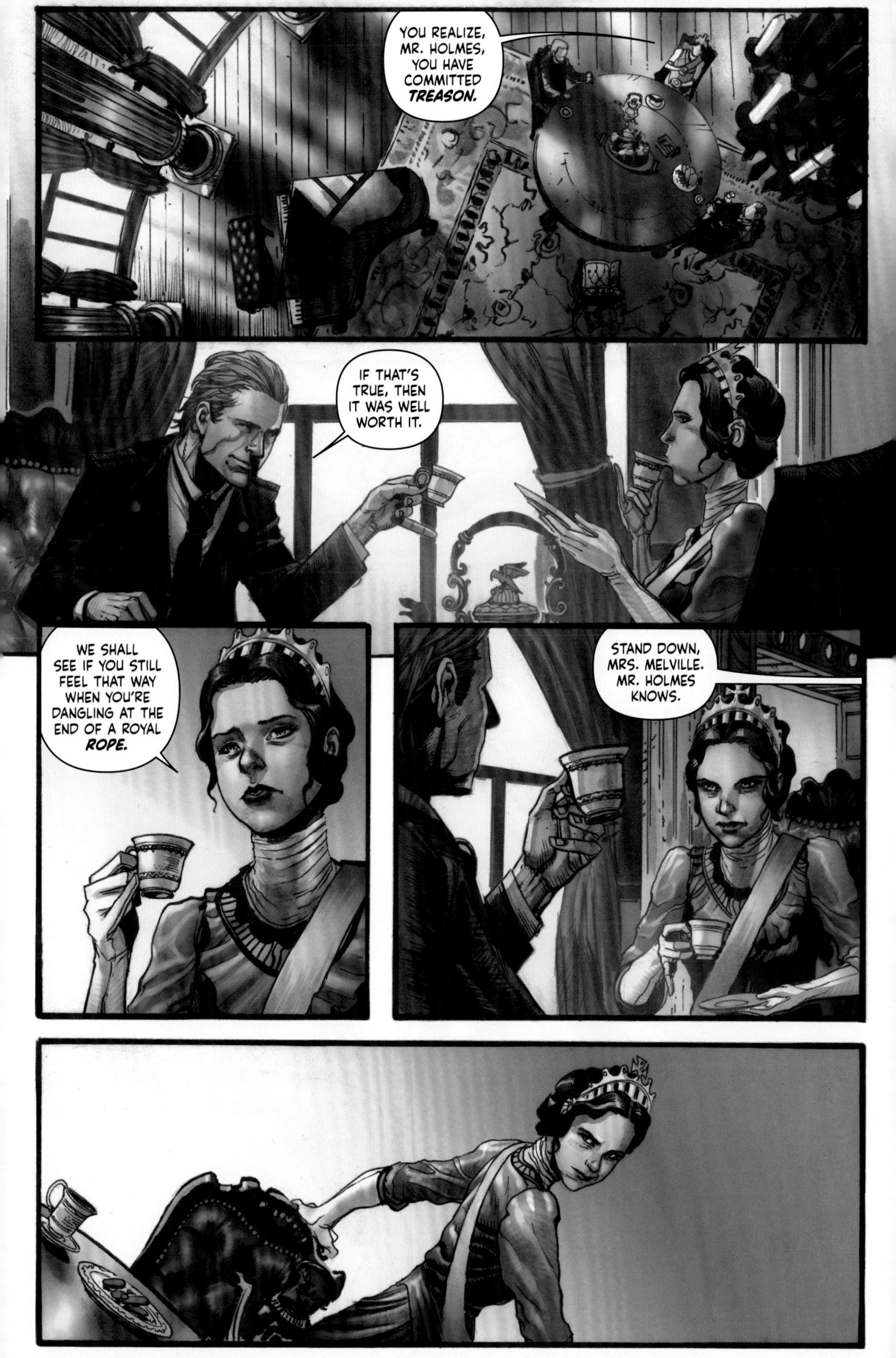
YOU REALIZE, MR. HOLMES, YOU HAVE COMMITTED TREASON.
IF THAT'S TRUE, THEN IT WAS WELL WORTH IT.
WE SHALL SEE IF YOU STILL FEEL THAT WAY WHEN YOU'RE DANGLING AT THE END OF A ROYAL ROPE.
STAND DOWN, MRS. MELVILLE. MR. HOLMES KNOWS.

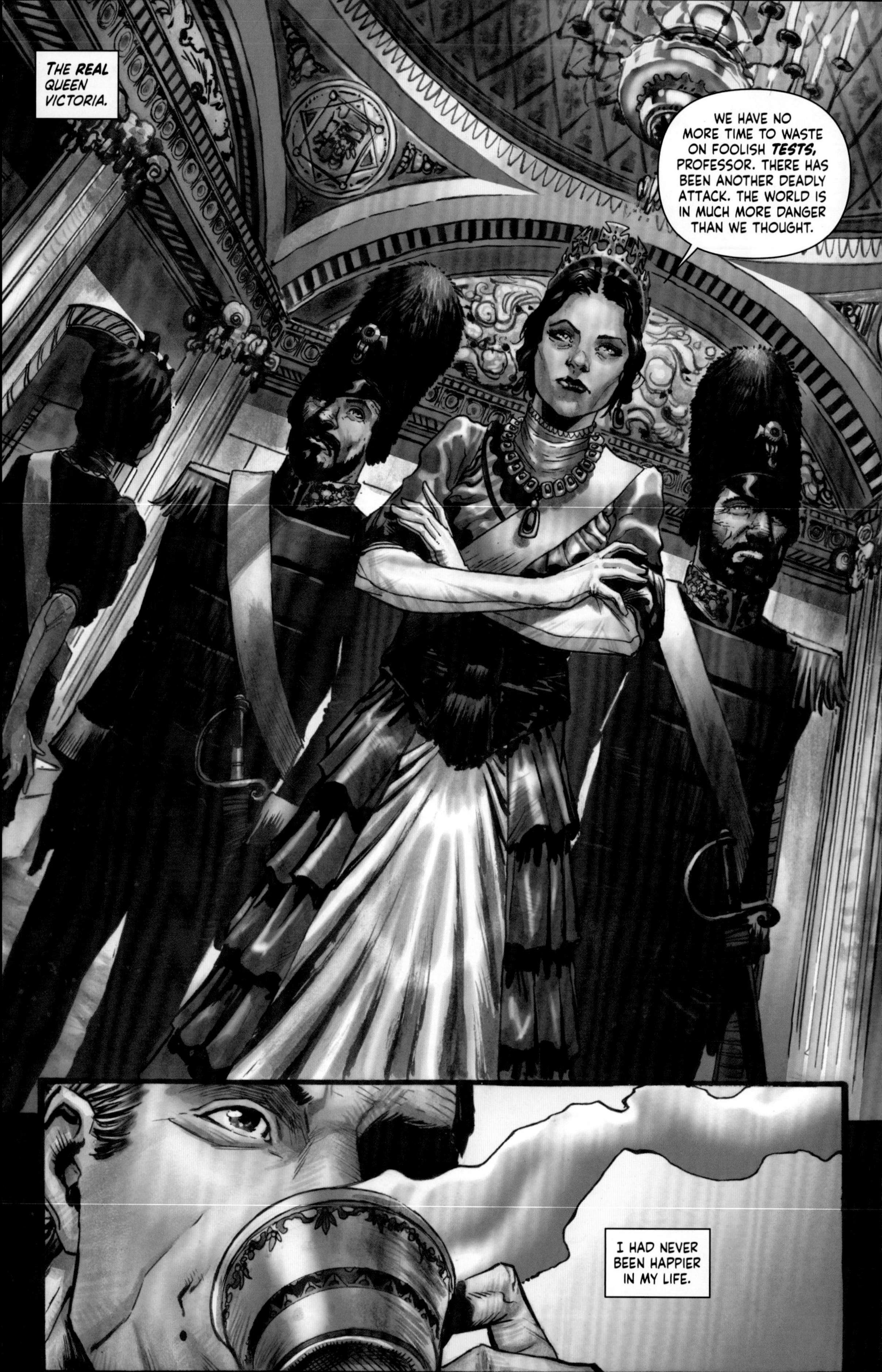
THE REAL QUEEN VICTORIA.
WE HAVE NO MORE TIME TO WASTE ON FOOLISH TESTS, PROFESSOR. THERE HAS BEEN ANOTHER DEADLY ATTACK. THE WORLD IS IN MUCH MORE DANGER THAN WE THOUGHT.
I HAD NEVER BEEN HAPPIER IN MY LIFE.

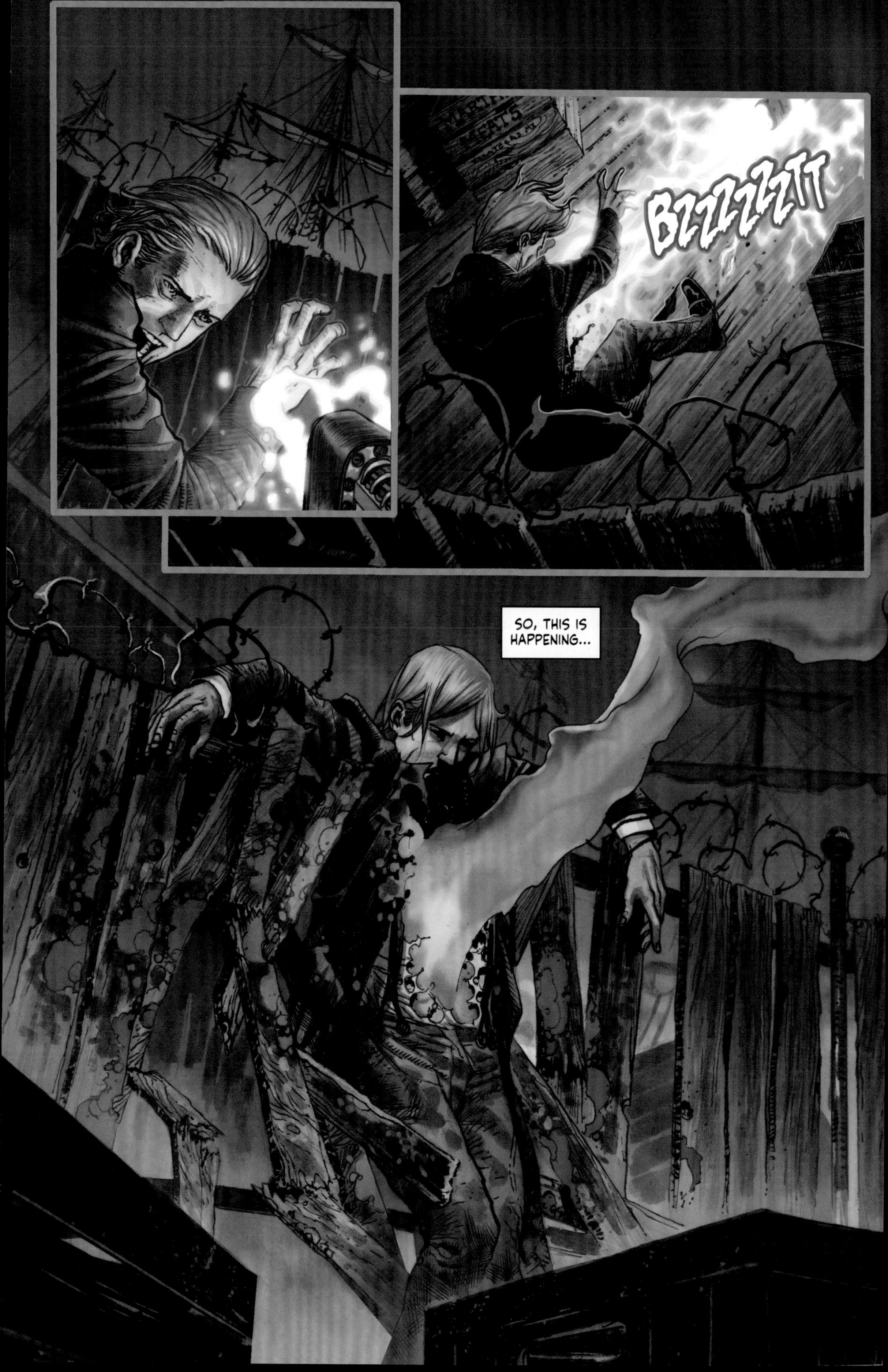
BZZZZZZTT
SO, THIS IS HAPPENING...

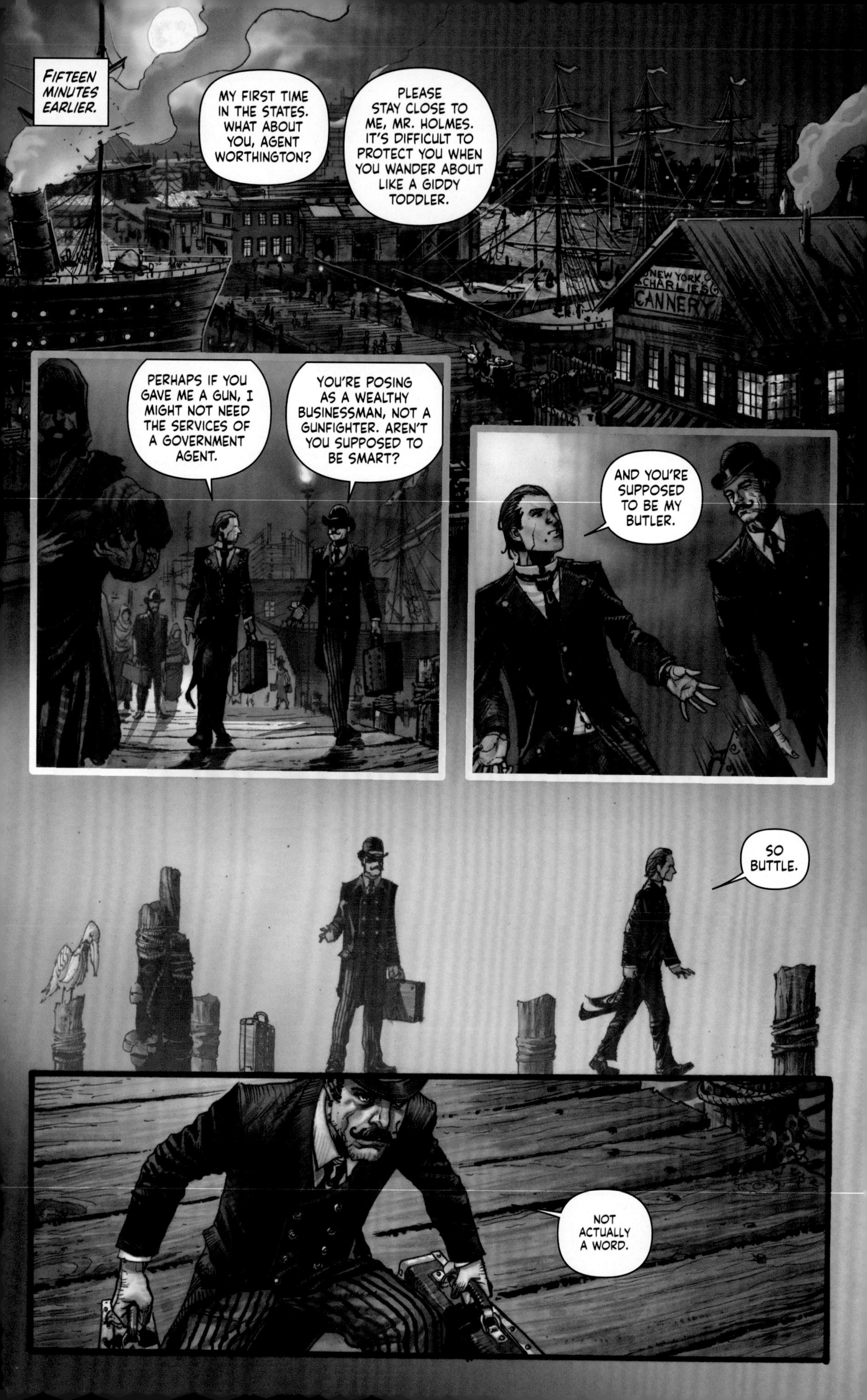
FIFTEEN MINUTES EARLIER.
MY FIRST TIME IN THE STATES. WHAT ABOUT YOU, AGENT WORTHINGTON?
PLEASE STAY CLOSE TO ME, MR. HOLMES. IT'S DIFFICULT TO PROTECT YOU WHEN YOU WANDER ABOUT LIKE A GIDDY TODDLER.
NEW YORK CHARLIE'S CANNERY
PERHAPS IF YOU GAVE ME A GUN, I MIGHT NOT NEED THE SERVICES OF A GOVERNMENT AGENT.
YOU'RE POSING AS A WEALTHY BUSINESSMAN, NOT A GUNFIGHTER. AREN'T YOU SUPPOSED TO BE SMART?
AND YOU'RE SUPPOSED TO BE MY BUTLER.
SO BUTTLE.
NOT ACTUALLY A WORD.

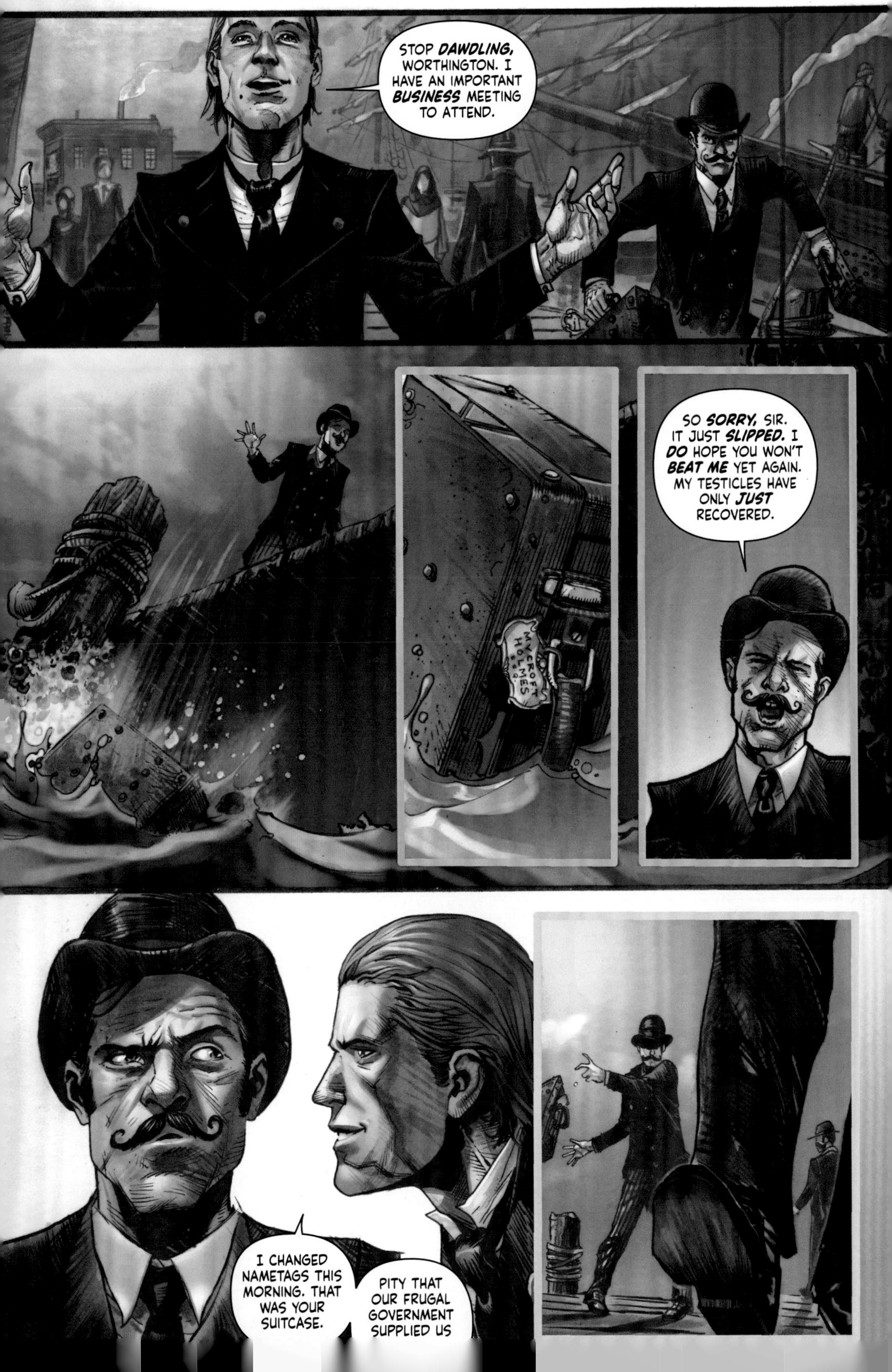
STOP DAWDLING, WORTHINGTON. I HAVE AN IMPORTANT BUSINESS MEETING TO ATTEND.
MYCROFT HOLMES, ESQ.
SO SORRY, SIR. IT JUST SLIPPED. I DO HOPE YOU WON'T BEAT ME YET AGAIN. MY TESTICLES HAVE ONLY JUST RECOVERED.
I CHANGED NAMETAGS THIS MORNING. THAT WAS YOUR SUITCASE.
PITY THAT OUR FRUGAL GOVERNMENT SUPPLIED US

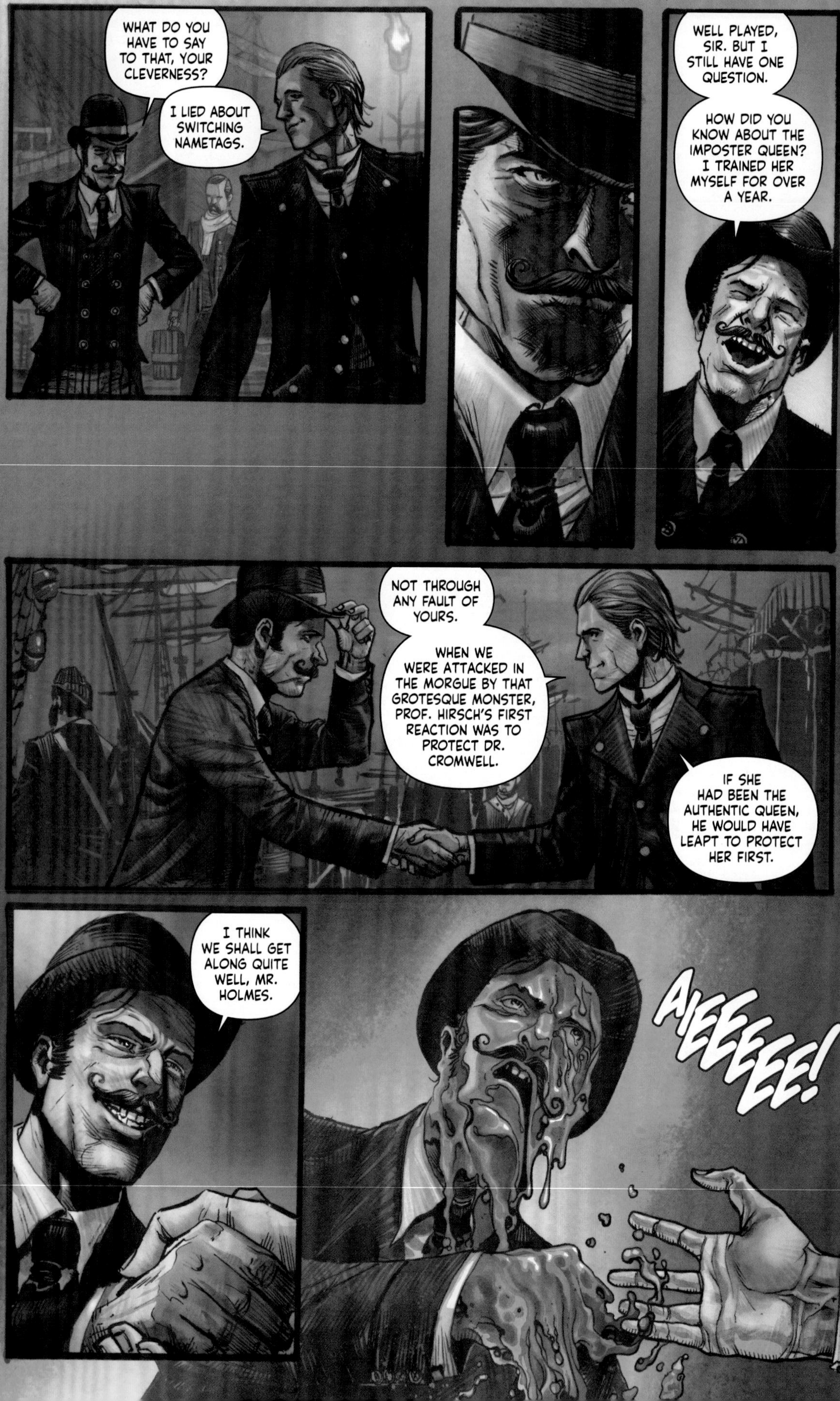
WHAT DO YOU HAVE TO SAY TO THAT, YOUR CLEVERNESS?
I LIED ABOUT SWITCHING NAMETAGS.
WELL PLAYED, SIR. BUT I STILL HAVE ONE QUESTION.
HOW DID YOU KNOW ABOUT THE IMPOSTER QUEEN? I TRAINED HER MYSELF FOR OVER A YEAR.
NOT THROUGH ANY FAULT OF YOURS.
WHEN WE WERE ATTACKED IN THE MORGUE BY THAT GROTESQUE MONSTER, PROF. HIRSCH'S FIRST REACTION WAS TO PROTECT DR. CROMWELL.
IF SHE HAD BEEN THE AUTHENTIC QUEEN, HE WOULD HAVE LEAPT TO PROTECT HER FIRST.
I THINK WE SHALL GET ALONG QUITE WELL, MR. HOLMES.
AIEEEEEEE!

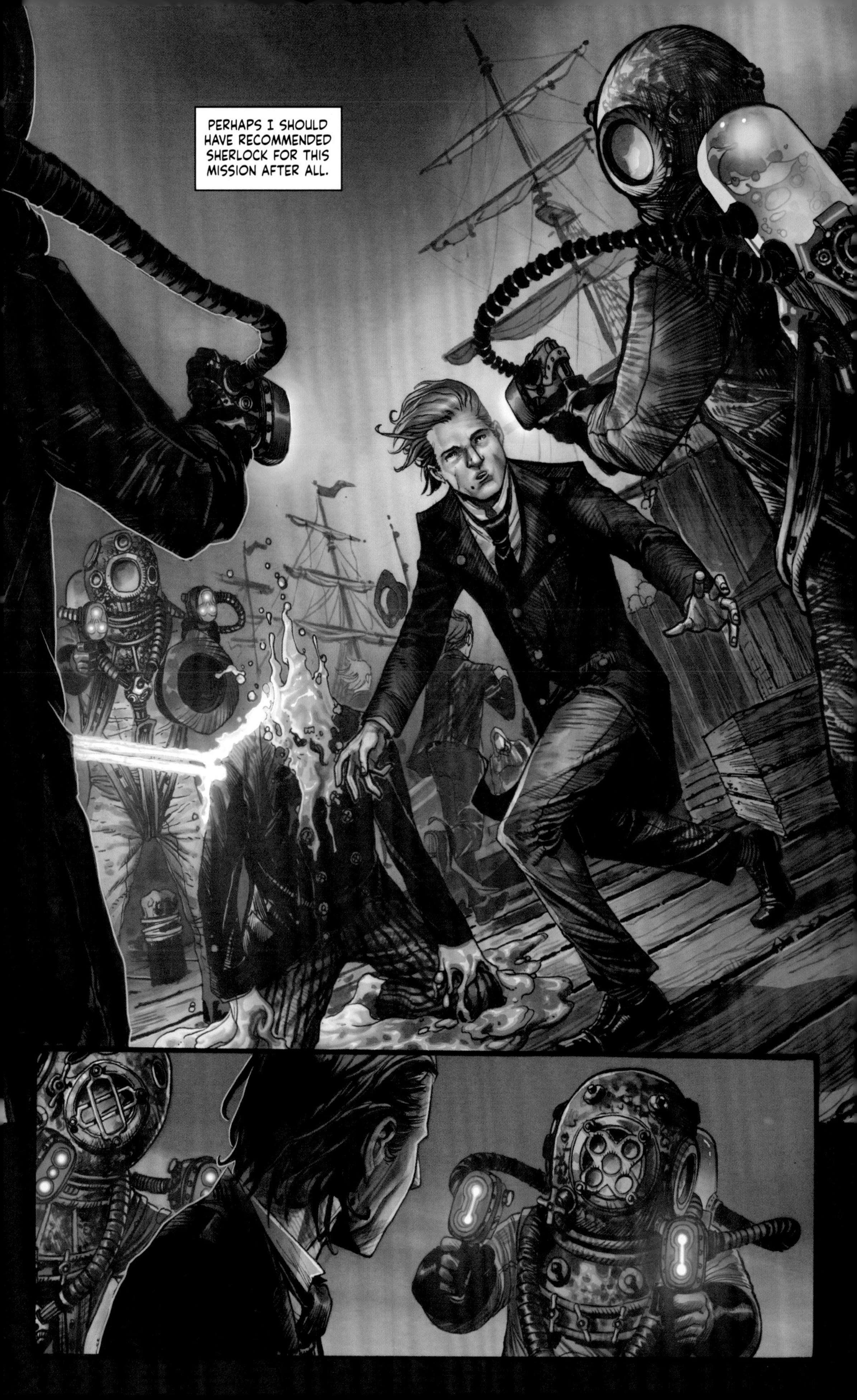
PERHAPS I SHOULD HAVE RECOMMENDED SHERLOCK FOR THIS MISSION AFTER ALL.

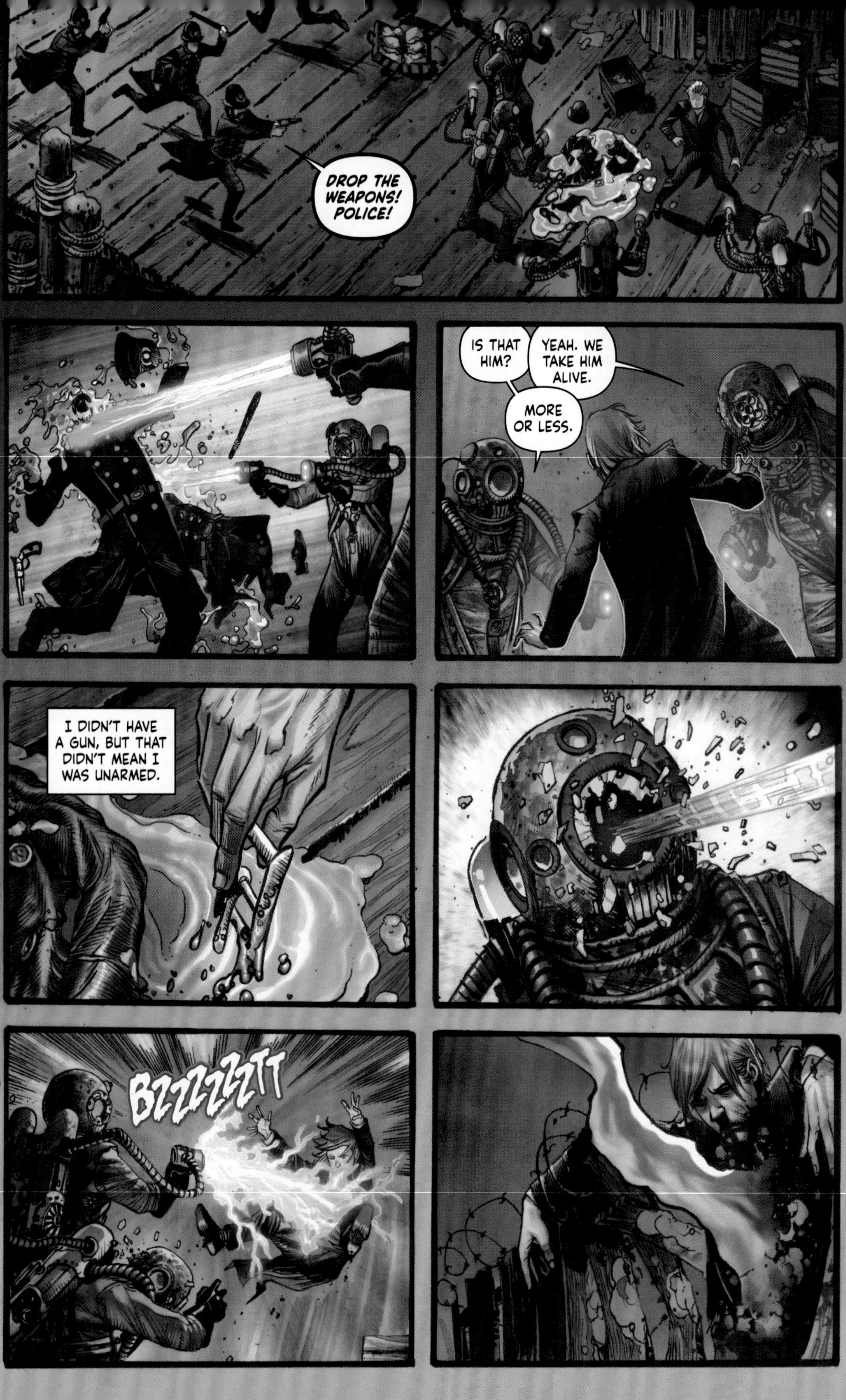
DROP THE WEAPONS! POLICE!
IS THAT HIM?
YEAH. WE TAKE HIM ALIVE.
MORE OR LESS.
I DIDN'T HAVE A GUN, BUT THAT DIDN'T MEAN I WAS UNARMED.
BZZZZZZTT

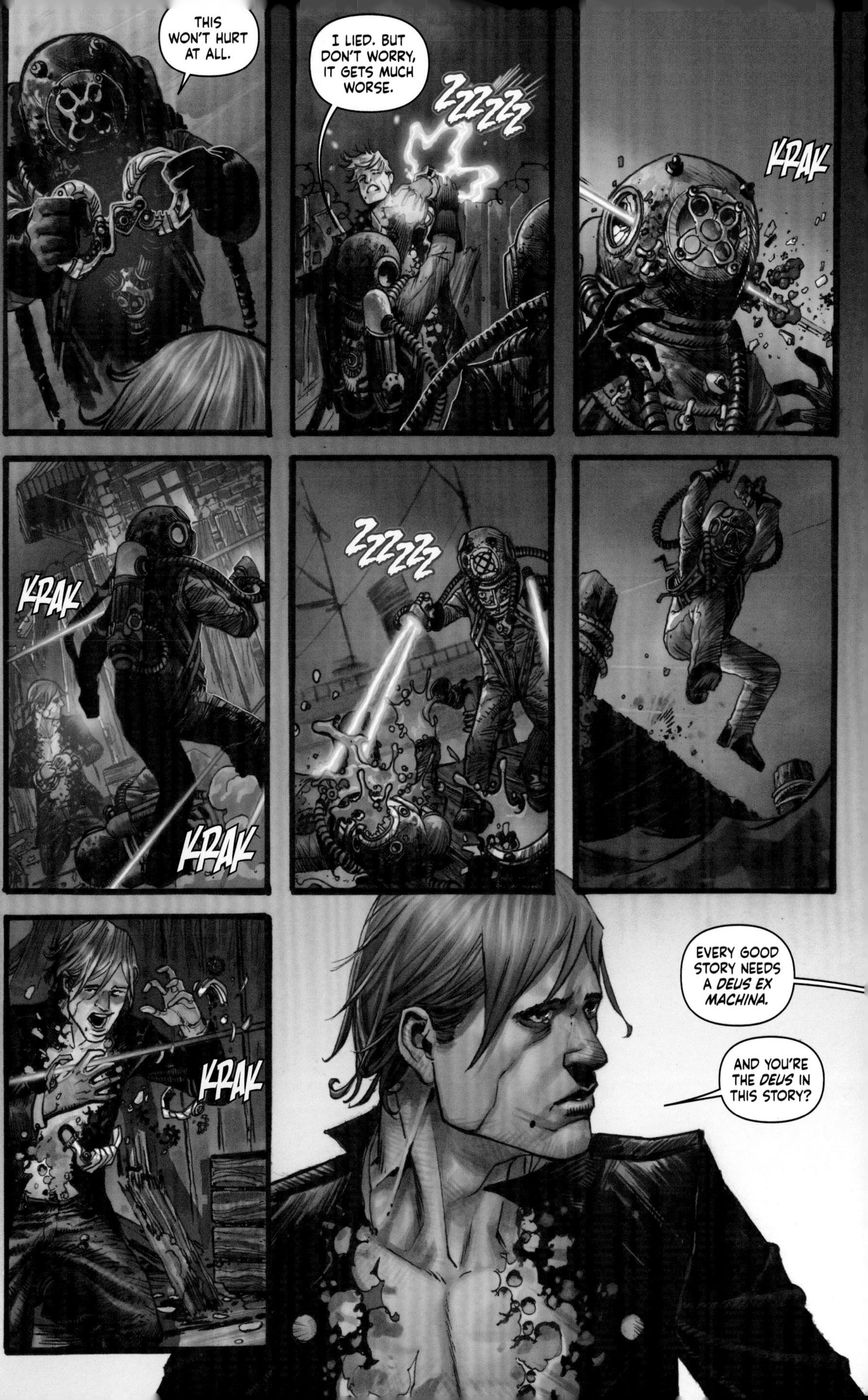

THIS WON'T HURT AT ALL.
I LIED. BUT DON'T WORRY, IT GETS MUCH WORSE.
ZZZZZZ
KRAK
KRAK
KRAK
ZZZZZZ
KRAK
EVERY GOOD STORY NEEDS A *DEUS EX MACHINA.*
AND YOU'RE THE *DEUS* IN THIS STORY?

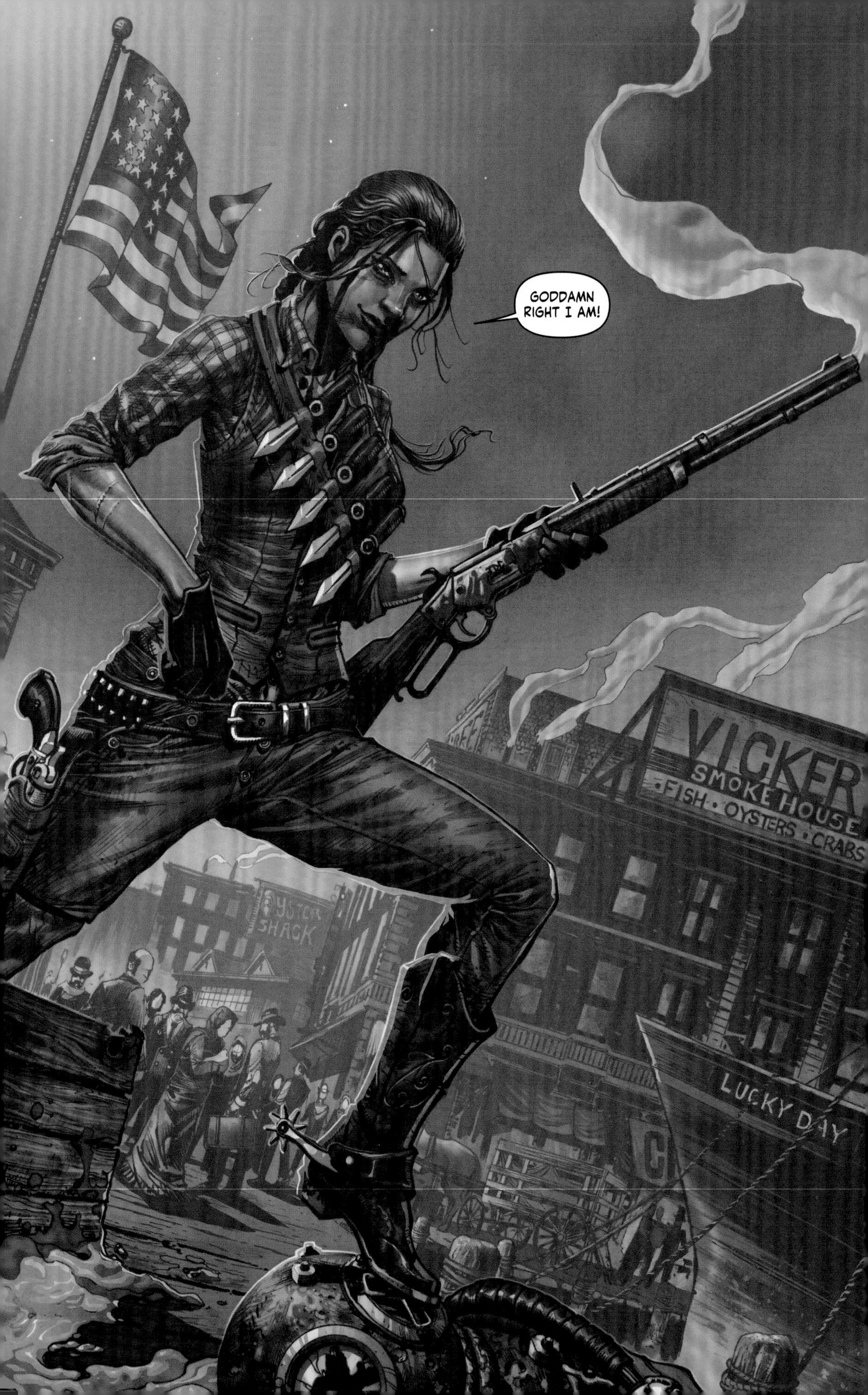
GODDAMN RIGHT I AM!
VICKER
SMOKE HOUSE
FISH · OYSTERS · CRABS
OYSTER SHACK
LUCKY DAY

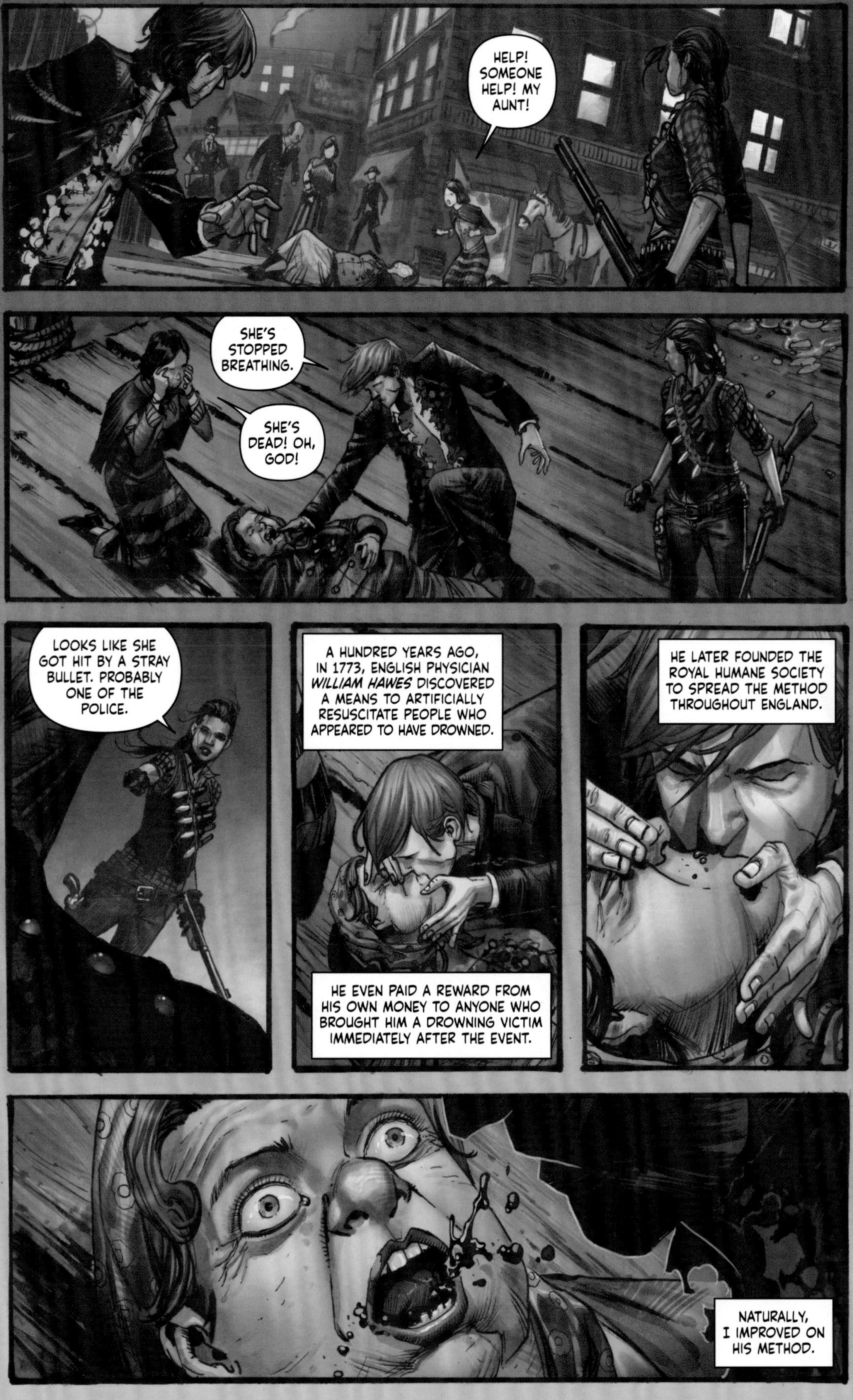
HELP! SOMEONE HELP! MY AUNT!
SHE'S STOPPED BREATHING.
SHE'S DEAD! OH, GOD!
LOOKS LIKE SHE GOT HIT BY A STRAY BULLET. PROBABLY ONE OF THE POLICE.
A HUNDRED YEARS AGO, IN 1773, ENGLISH PHYSICIAN WILLIAM HAWES DISCOVERED A MEANS TO ARTIFICIALLY RESUSCITATE PEOPLE WHO APPEARED TO HAVE DROWNED.
HE EVEN PAID A REWARD FROM HIS OWN MONEY TO ANYONE WHO BROUGHT HIM A DROWNING VICTIM IMMEDIATELY AFTER THE EVENT.
HE LATER FOUNDED THE ROYAL HUMANE SOCIETY TO SPREAD THE METHOD THROUGHOUT ENGLAND.
NATURALLY, I IMPROVED ON HIS METHOD.

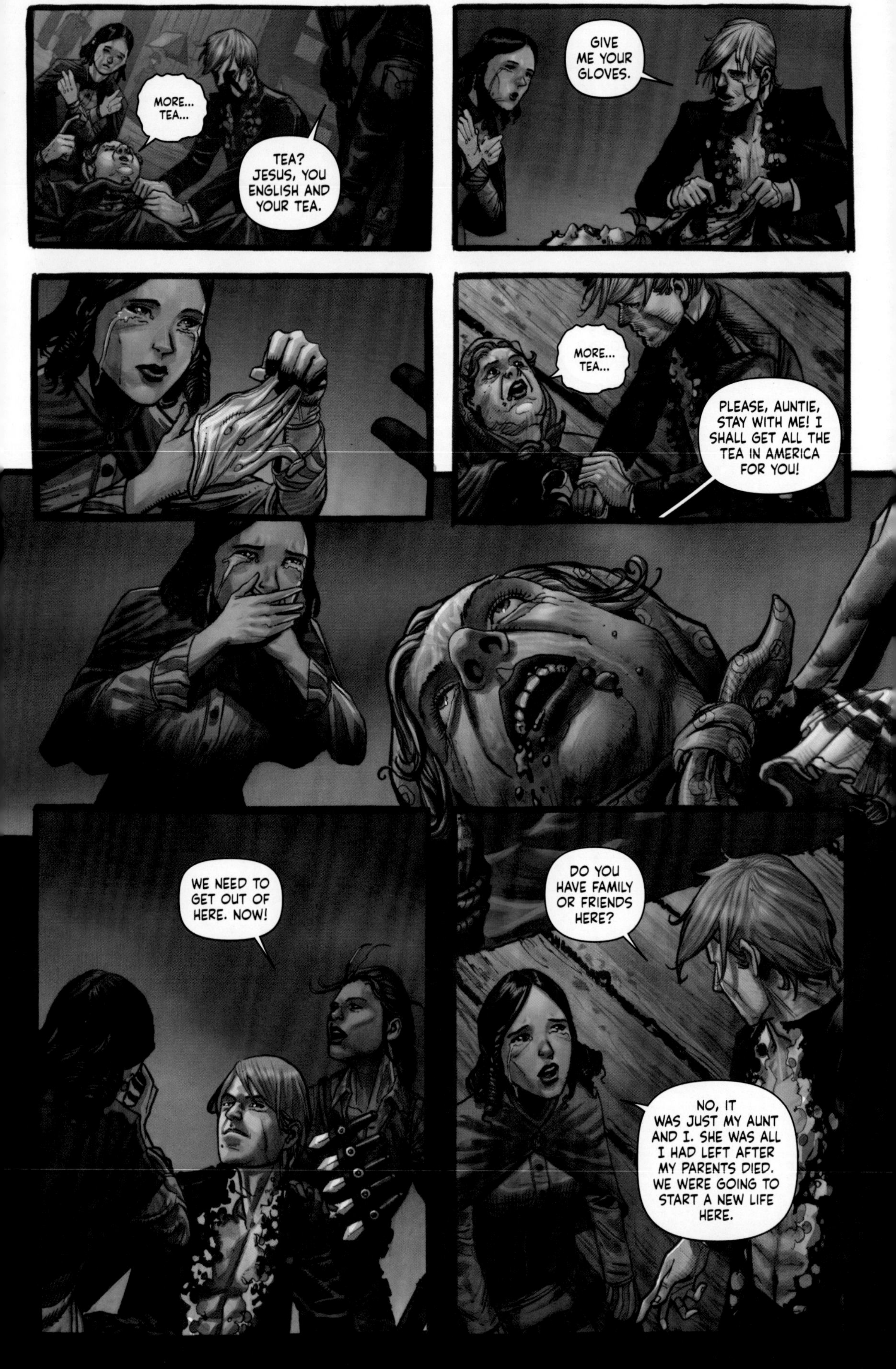
MORE... TEA...
TEA? JESUS, YOU ENGLISH AND YOUR TEA.
GIVE ME YOUR GLOVES.
MORE... TEA...
PLEASE, AUNTIE, STAY WITH ME! I SHALL GET ALL THE TEA IN AMERICA FOR YOU!
WE NEED TO GET OUT OF HERE. NOW!
DO YOU HAVE FAMILY OR FRIENDS HERE?
NO, IT WAS JUST MY AUNT AND I. SHE WAS ALL I HAD LEFT AFTER MY PARENTS DIED. WE WERE GOING TO START A NEW LIFE HERE.

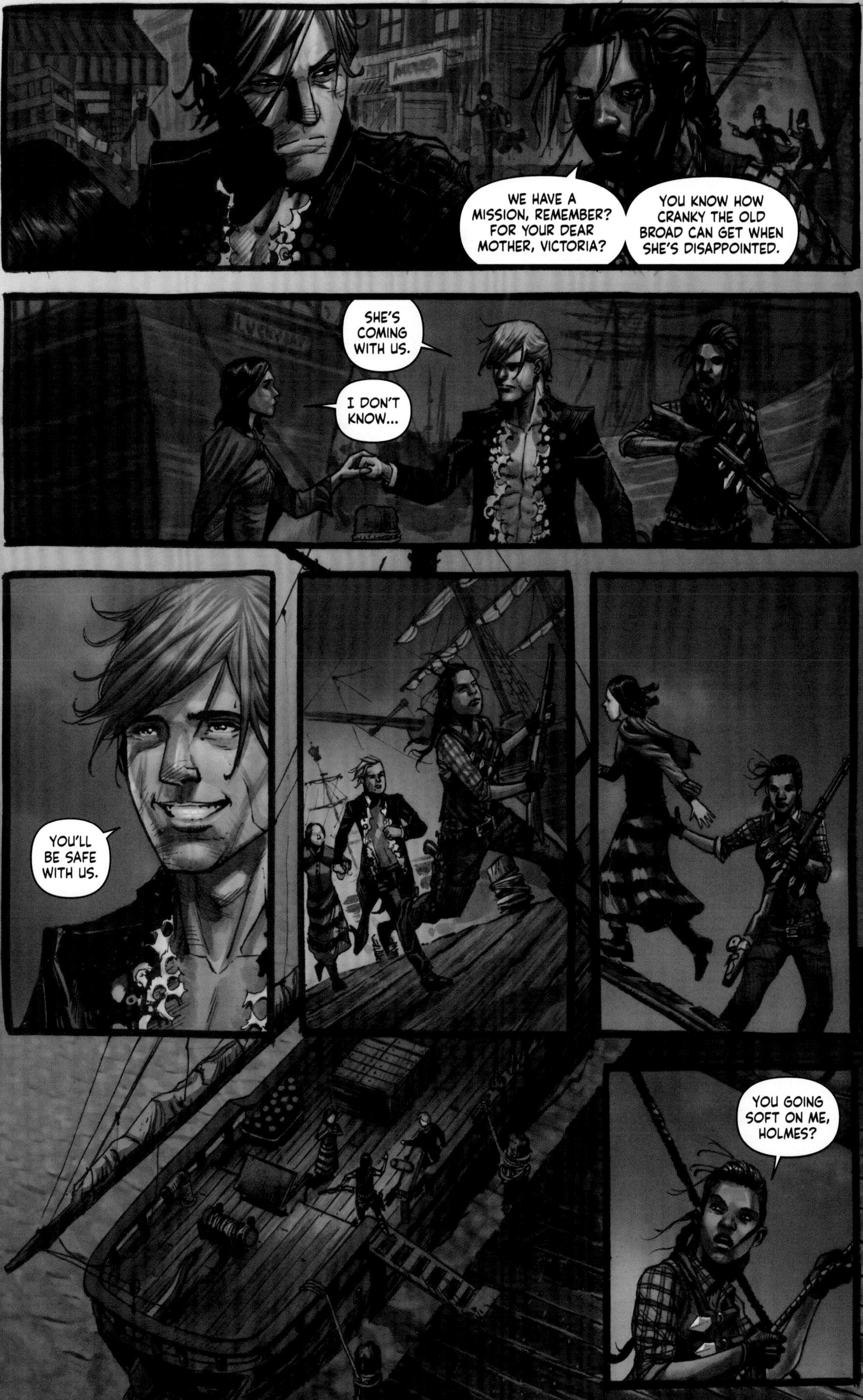
WE HAVE A MISSION, REMEMBER? FOR YOUR DEAR MOTHER, VICTORIA?
YOU KNOW HOW CRANKY THE OLD BROAD CAN GET WHEN SHE'S DISAPPOINTED.
SHE'S COMING WITH US.
I DON'T KNOW...
YOU'LL BE SAFE WITH US.
YOU GOING SOFT ON ME, HOLMES?

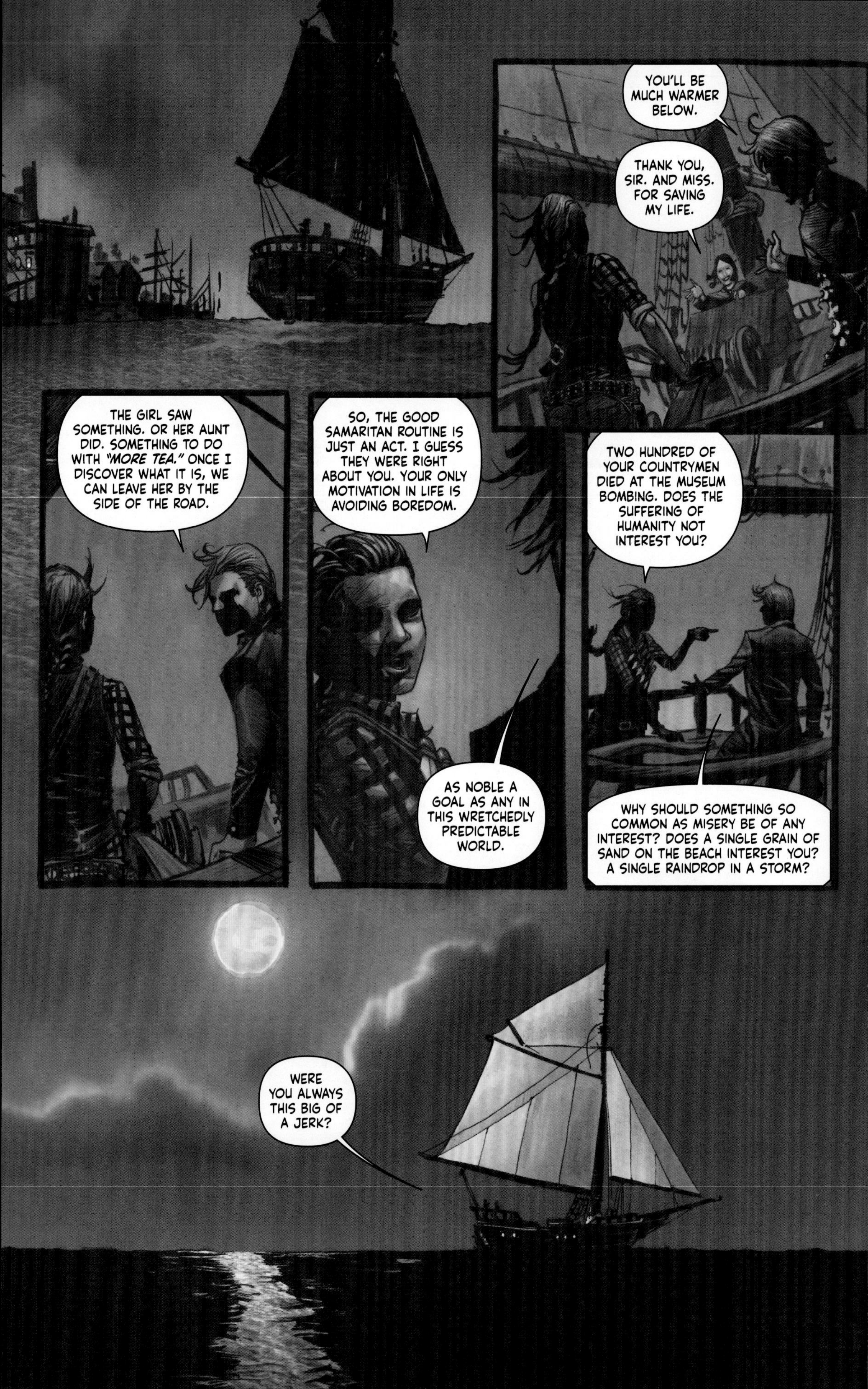
YOU'LL BE MUCH WARMER BELOW.
THANK YOU, SIR. AND MISS. FOR SAVING MY LIFE.
THE GIRL SAW SOMETHING. OR HER AUNT DID. SOMETHING TO DO WITH "MORE TEA." ONCE I DISCOVER WHAT IT IS, WE CAN LEAVE HER BY THE SIDE OF THE ROAD.
SO, THE GOOD SAMARITAN ROUTINE IS JUST AN ACT. I GUESS THEY WERE RIGHT ABOUT YOU. YOUR ONLY MOTIVATION IN LIFE IS AVOIDING BOREDOM.
AS NOBLE A GOAL AS ANY IN THIS WRETCHEDLY PREDICTABLE WORLD.
TWO HUNDRED OF YOUR COUNTRYMEN DIED AT THE MUSEUM BOMBING. DOES THE SUFFERING OF HUMANITY NOT INTEREST YOU?
WHY SHOULD SOMETHING SO COMMON AS MISERY BE OF ANY INTEREST? DOES A SINGLE GRAIN OF SAND ON THE BEACH INTEREST YOU? A SINGLE RAINDROP IN A STORM?
WERE YOU ALWAYS THIS BIG OF A JERK?

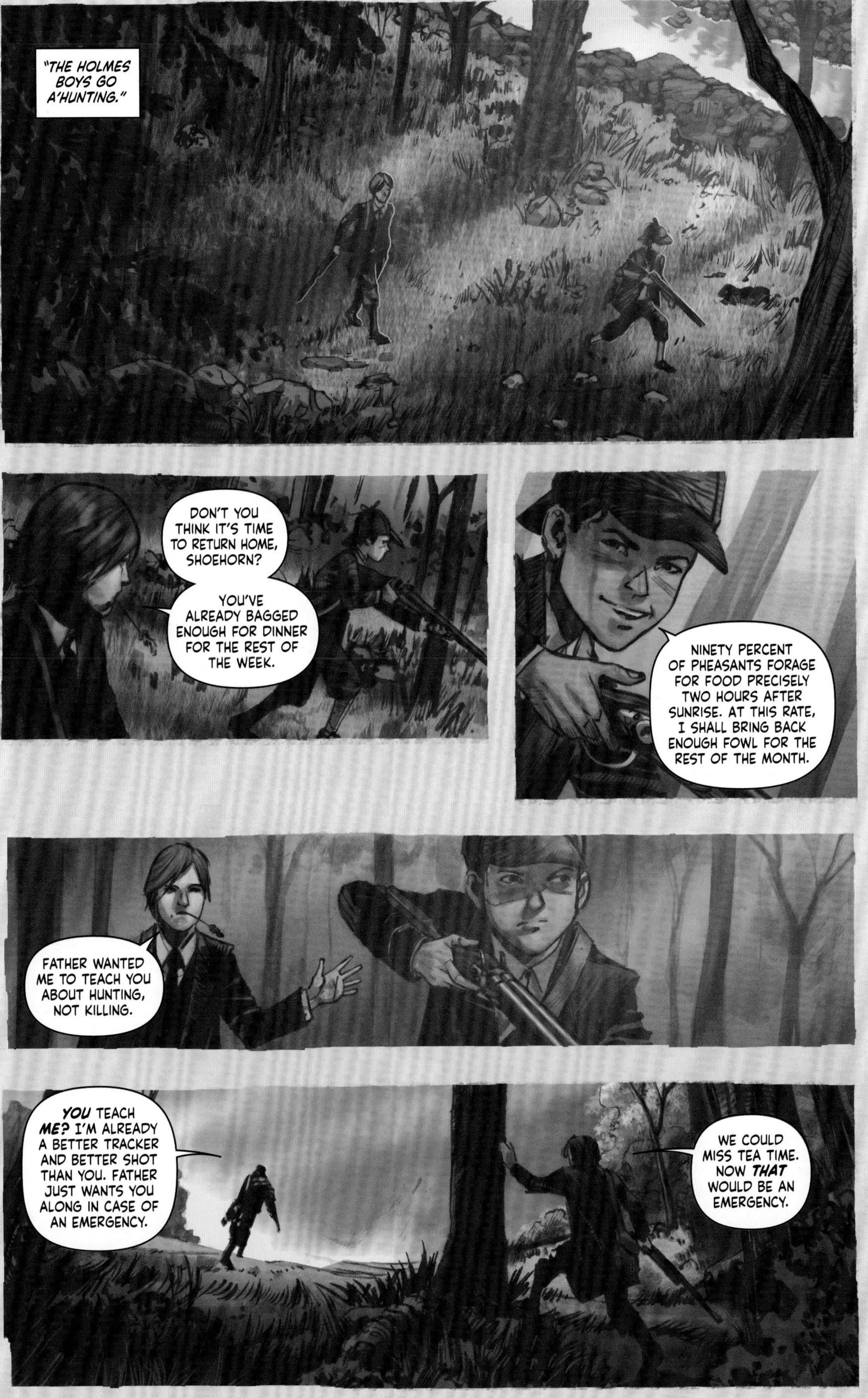
"THE HOLMES BOYS GO A'HUNTING."
DON'T YOU THINK IT'S TIME TO RETURN HOME, SHOEHORN?
YOU'VE ALREADY BAGGED ENOUGH FOR DINNER FOR THE REST OF THE WEEK.
NINETY PERCENT OF PHEASANTS FORAGE FOR FOOD PRECISELY TWO HOURS AFTER SUNRISE. AT THIS RATE, I SHALL BRING BACK ENOUGH FOWL FOR THE REST OF THE MONTH.
FATHER WANTED ME TO TEACH YOU ABOUT HUNTING, NOT KILLING.
YOU TEACH ME? I'M ALREADY A BETTER TRACKER AND BETTER SHOT THAN YOU. FATHER JUST WANTS YOU ALONG IN CASE OF AN EMERGENCY.
WE COULD MISS TEA TIME. NOW THAT WOULD BE AN EMERGENCY.

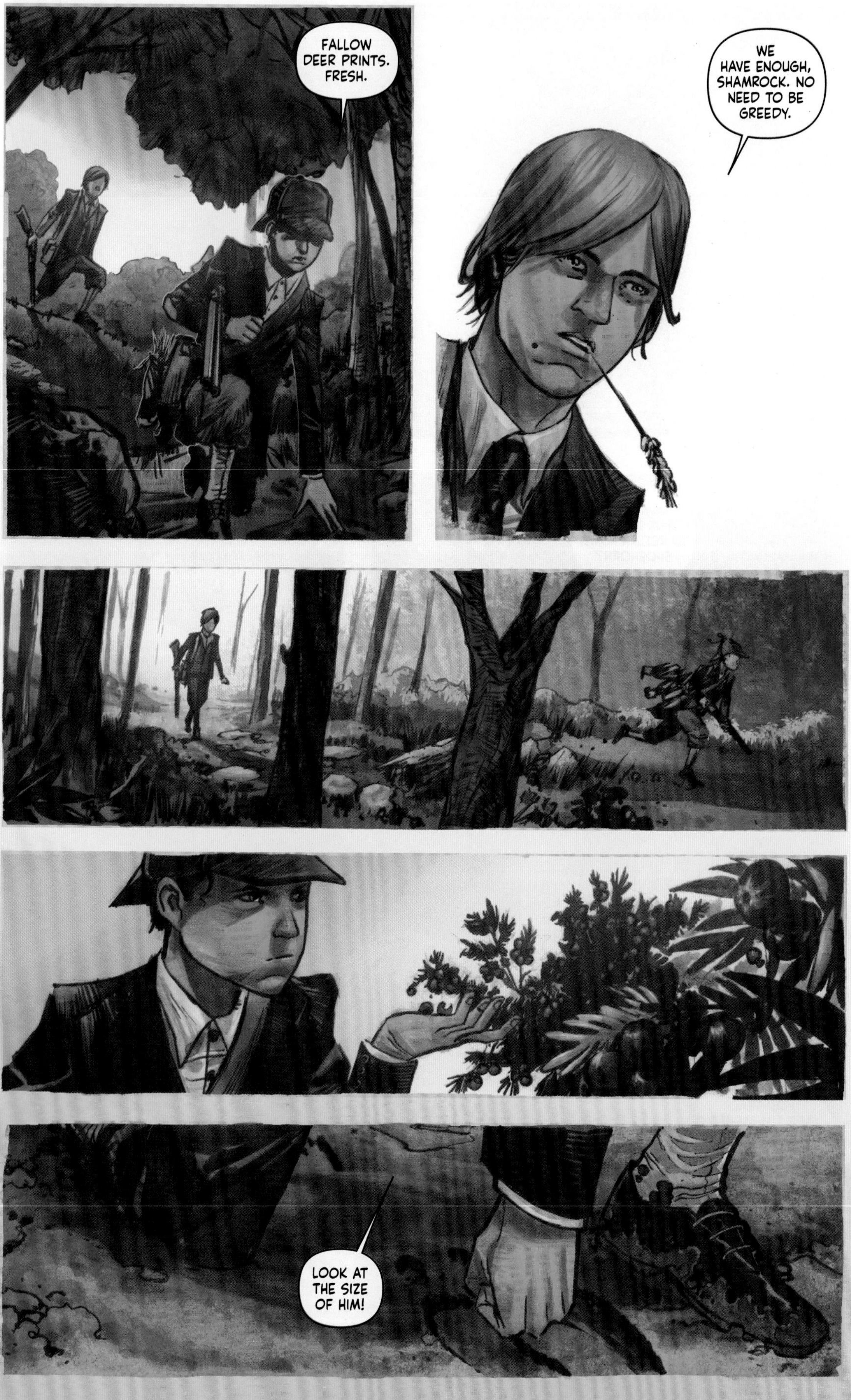
FALLOW DEER PRINTS. FRESH.
WE HAVE ENOUGH, SHAMROCK. NO NEED TO BE GREEDY.
LOOK AT THE SIZE OF HIM!

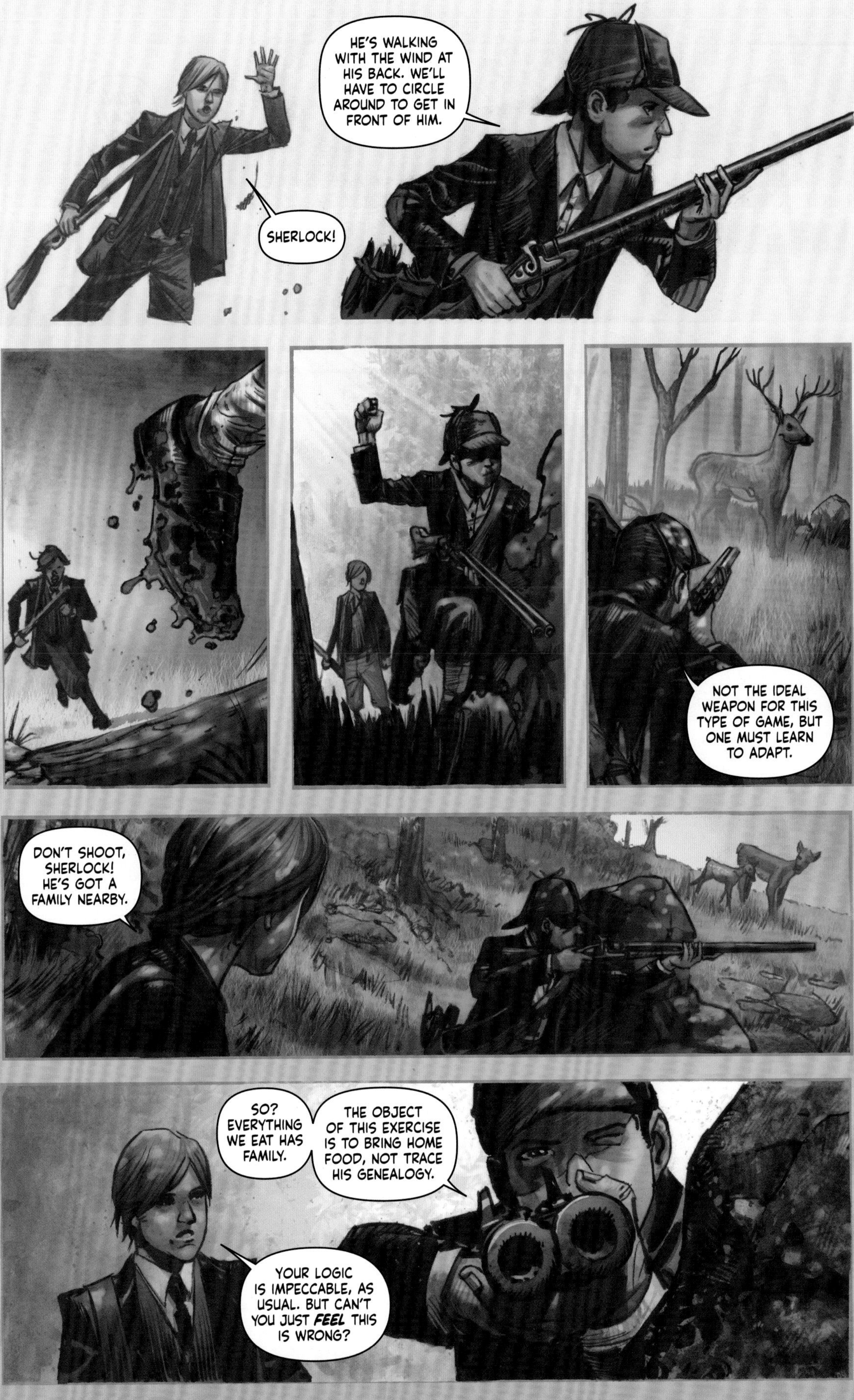
HE'S WALKING WITH THE WIND AT HIS BACK. WE'LL HAVE TO CIRCLE AROUND TO GET IN FRONT OF HIM.
SHERLOCK!
NOT THE IDEAL WEAPON FOR THIS TYPE OF GAME, BUT ONE MUST LEARN TO ADAPT.
DON'T SHOOT, SHERLOCK! HE'S GOT A FAMILY NEARBY.
SO? EVERYTHING WE EAT HAS FAMILY.
THE OBJECT OF THIS EXERCISE IS TO BRING HOME FOOD, NOT TRACE HIS GENEALOGY.
YOUR LOGIC IS IMPECCABLE, AS USUAL. BUT CAN'T YOU JUST *FEEL* THIS IS WRONG?

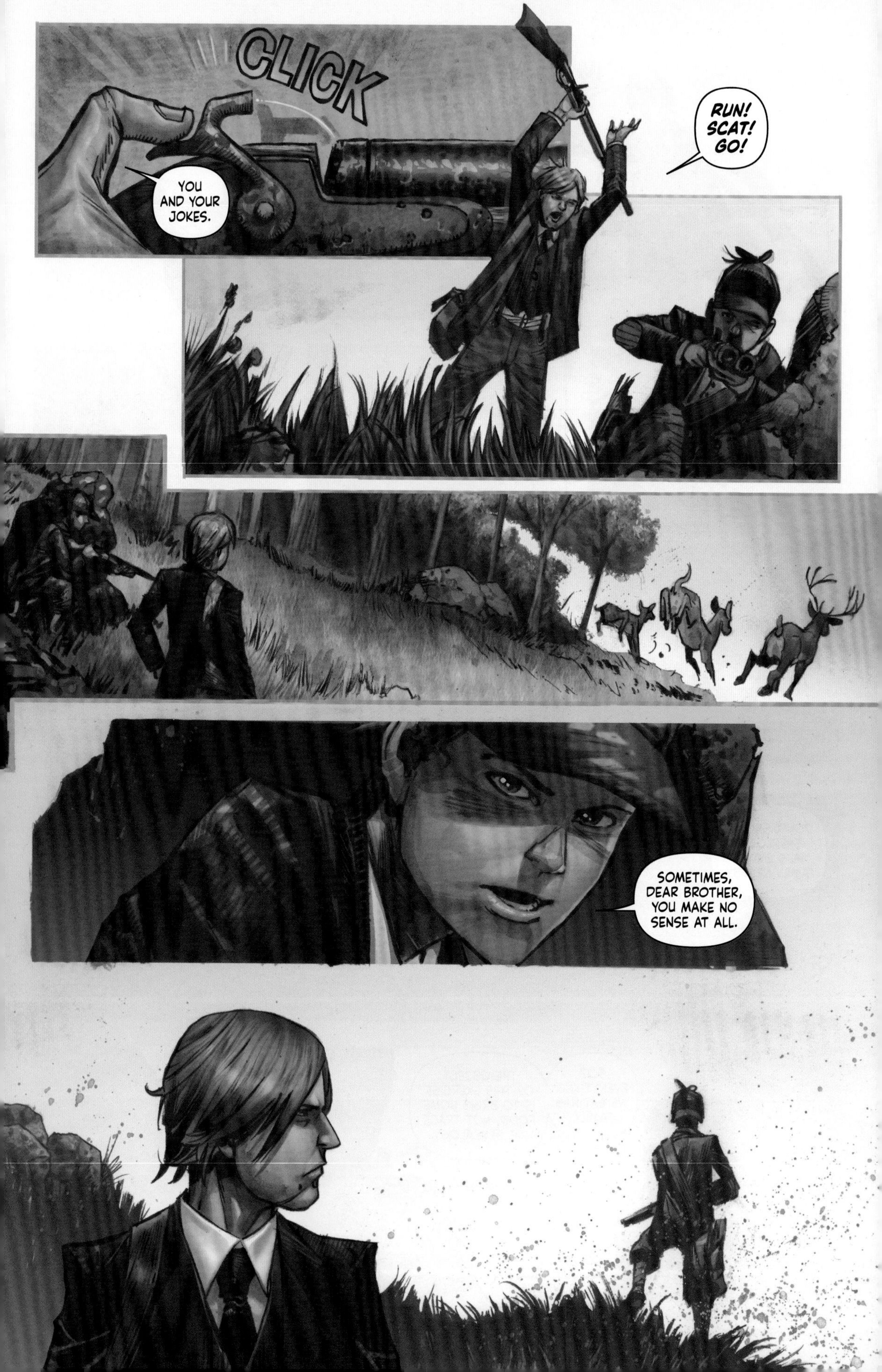
CLICK
YOU AND YOUR JOKES.
RUN! SCAT! GO!
SOMETIMES, DEAR BROTHER, YOU MAKE NO SENSE AT ALL.

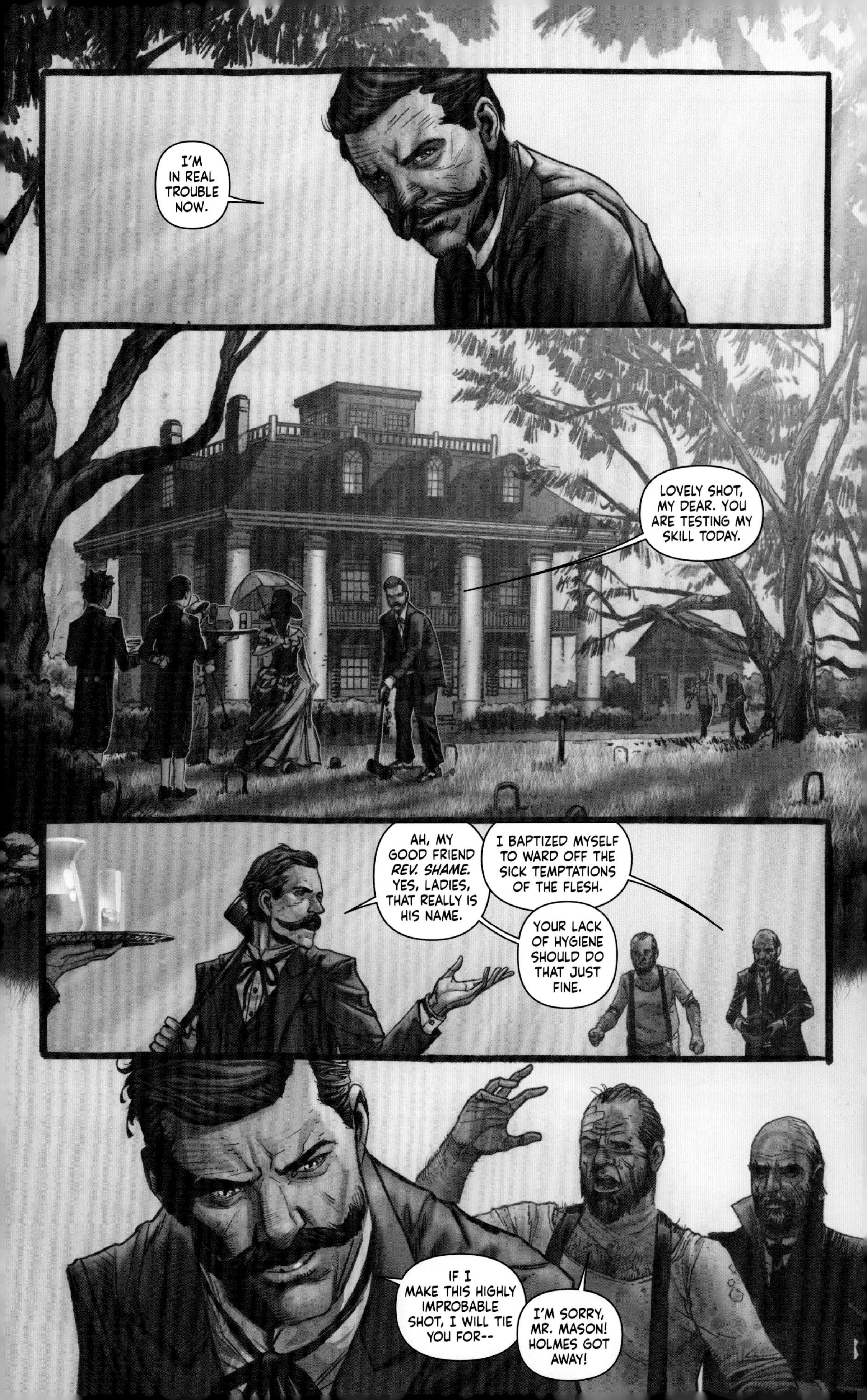
I'M IN REAL TROUBLE NOW.
LOVELY SHOT, MY DEAR. YOU ARE TESTING MY SKILL TODAY.
AH, MY GOOD FRIEND *REV. SHAME.* YES, LADIES, THAT REALLY IS HIS NAME.
I BAPTIZED MYSELF TO WARD OFF THE SICK TEMPTATIONS OF THE FLESH.
YOUR LACK OF HYGIENE SHOULD DO THAT JUST FINE.
IF I MAKE THIS HIGHLY IMPROBABLE SHOT, I WILL TIE YOU FOR--
I'M SORRY, MR. MASON! HOLMES GOT AWAY!

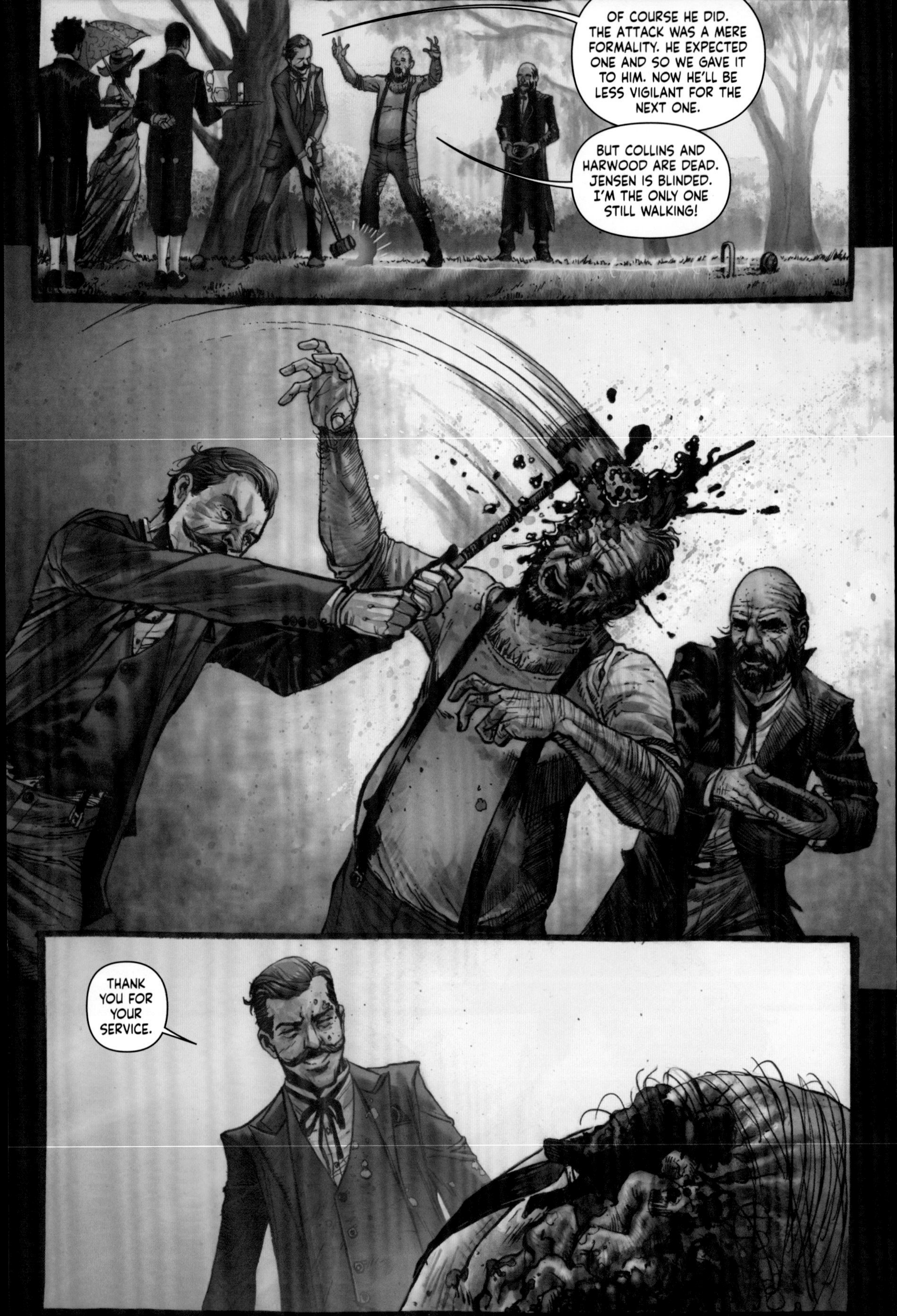
OF COURSE HE DID. THE ATTACK WAS A MERE FORMALITY. HE EXPECTED ONE AND SO WE GAVE IT TO HIM. NOW HE'LL BE LESS VIGILANT FOR THE NEXT ONE.
BUT COLLINS AND HARWOOD ARE DEAD. JENSEN IS BLINDED. I'M THE ONLY ONE STILL WALKING!
THANK YOU FOR YOUR SERVICE.

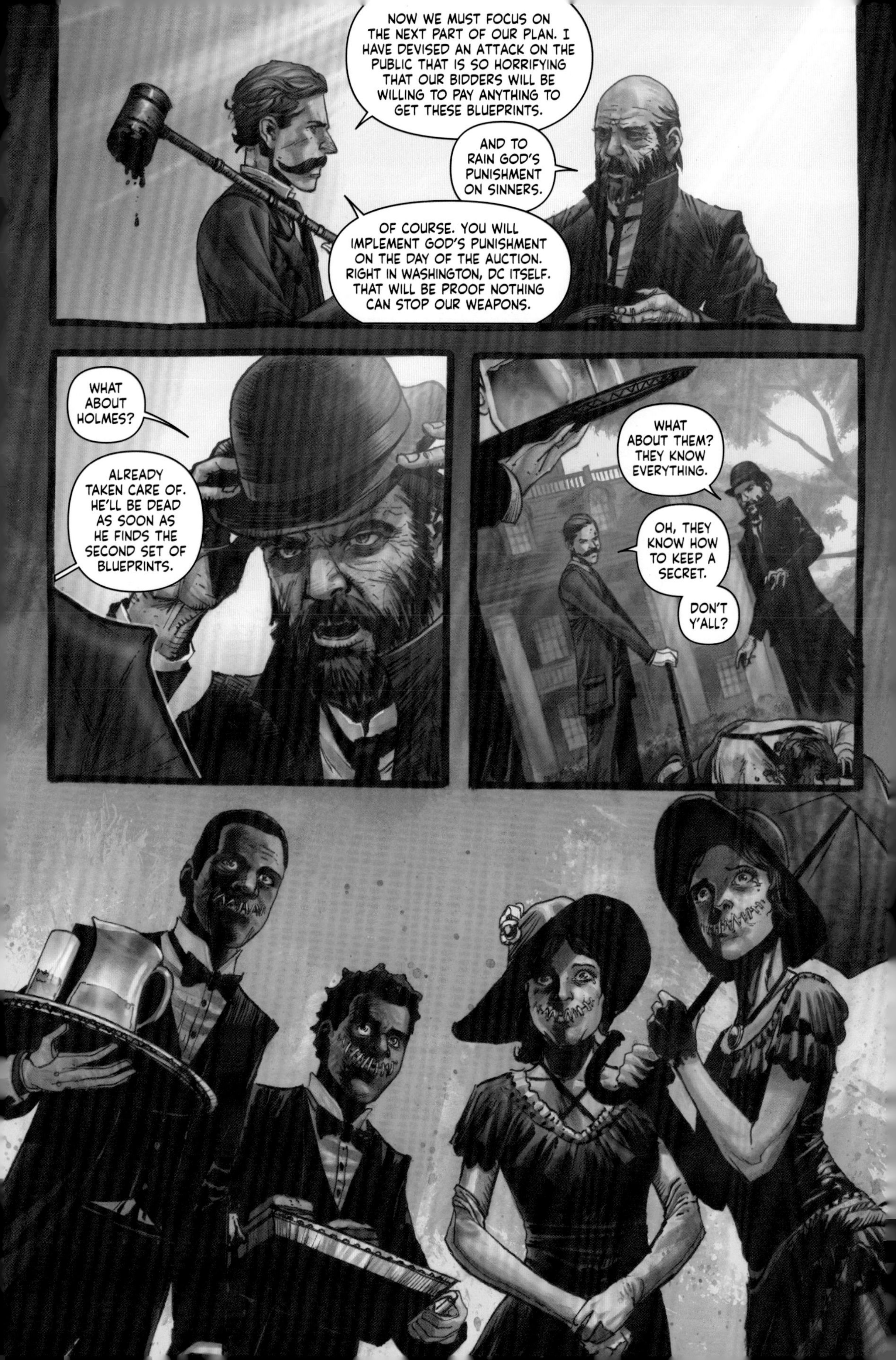
NOW WE MUST FOCUS ON THE NEXT PART OF OUR PLAN. I HAVE DEVISED AN ATTACK ON THE PUBLIC THAT IS SO HORRIFYING THAT OUR BIDDERS WILL BE WILLING TO PAY ANYTHING TO GET THESE BLUEPRINTS.
AND TO RAIN GOD'S PUNISHMENT ON SINNERS.
OF COURSE. YOU WILL IMPLEMENT GOD'S PUNISHMENT ON THE DAY OF THE AUCTION. RIGHT IN WASHINGTON, DC ITSELF. THAT WILL BE PROOF NOTHING CAN STOP OUR WEAPONS.
WHAT ABOUT HOLMES?
ALREADY TAKEN CARE OF. HE'LL BE DEAD AS SOON AS HE FINDS THE SECOND SET OF BLUEPRINTS.
WHAT ABOUT THEM? THEY KNOW EVERYTHING.
OH, THEY KNOW HOW TO KEEP A SECRET.
DON'T Y'ALL?

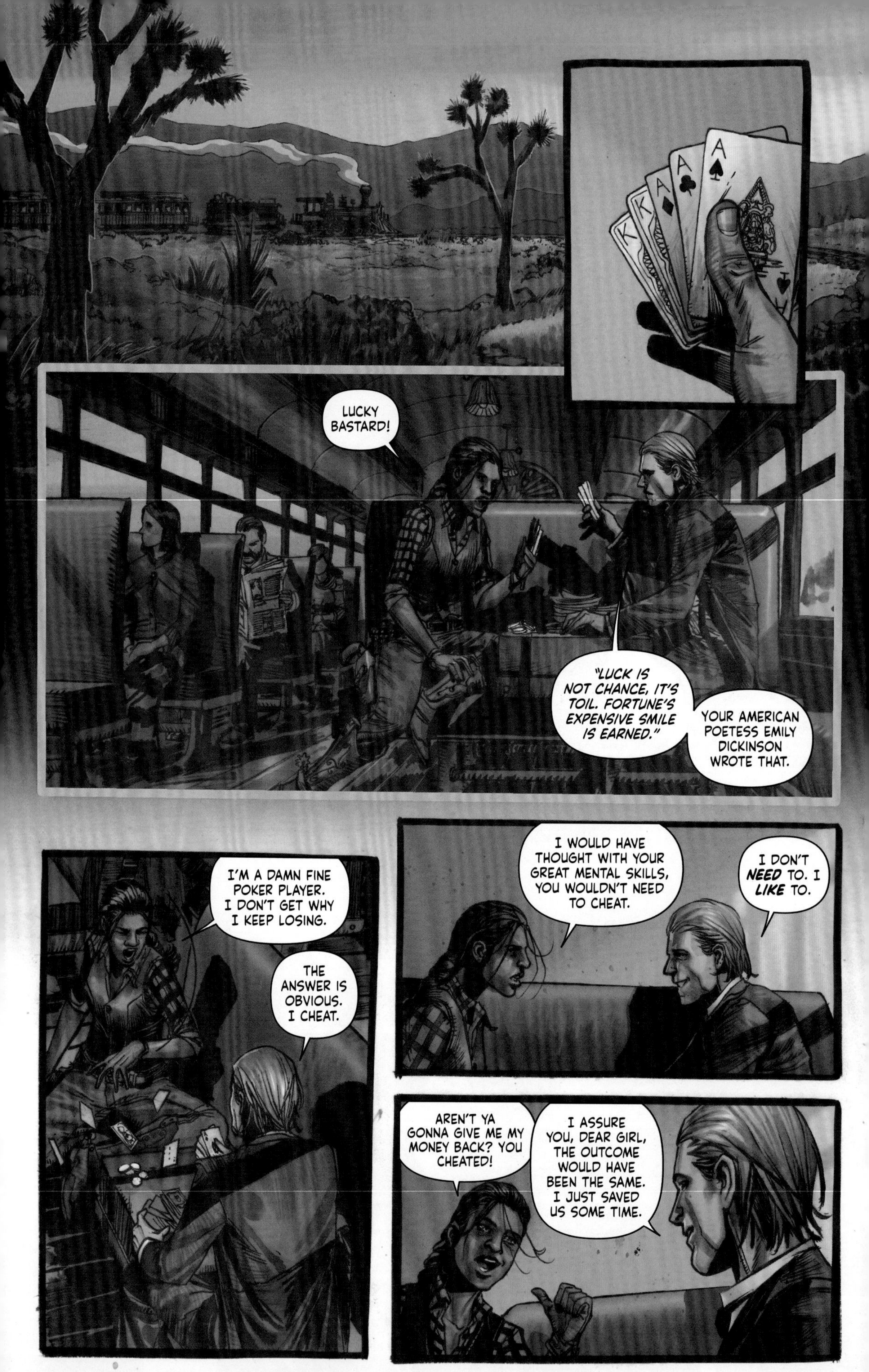

LUCKY BASTARD!
"LUCK IS NOT CHANCE, IT'S TOIL. FORTUNE'S EXPENSIVE SMILE IS EARNED."
YOUR AMERICAN POETESS EMILY DICKINSON WROTE THAT.
I'M A DAMN FINE POKER PLAYER. I DON'T GET WHY I KEEP LOSING.
THE ANSWER IS OBVIOUS. I CHEAT.
I WOULD HAVE THOUGHT WITH YOUR GREAT MENTAL SKILLS, YOU WOULDN'T NEED TO CHEAT.
I DON'T NEED TO. I LIKE TO.
AREN'T YA GONNA GIVE ME MY MONEY BACK? YOU CHEATED!
I ASSURE YOU, DEAR GIRL, THE OUTCOME WOULD HAVE BEEN THE SAME. I JUST SAVED US SOME TIME.

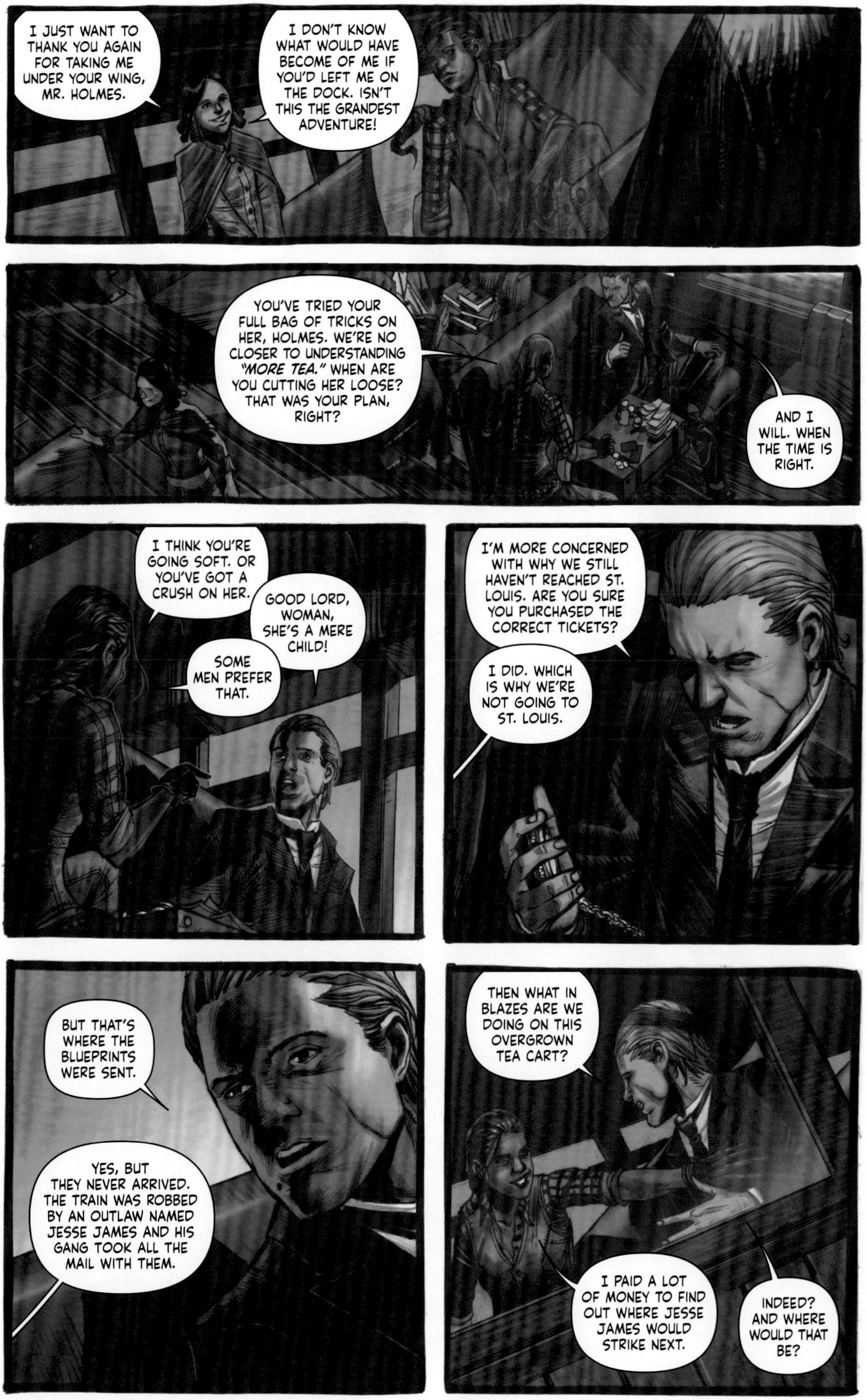
I JUST WANT TO THANK YOU AGAIN FOR TAKING ME UNDER YOUR WING, MR. HOLMES.
I DON'T KNOW WHAT WOULD HAVE BECOME OF ME IF YOU'D LEFT ME ON THE DOCK. ISN'T THIS THE GRANDEST ADVENTURE!
YOU'VE TRIED YOUR FULL BAG OF TRICKS ON HER, HOLMES. WE'RE NO CLOSER TO UNDERSTANDING *"MORE TEA."* WHEN ARE YOU CUTTING HER LOOSE? THAT WAS YOUR PLAN, RIGHT?
AND I WILL. WHEN THE TIME IS RIGHT.
I THINK YOU'RE GOING SOFT. OR YOU'VE GOT A CRUSH ON HER.
GOOD LORD, WOMAN, SHE'S A MERE CHILD!
SOME MEN PREFER THAT.
I'M MORE CONCERNED WITH WHY WE STILL HAVEN'T REACHED ST. LOUIS. ARE YOU SURE YOU PURCHASED THE CORRECT TICKETS?
I DID. WHICH IS WHY WE'RE NOT GOING TO ST. LOUIS.
BUT THAT'S WHERE THE BLUEPRINTS WERE SENT.
YES, BUT THEY NEVER ARRIVED. THE TRAIN WAS ROBBED BY AN OUTLAW NAMED JESSE JAMES AND HIS GANG TOOK ALL THE MAIL WITH THEM.
THEN WHAT IN BLAZES ARE WE DOING ON THIS OVERGROWN TEA CART?
I PAID A LOT OF MONEY TO FIND OUT WHERE JESSE JAMES WOULD STRIKE NEXT.
INDEED? AND WHERE WOULD THAT BE?

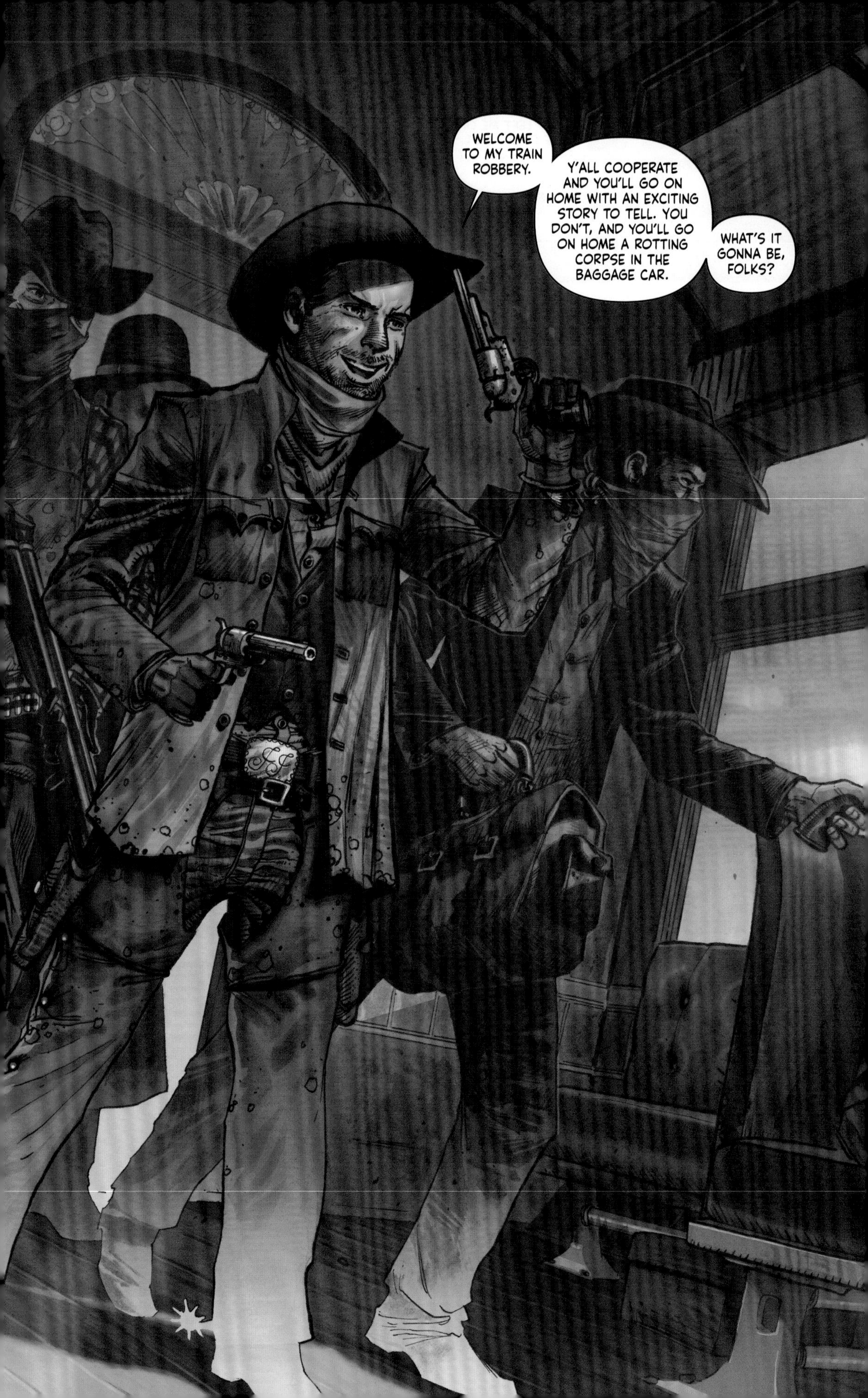
WELCOME TO MY TRAIN ROBBERY.
Y'ALL COOPERATE AND YOU'LL GO ON HOME WITH AN EXCITING STORY TO TELL. YOU DON'T, AND YOU'LL GO ON HOME A ROTTING CORPSE IN THE BAGGAGE CAR.
WHAT'S IT GONNA BE, FOLKS?

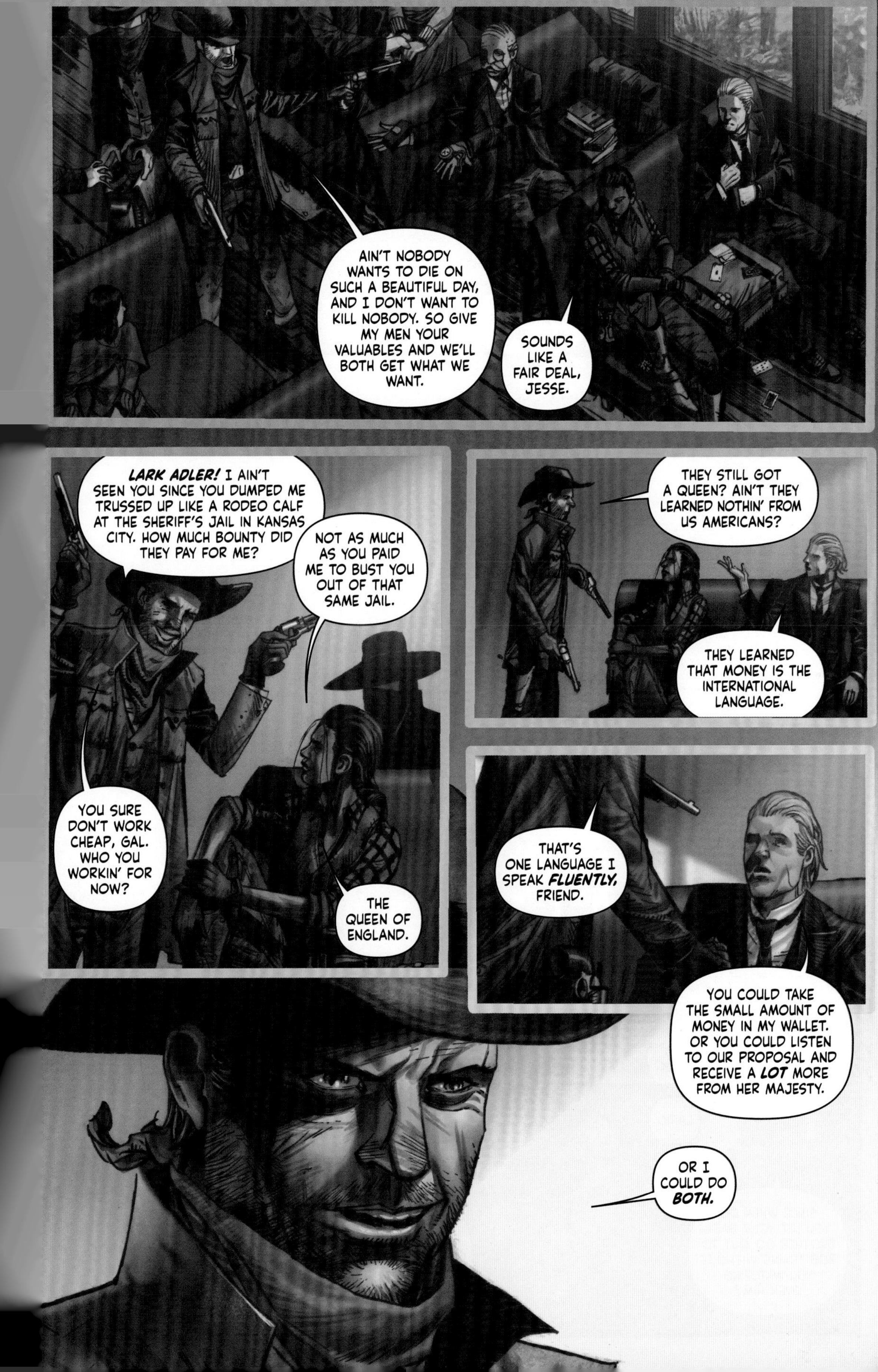
AIN'T NOBODY WANTS TO DIE ON SUCH A BEAUTIFUL DAY, AND I DON'T WANT TO KILL NOBODY. SO GIVE MY MEN YOUR VALUABLES AND WE'LL BOTH GET WHAT WE WANT.
SOUNDS LIKE A FAIR DEAL, JESSE.
LARK ADLER! I AIN'T SEEN YOU SINCE YOU DUMPED ME TRUSSED UP LIKE A RODEO CALF AT THE SHERIFF'S JAIL IN KANSAS CITY. HOW MUCH BOUNTY DID THEY PAY FOR ME?
NOT AS MUCH AS YOU PAID ME TO BUST YOU OUT OF THAT SAME JAIL.
YOU SURE DON'T WORK CHEAP, GAL. WHO YOU WORKIN' FOR NOW?
THE QUEEN OF ENGLAND.
THEY STILL GOT A QUEEN? AIN'T THEY LEARNED NOTHIN' FROM US AMERICANS?
THEY LEARNED THAT MONEY IS THE INTERNATIONAL LANGUAGE.
THAT'S ONE LANGUAGE I SPEAK ***FLUENTLY,*** FRIEND.
YOU COULD TAKE THE SMALL AMOUNT OF MONEY IN MY WALLET. OR YOU COULD LISTEN TO OUR PROPOSAL AND RECEIVE A ***LOT*** MORE FROM HER MAJESTY.
OR I COULD DO ***BOTH.***

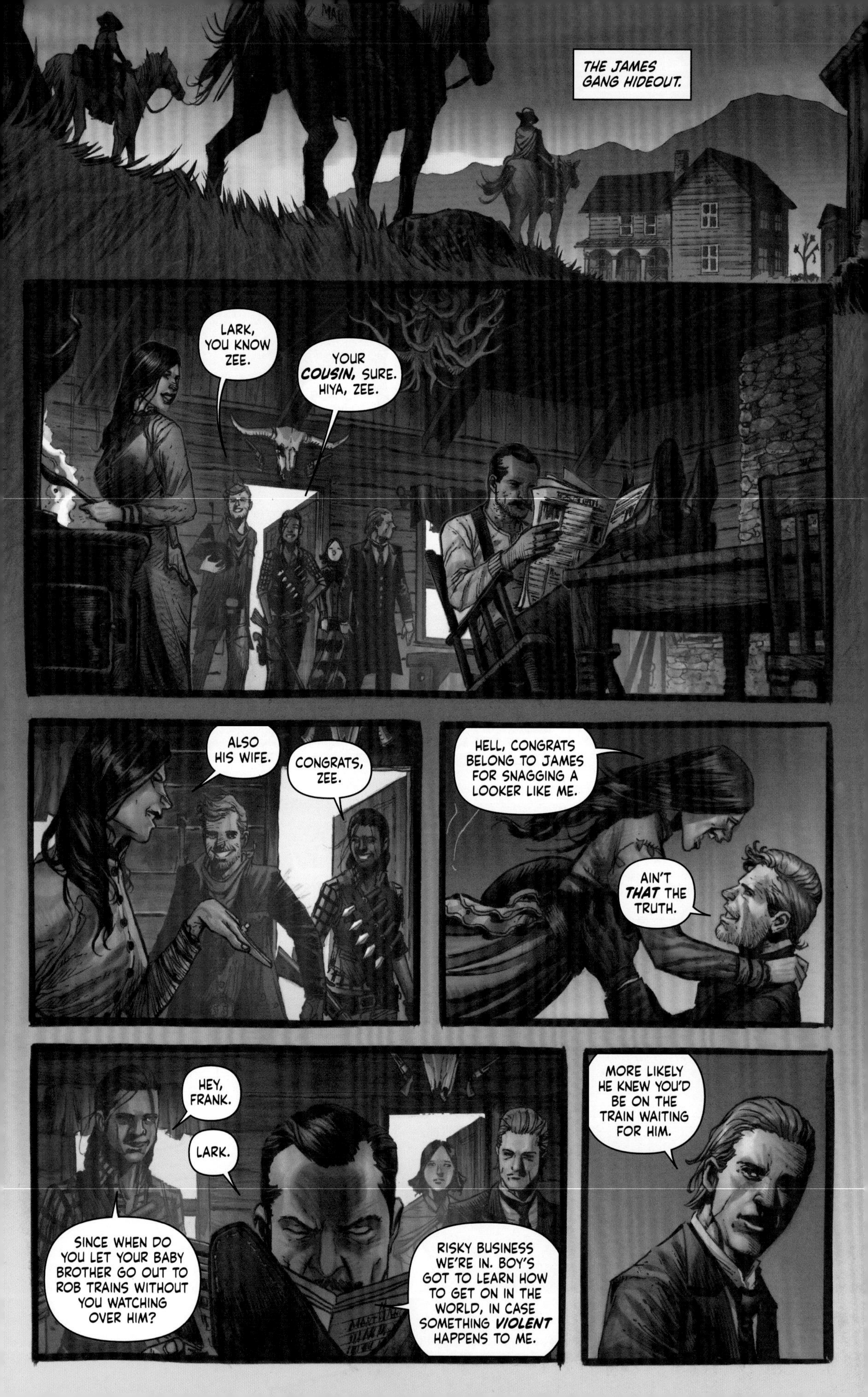
THE JAMES GANG HIDEOUT.
LARK, YOU KNOW ZEE.
YOUR *COUSIN,* SURE. HIYA, ZEE.
ALSO HIS WIFE.
CONGRATS, ZEE.
HELL, CONGRATS BELONG TO JAMES FOR SNAGGING A LOOKER LIKE ME.
AIN'T *THAT* THE TRUTH.
HEY, FRANK.
LARK.
SINCE WHEN DO YOU LET YOUR BABY BROTHER GO OUT TO ROB TRAINS WITHOUT YOU WATCHING OVER HIM?
RISKY BUSINESS WE'RE IN. BOY'S GOT TO LEARN HOW TO GET ON IN THE WORLD, IN CASE SOMETHING *VIOLENT* HAPPENS TO ME.
MORE LIKELY HE KNEW YOU'D BE ON THE TRAIN WAITING FOR HIM.

WHO'S THE DUDE?

LARK'S INQUIRIES ABOUT YOUR NEXT HEIST MUST HAVE GOTTEN BACK TO YOU VIA THE LOCAL CRIMINAL UNDERGROUND.

YOU **KNEW** THAT SHE WOULD BE ON THE TRAIN, AND SINCE SHE WAS LOOKING FOR THE **TWO** OF YOU, SHE WOULD HAVE PAID OFF ANY GUARDS THAT MIGHT HAVE INTERFERED WITH THE ROBBERY. SO, THERE WAS NO ACTUAL RISK TO THE GANG. NO REASON FOR YOU TO PARTICIPATE.

THAT **TRUE,** FRANK?

CLOSE ENOUGH.

GOODNESS, FRANK, I DIDN'T GIVE YOU CREDIT FOR BEING THAT SMART.

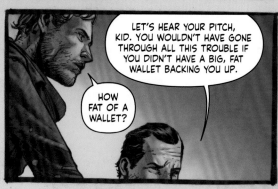

LET'S HEAR YOUR PITCH, KID. YOU WOULDN'T HAVE GONE THROUGH ALL THIS TROUBLE IF YOU DIDN'T HAVE A BIG, FAT WALLET BACKING YOU UP.

HOW FAT OF A WALLET?

YOU ROBBED A TRAIN BOUND FOR CHICAGO SOME MONTHS BACK AND TOOK A BUNCH A MAIL POUCHES.

WE **ALWAYS** TAKE THE MAIL.

YOU NEVER KNOW WHAT VALUABLES PEOPLE SEND TO EACH OTHER. WE'VE GOTTEN GOLD WATCHES, ENGAGEMENT RINGS FROM LADIES BREAKING IT OFF, ALL KINDS OF TREASURES.

GOT A FULL SET OF FALSE TEETH ONCE. REMEMBER THAT, JESSE?

THIS WASN'T VALUABLE LIKE THAT. JUST SOME PAPERS.

WHAT **KIND** OF PAPERS?

DO YOU DESTROY THE MAIL AFTER YOU'VE RANSACKED IT?

WHO **IS** THIS JACKASS, AGAIN -- AND WHY HASN'T SOMEBODY SHOT HIM?

HE'S WITH **ME.** THAT'S WHY.

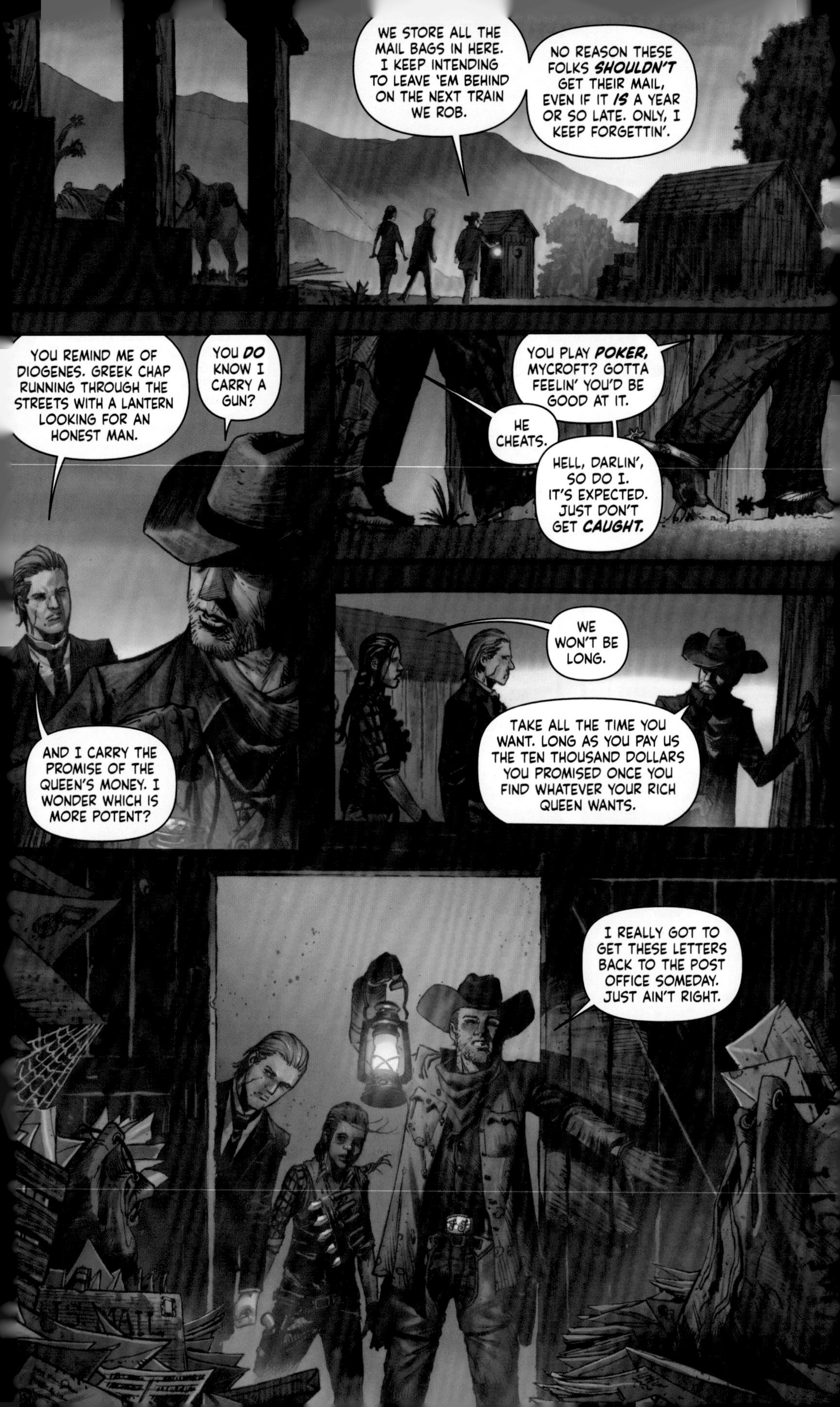
WE STORE ALL THE MAIL BAGS IN HERE. I KEEP INTENDING TO LEAVE 'EM BEHIND ON THE NEXT TRAIN WE ROB.
NO REASON THESE FOLKS SHOULDN'T GET THEIR MAIL, EVEN IF IT IS A YEAR OR SO LATE. ONLY, I KEEP FORGETTIN'.
YOU REMIND ME OF DIOGENES. GREEK CHAP RUNNING THROUGH THE STREETS WITH A LANTERN LOOKING FOR AN HONEST MAN.
YOU DO KNOW I CARRY A GUN?
AND I CARRY THE PROMISE OF THE QUEEN'S MONEY. I WONDER WHICH IS MORE POTENT?
YOU PLAY POKER, MYCROFT? GOTTA FEELIN' YOU'D BE GOOD AT IT.
HE CHEATS.
HELL, DARLIN', SO DO I. IT'S EXPECTED. JUST DON'T GET CAUGHT.
WE WON'T BE LONG.
TAKE ALL THE TIME YOU WANT. LONG AS YOU PAY US THE TEN THOUSAND DOLLARS YOU PROMISED ONCE YOU FIND WHATEVER YOUR RICH QUEEN WANTS.
I REALLY GOT TO GET THESE LETTERS BACK TO THE POST OFFICE SOMEDAY. JUST AIN'T RIGHT.

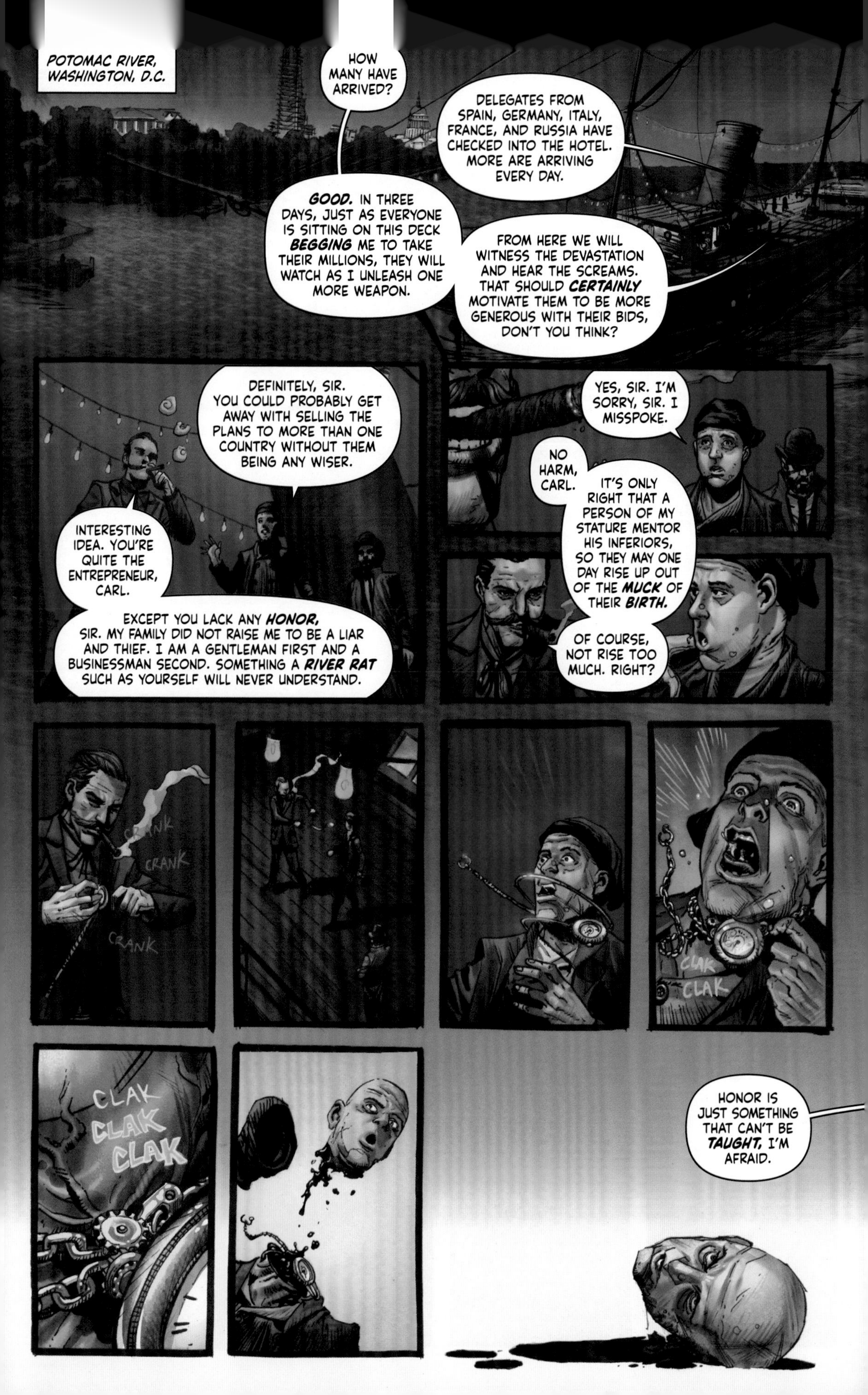
POTOMAC RIVER, WASHINGTON, D.C.
HOW MANY HAVE ARRIVED?
DELEGATES FROM SPAIN, GERMANY, ITALY, FRANCE, AND RUSSIA HAVE CHECKED INTO THE HOTEL. MORE ARE ARRIVING EVERY DAY.
GOOD. IN THREE DAYS, JUST AS EVERYONE IS SITTING ON THIS DECK BEGGING ME TO TAKE THEIR MILLIONS, THEY WILL WATCH AS I UNLEASH ONE MORE WEAPON.
FROM HERE WE WILL WITNESS THE DEVASTATION AND HEAR THE SCREAMS. THAT SHOULD CERTAINLY MOTIVATE THEM TO BE MORE GENEROUS WITH THEIR BIDS, DON'T YOU THINK?
DEFINITELY, SIR. YOU COULD PROBABLY GET AWAY WITH SELLING THE PLANS TO MORE THAN ONE COUNTRY WITHOUT THEM BEING ANY WISER.
INTERESTING IDEA. YOU'RE QUITE THE ENTREPRENEUR, CARL.
EXCEPT YOU LACK ANY HONOR, SIR. MY FAMILY DID NOT RAISE ME TO BE A LIAR AND THIEF. I AM A GENTLEMAN FIRST AND A BUSINESSMAN SECOND. SOMETHING A RIVER RAT SUCH AS YOURSELF WILL NEVER UNDERSTAND.
YES, SIR. I'M SORRY, SIR. I MISSPOKE.
NO HARM, CARL.
IT'S ONLY RIGHT THAT A PERSON OF MY STATURE MENTOR HIS INFERIORS, SO THEY MAY ONE DAY RISE UP OUT OF THE MUCK OF THEIR BIRTH.
OF COURSE, NOT RISE TOO MUCH. RIGHT?
CRANK
CRANK
CRANK
CLAK
CLAK
CLAK
CLAK
CLAK
HONOR IS JUST SOMETHING THAT CAN'T BE TAUGHT, I'M AFRAID.

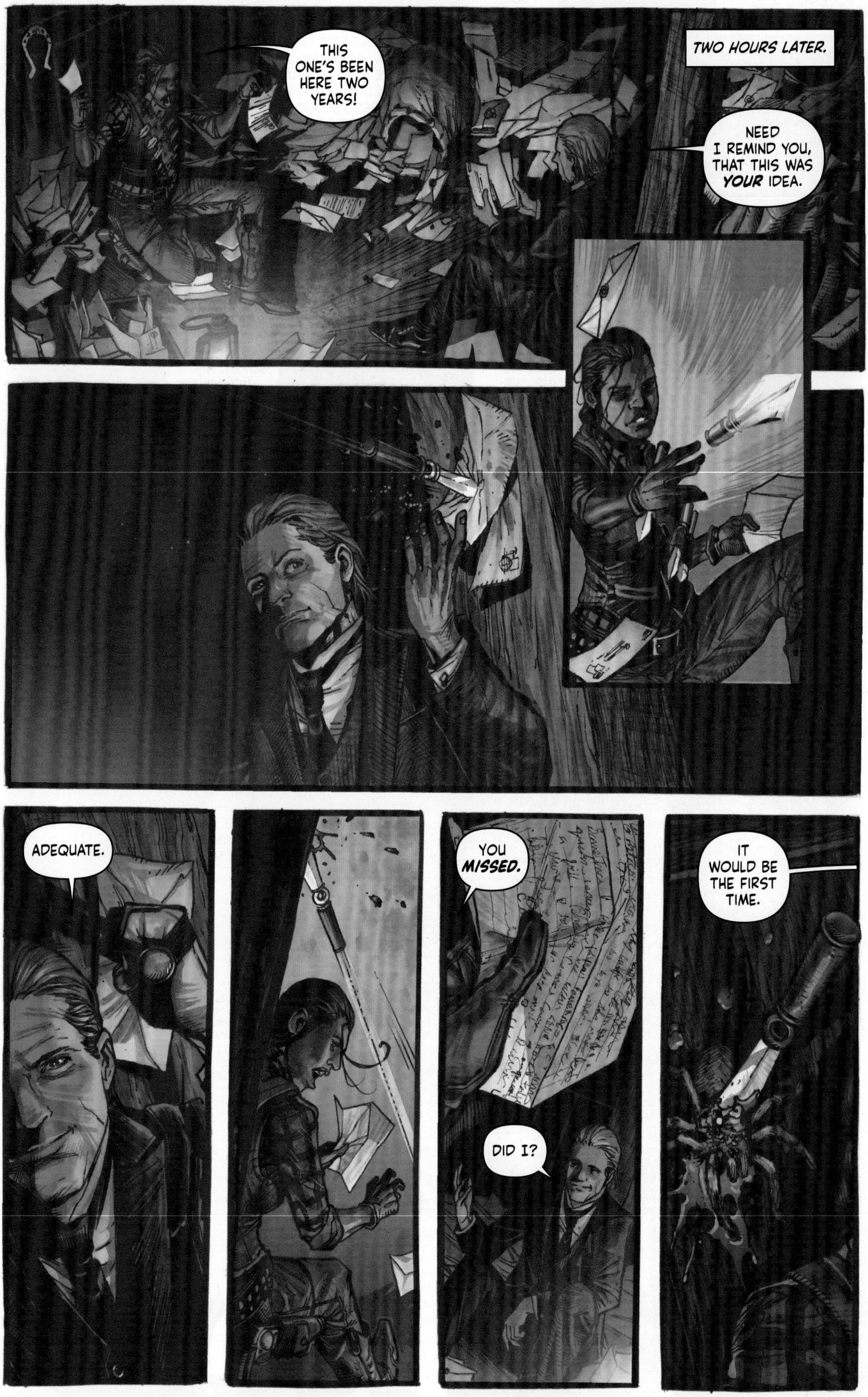
THIS ONE'S BEEN HERE TWO YEARS!
TWO HOURS LATER.
NEED I REMIND YOU, THAT THIS WAS YOUR IDEA.
ADEQUATE.
YOU MISSED.
DID I?
IT WOULD BE THE FIRST TIME.

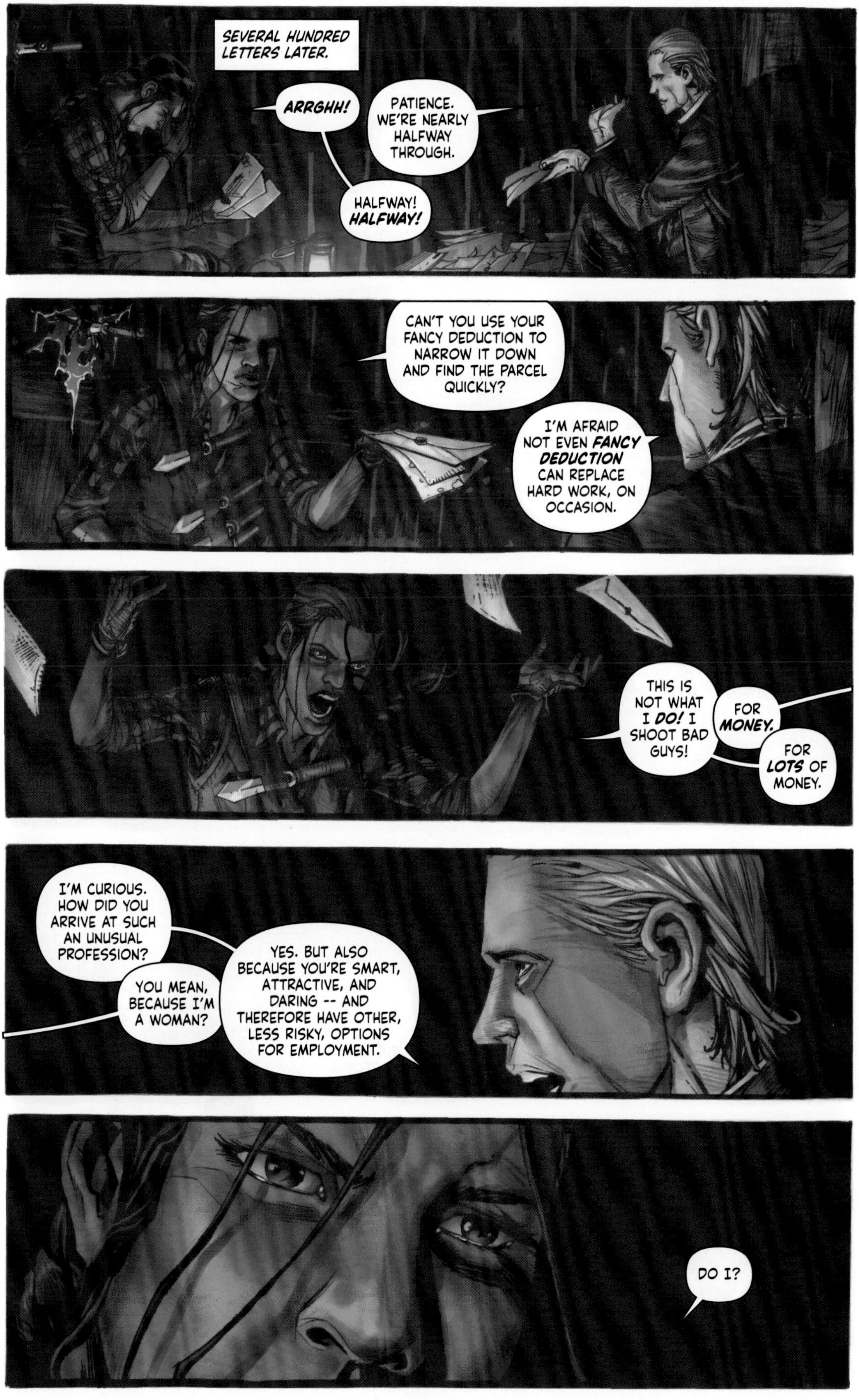
SEVERAL HUNDRED LETTERS LATER.
ARRGHH!
PATIENCE. WE'RE NEARLY HALFWAY THROUGH.
HALFWAY! HALFWAY!
CAN'T YOU USE YOUR FANCY DEDUCTION TO NARROW IT DOWN AND FIND THE PARCEL QUICKLY?
I'M AFRAID NOT EVEN FANCY DEDUCTION CAN REPLACE HARD WORK, ON OCCASION.
THIS IS NOT WHAT I DO! I SHOOT BAD GUYS!
FOR MONEY.
FOR LOTS OF MONEY.
I'M CURIOUS. HOW DID YOU ARRIVE AT SUCH AN UNUSUAL PROFESSION?
YOU MEAN, BECAUSE I'M A WOMAN?
YES. BUT ALSO BECAUSE YOU'RE SMART, ATTRACTIVE, AND DARING -- AND THEREFORE HAVE OTHER, LESS RISKY, OPTIONS FOR EMPLOYMENT.
DO I?

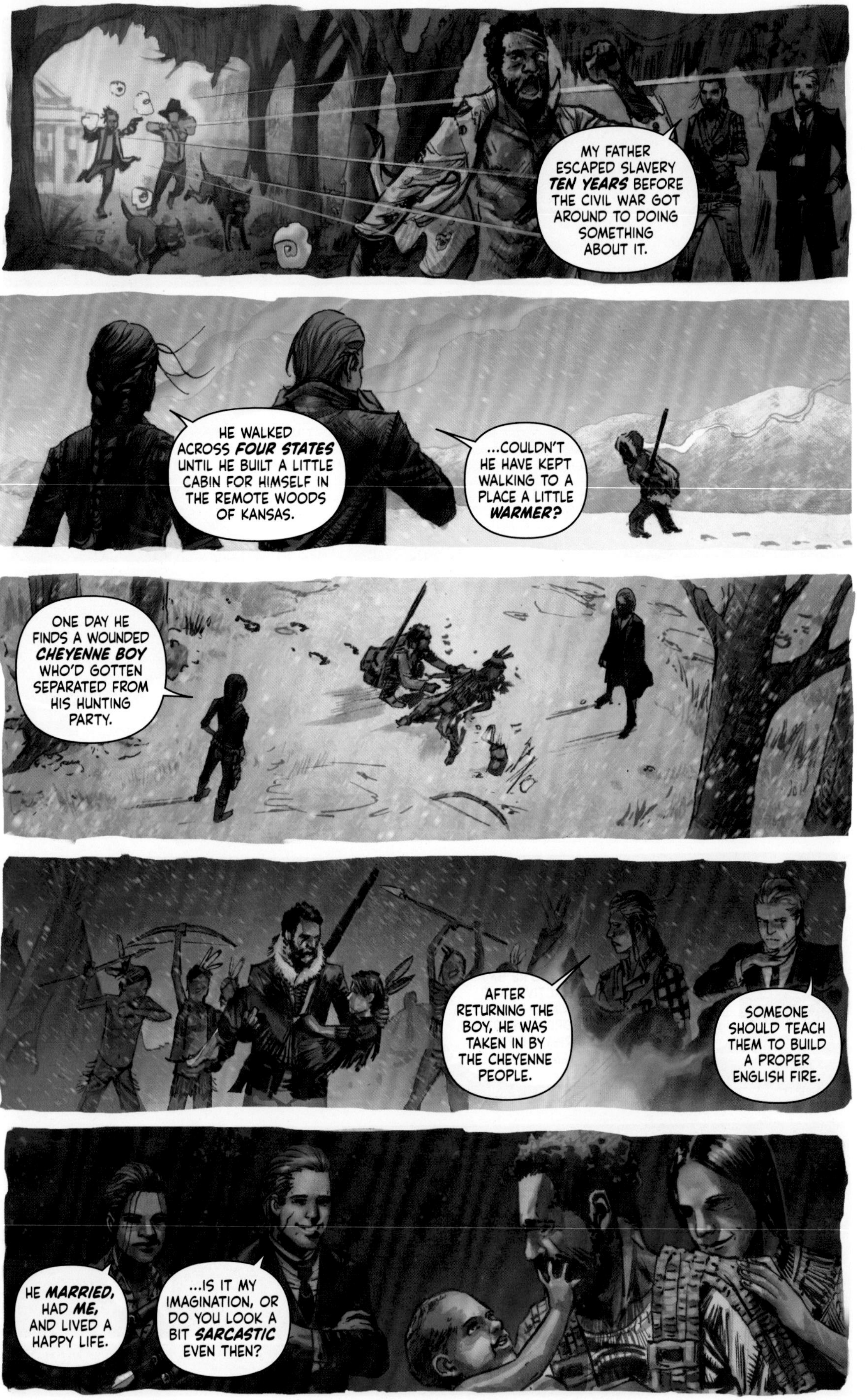

MY FATHER ESCAPED SLAVERY **TEN YEARS** BEFORE THE CIVIL WAR GOT AROUND TO DOING SOMETHING ABOUT IT.
HE WALKED ACROSS **FOUR STATES** UNTIL HE BUILT A LITTLE CABIN FOR HIMSELF IN THE REMOTE WOODS OF KANSAS.
...COULDN'T HE HAVE KEPT WALKING TO A PLACE A LITTLE **WARMER?**
ONE DAY HE FINDS A WOUNDED **CHEYENNE BOY** WHO'D GOTTEN SEPARATED FROM HIS HUNTING PARTY.
AFTER RETURNING THE BOY, HE WAS TAKEN IN BY THE CHEYENNE PEOPLE.
SOMEONE SHOULD TEACH THEM TO BUILD A PROPER ENGLISH FIRE.
HE **MARRIED,** HAD **ME,** AND LIVED A HAPPY LIFE.
...IS IT MY IMAGINATION, OR DO YOU LOOK A BIT **SARCASTIC** EVEN THEN?

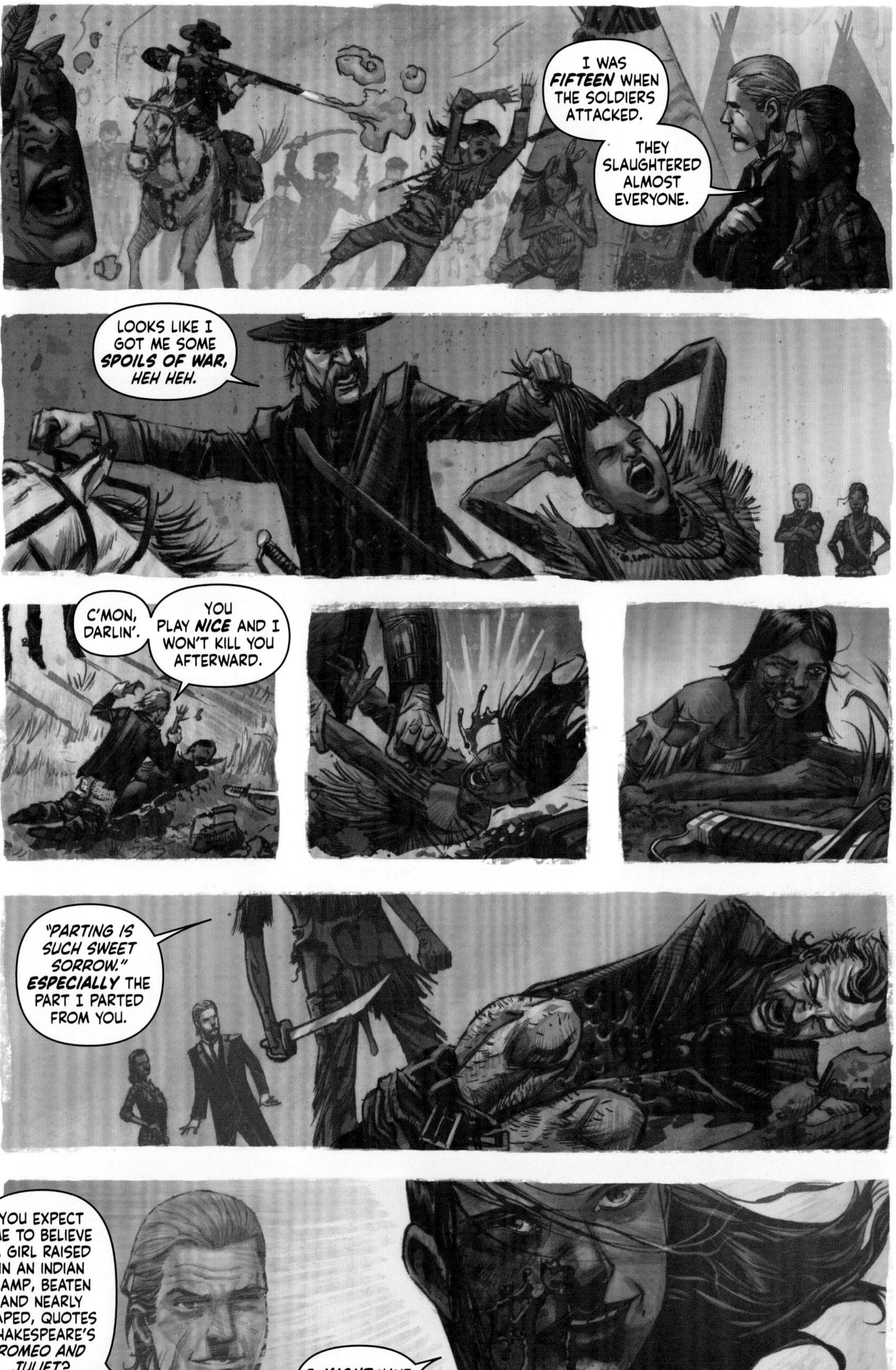
I WAS FIFTEEN WHEN THE SOLDIERS ATTACKED.
THEY SLAUGHTERED ALMOST EVERYONE.
LOOKS LIKE I GOT ME SOME SPOILS OF WAR, HEH HEH.
C'MON, DARLIN'.
YOU PLAY NICE AND I WON'T KILL YOU AFTERWARD.
"PARTING IS SUCH SWEET SORROW." ESPECIALLY THE PART I PARTED FROM YOU.
YOU EXPECT ME TO BELIEVE A GIRL RAISED IN AN INDIAN CAMP, BEATEN AND NEARLY RAPED, QUOTES SHAKESPEARE'S ROMEO AND JULIET?
I MIGHT HAVE EMBELLISHED FOR DRAMATIC EFFECT.

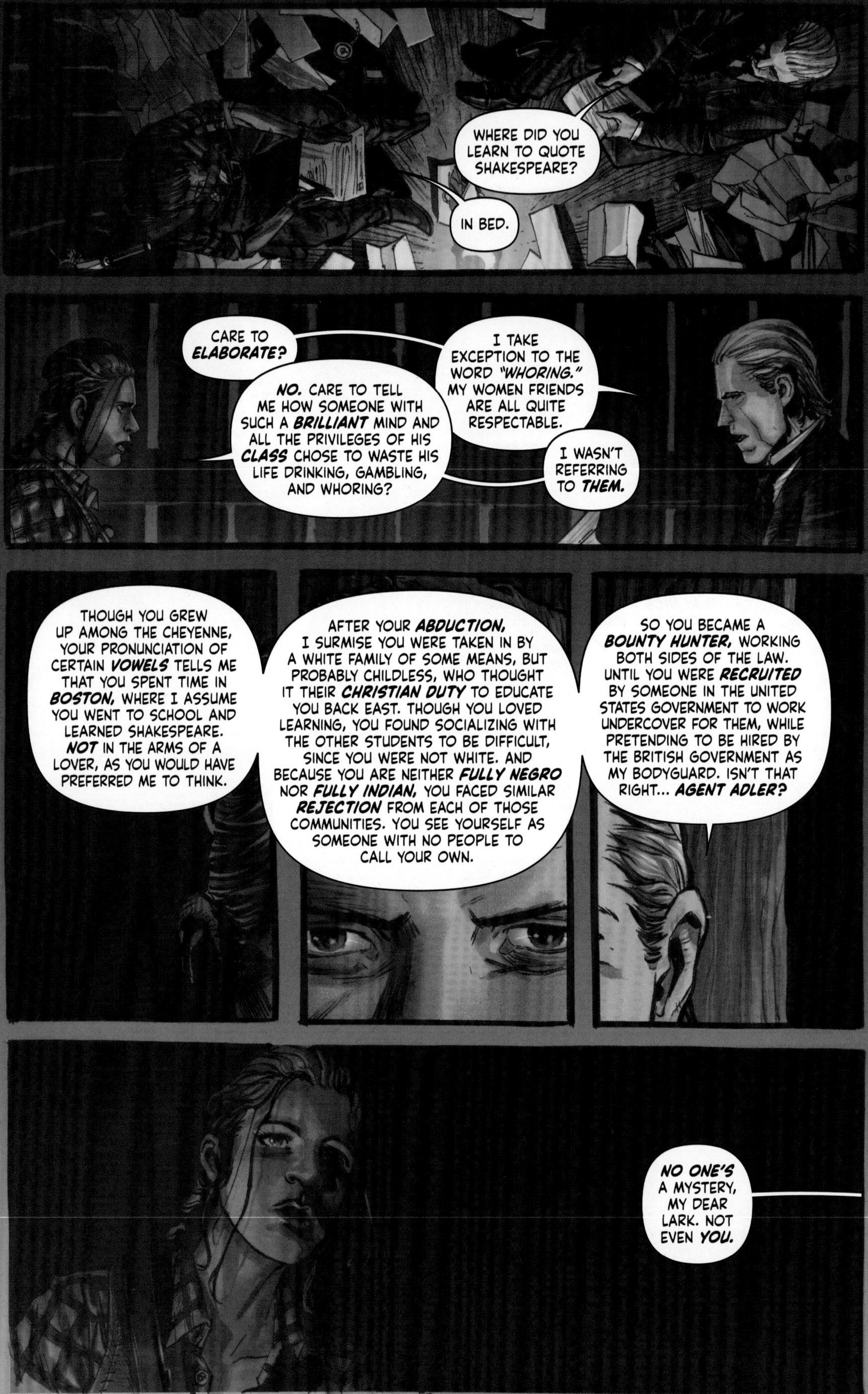
WHERE DID YOU LEARN TO QUOTE SHAKESPEARE?
IN BED.
CARE TO ELABORATE?
NO. CARE TO TELL ME HOW SOMEONE WITH SUCH A BRILLIANT MIND AND ALL THE PRIVILEGES OF HIS CLASS CHOSE TO WASTE HIS LIFE DRINKING, GAMBLING, AND WHORING?
I TAKE EXCEPTION TO THE WORD "WHORING." MY WOMEN FRIENDS ARE ALL QUITE RESPECTABLE.
I WASN'T REFERRING TO THEM.
THOUGH YOU GREW UP AMONG THE CHEYENNE, YOUR PRONUNCIATION OF CERTAIN VOWELS TELLS ME THAT YOU SPENT TIME IN BOSTON, WHERE I ASSUME YOU WENT TO SCHOOL AND LEARNED SHAKESPEARE. NOT IN THE ARMS OF A LOVER, AS YOU WOULD HAVE PREFERRED ME TO THINK.
AFTER YOUR ABDUCTION, I SURMISE YOU WERE TAKEN IN BY A WHITE FAMILY OF SOME MEANS, BUT PROBABLY CHILDLESS, WHO THOUGHT IT THEIR CHRISTIAN DUTY TO EDUCATE YOU BACK EAST. THOUGH YOU LOVED LEARNING, YOU FOUND SOCIALIZING WITH THE OTHER STUDENTS TO BE DIFFICULT, SINCE YOU WERE NOT WHITE. AND BECAUSE YOU ARE NEITHER FULLY NEGRO NOR FULLY INDIAN, YOU FACED SIMILAR REJECTION FROM EACH OF THOSE COMMUNITIES. YOU SEE YOURSELF AS SOMEONE WITH NO PEOPLE TO CALL YOUR OWN.
SO YOU BECAME A BOUNTY HUNTER, WORKING BOTH SIDES OF THE LAW. UNTIL YOU WERE RECRUITED BY SOMEONE IN THE UNITED STATES GOVERNMENT TO WORK UNDERCOVER FOR THEM, WHILE PRETENDING TO BE HIRED BY THE BRITISH GOVERNMENT AS MY BODYGUARD. ISN'T THAT RIGHT... AGENT ADLER?
NO ONE'S A MYSTERY, MY DEAR LARK. NOT EVEN YOU.

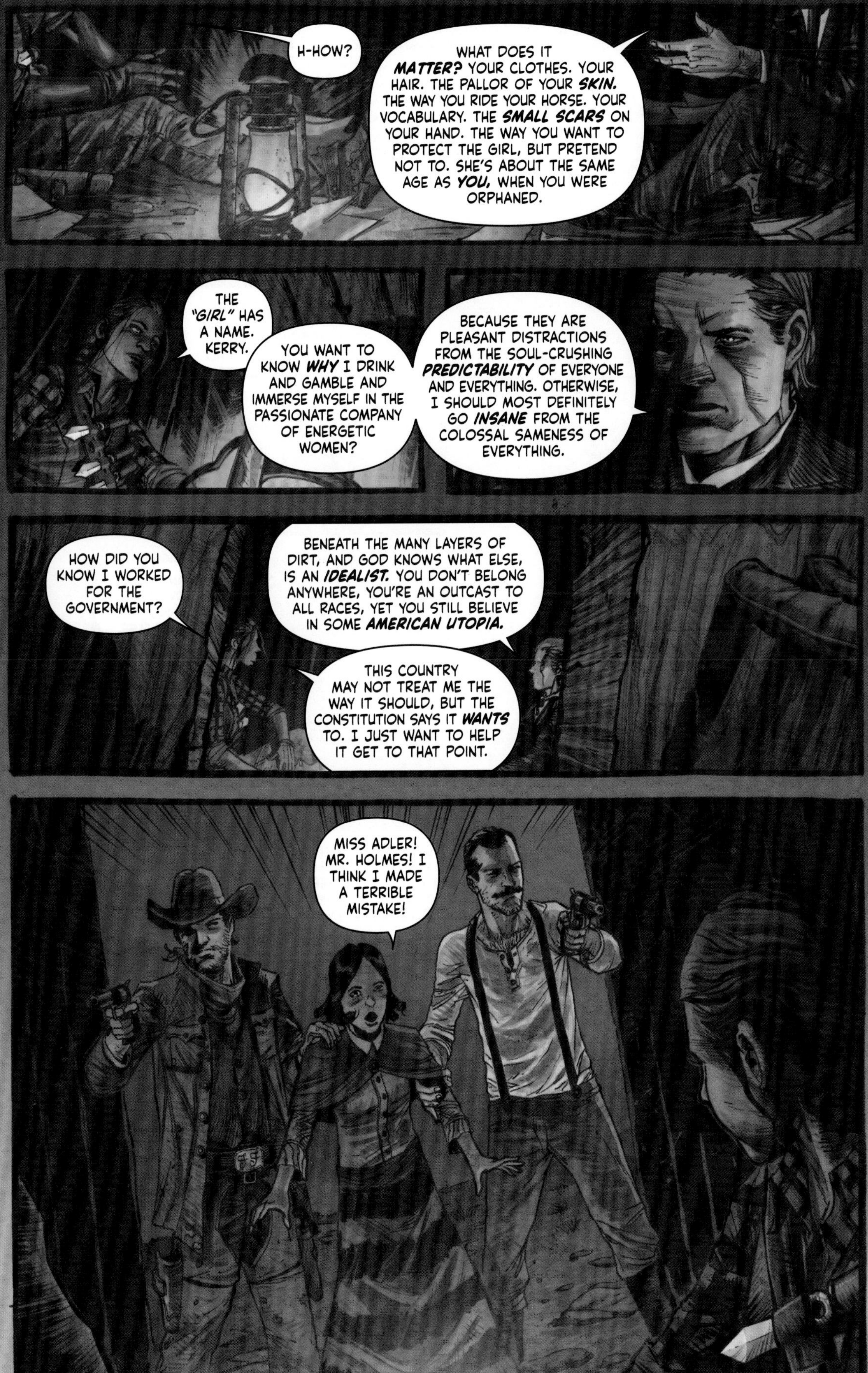
H-HOW?
WHAT DOES IT MATTER? YOUR CLOTHES. YOUR HAIR. THE PALLOR OF YOUR SKIN. THE WAY YOU RIDE YOUR HORSE. YOUR VOCABULARY. THE SMALL SCARS ON YOUR HAND. THE WAY YOU WANT TO PROTECT THE GIRL, BUT PRETEND NOT TO. SHE'S ABOUT THE SAME AGE AS YOU, WHEN YOU WERE ORPHANED.
THE "GIRL" HAS A NAME. KERRY.
YOU WANT TO KNOW WHY I DRINK AND GAMBLE AND IMMERSE MYSELF IN THE PASSIONATE COMPANY OF ENERGETIC WOMEN?
BECAUSE THEY ARE PLEASANT DISTRACTIONS FROM THE SOUL-CRUSHING PREDICTABILITY OF EVERYONE AND EVERYTHING. OTHERWISE, I SHOULD MOST DEFINITELY GO INSANE FROM THE COLOSSAL SAMENESS OF EVERYTHING.
HOW DID YOU KNOW I WORKED FOR THE GOVERNMENT?
BENEATH THE MANY LAYERS OF DIRT, AND GOD KNOWS WHAT ELSE, IS AN IDEALIST. YOU DON'T BELONG ANYWHERE, YOU'RE AN OUTCAST TO ALL RACES, YET YOU STILL BELIEVE IN SOME AMERICAN UTOPIA.
THIS COUNTRY MAY NOT TREAT ME THE WAY IT SHOULD, BUT THE CONSTITUTION SAYS IT WANTS TO. I JUST WANT TO HELP IT GET TO THAT POINT.
MISS ADLER! MR. HOLMES! I THINK I MADE A TERRIBLE MISTAKE!

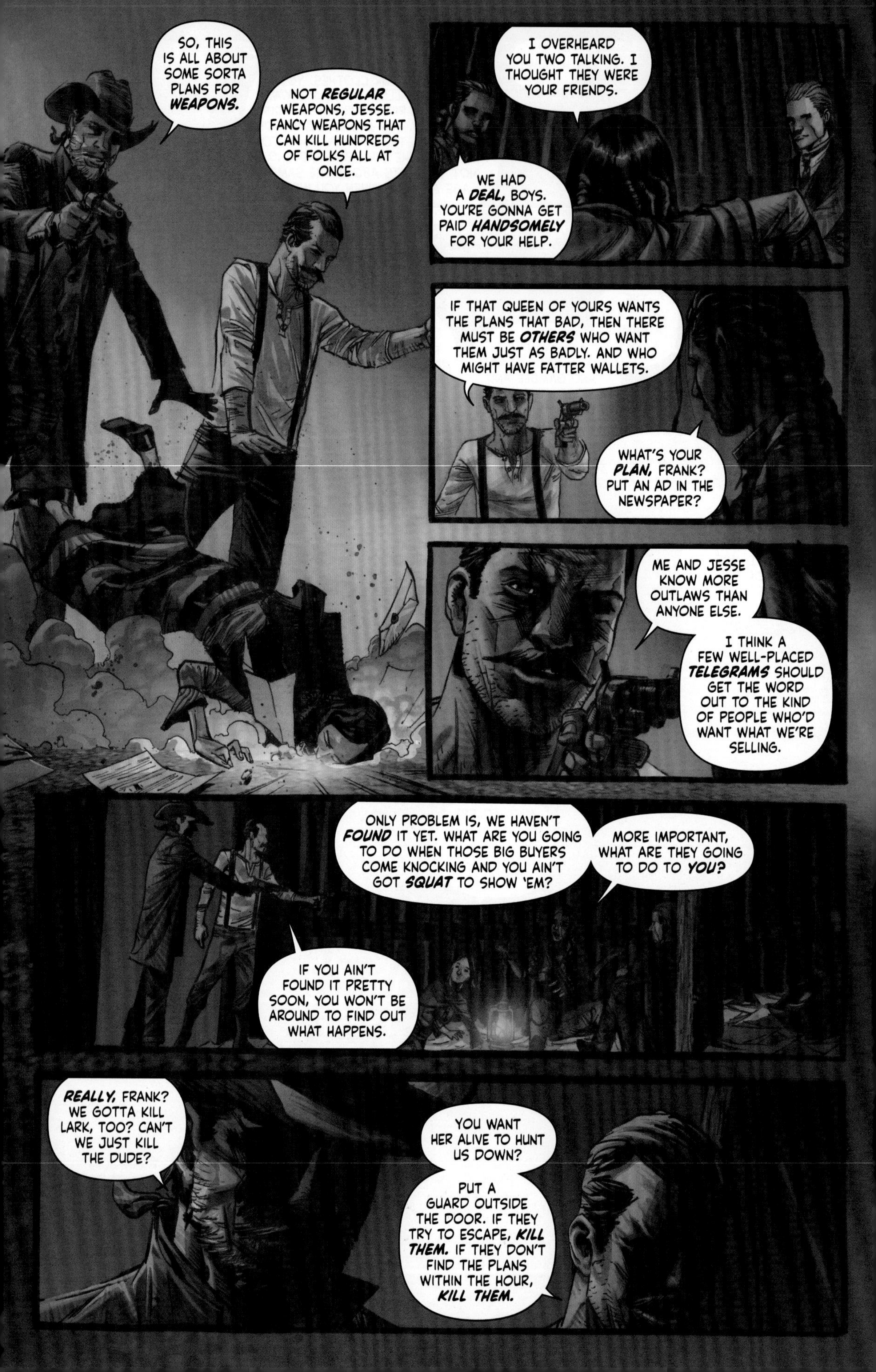
SO, THIS IS ALL ABOUT SOME SORTA PLANS FOR WEAPONS.
NOT REGULAR WEAPONS, JESSE. FANCY WEAPONS THAT CAN KILL HUNDREDS OF FOLKS ALL AT ONCE.
I OVERHEARD YOU TWO TALKING. I THOUGHT THEY WERE YOUR FRIENDS.
WE HAD A DEAL, BOYS. YOU'RE GONNA GET PAID HANDSOMELY FOR YOUR HELP.
IF THAT QUEEN OF YOURS WANTS THE PLANS THAT BAD, THEN THERE MUST BE OTHERS WHO WANT THEM JUST AS BADLY. AND WHO MIGHT HAVE FATTER WALLETS.
WHAT'S YOUR PLAN, FRANK? PUT AN AD IN THE NEWSPAPER?
ME AND JESSE KNOW MORE OUTLAWS THAN ANYONE ELSE.
I THINK A FEW WELL-PLACED TELEGRAMS SHOULD GET THE WORD OUT TO THE KIND OF PEOPLE WHO'D WANT WHAT WE'RE SELLING.
ONLY PROBLEM IS, WE HAVEN'T FOUND IT YET. WHAT ARE YOU GOING TO DO WHEN THOSE BIG BUYERS COME KNOCKING AND YOU AIN'T GOT SQUAT TO SHOW 'EM?
MORE IMPORTANT, WHAT ARE THEY GOING TO DO TO YOU?
IF YOU AIN'T FOUND IT PRETTY SOON, YOU WON'T BE AROUND TO FIND OUT WHAT HAPPENS.
REALLY, FRANK? WE GOTTA KILL LARK, TOO? CAN'T WE JUST KILL THE DUDE?
YOU WANT HER ALIVE TO HUNT US DOWN?
PUT A GUARD OUTSIDE THE DOOR. IF THEY TRY TO ESCAPE, KILL THEM. IF THEY DON'T FIND THE PLANS WITHIN THE HOUR, KILL THEM.

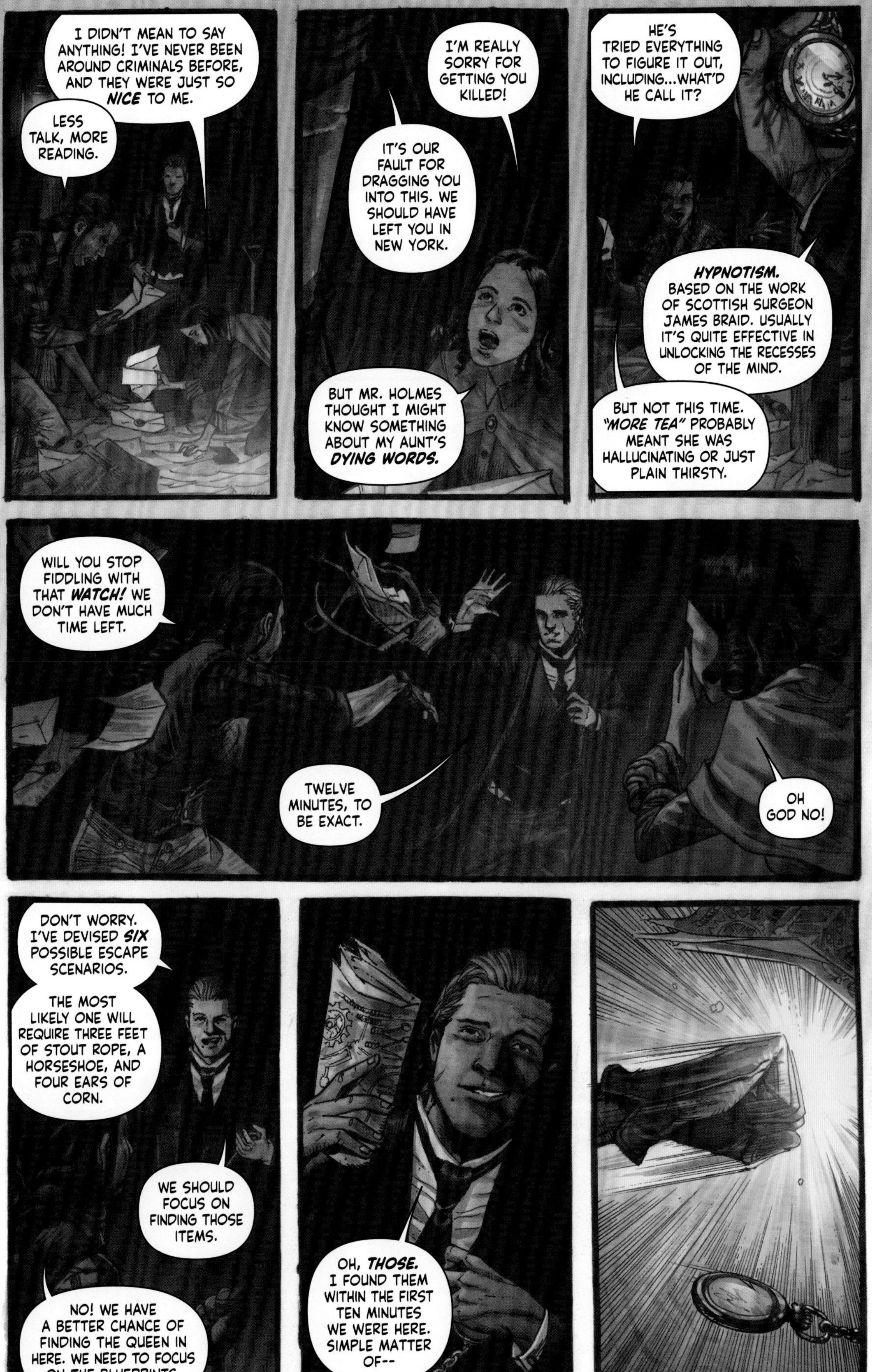
I DIDN'T MEAN TO SAY ANYTHING! I'VE NEVER BEEN AROUND CRIMINALS BEFORE, AND THEY WERE JUST SO *NICE* TO ME.
LESS TALK, MORE READING.
I'M REALLY SORRY FOR GETTING YOU KILLED!
IT'S OUR FAULT FOR DRAGGING YOU INTO THIS. WE SHOULD HAVE LEFT YOU IN NEW YORK.
BUT MR. HOLMES THOUGHT I MIGHT KNOW SOMETHING ABOUT MY AUNT'S *DYING WORDS.*
HE'S TRIED EVERYTHING TO FIGURE IT OUT, INCLUDING...WHAT'D HE CALL IT?
HYPNOTISM. BASED ON THE WORK OF SCOTTISH SURGEON JAMES BRAID. USUALLY IT'S QUITE EFFECTIVE IN UNLOCKING THE RECESSES OF THE MIND.
BUT NOT THIS TIME. *"MORE TEA"* PROBABLY MEANT SHE WAS HALLUCINATING OR JUST PLAIN THIRSTY.
WILL YOU STOP FIDDLING WITH THAT *WATCH!* WE DON'T HAVE MUCH TIME LEFT.
TWELVE MINUTES, TO BE EXACT.
OH GOD NO!
DON'T WORRY. I'VE DEVISED *SIX* POSSIBLE ESCAPE SCENARIOS.
THE MOST LIKELY ONE WILL REQUIRE THREE FEET OF STOUT ROPE, A HORSESHOE, AND FOUR EARS OF CORN.
WE SHOULD FOCUS ON FINDING THOSE ITEMS.
NO! WE HAVE A BETTER CHANCE OF FINDING THE QUEEN IN HERE. WE NEED TO FOCUS ON THE BLUEPRINTS.
OH, *THOSE.* I FOUND THEM WITHIN THE FIRST TEN MINUTES WE WERE HERE. SIMPLE MATTER OF--

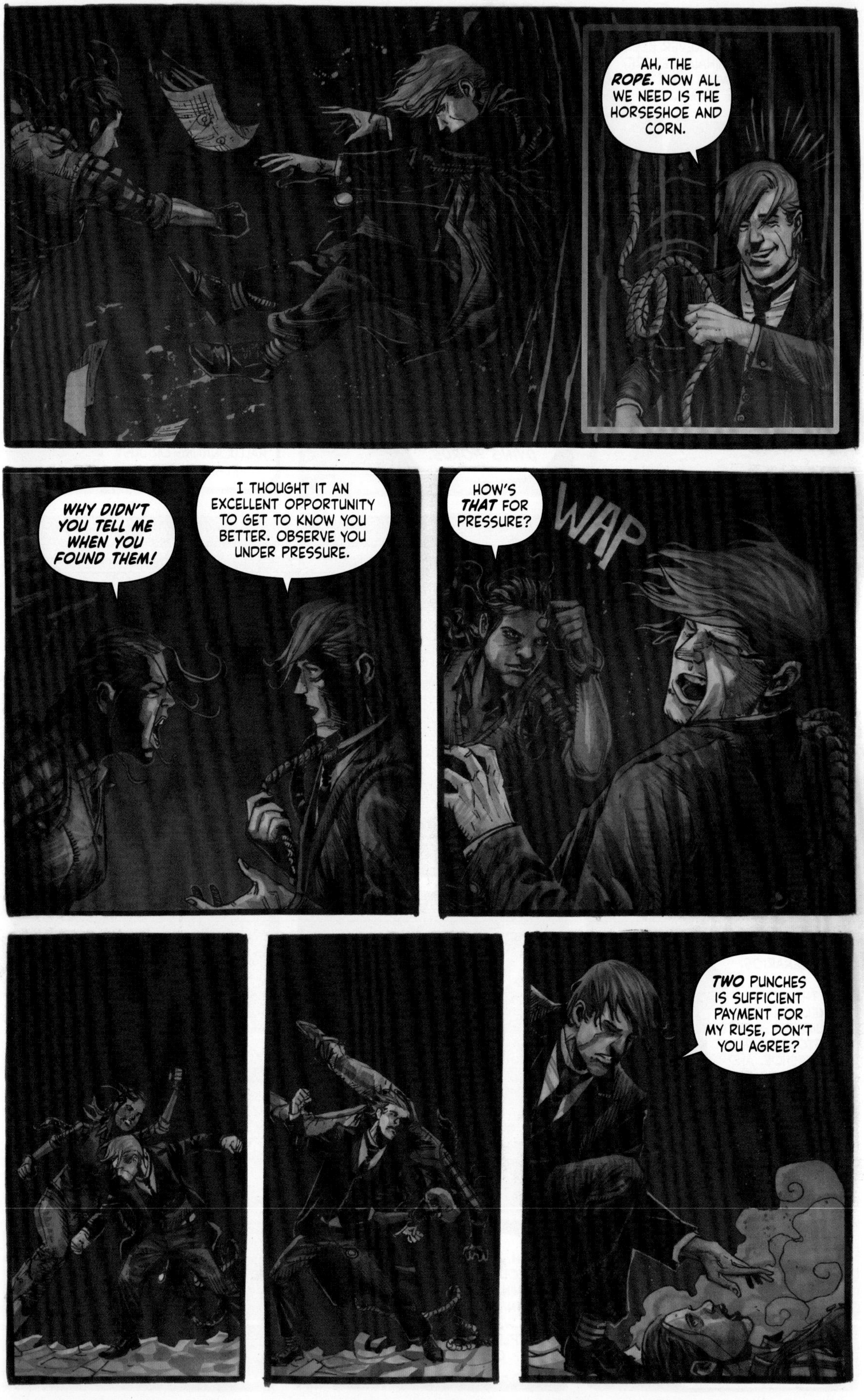
AH, THE ROPE. NOW ALL WE NEED IS THE HORSESHOE AND CORN.
WHY DIDN'T YOU TELL ME WHEN YOU FOUND THEM!
I THOUGHT IT AN EXCELLENT OPPORTUNITY TO GET TO KNOW YOU BETTER. OBSERVE YOU UNDER PRESSURE.
HOW'S THAT FOR PRESSURE?
WAP
TWO PUNCHES IS SUFFICIENT PAYMENT FOR MY RUSE, DON'T YOU AGREE?

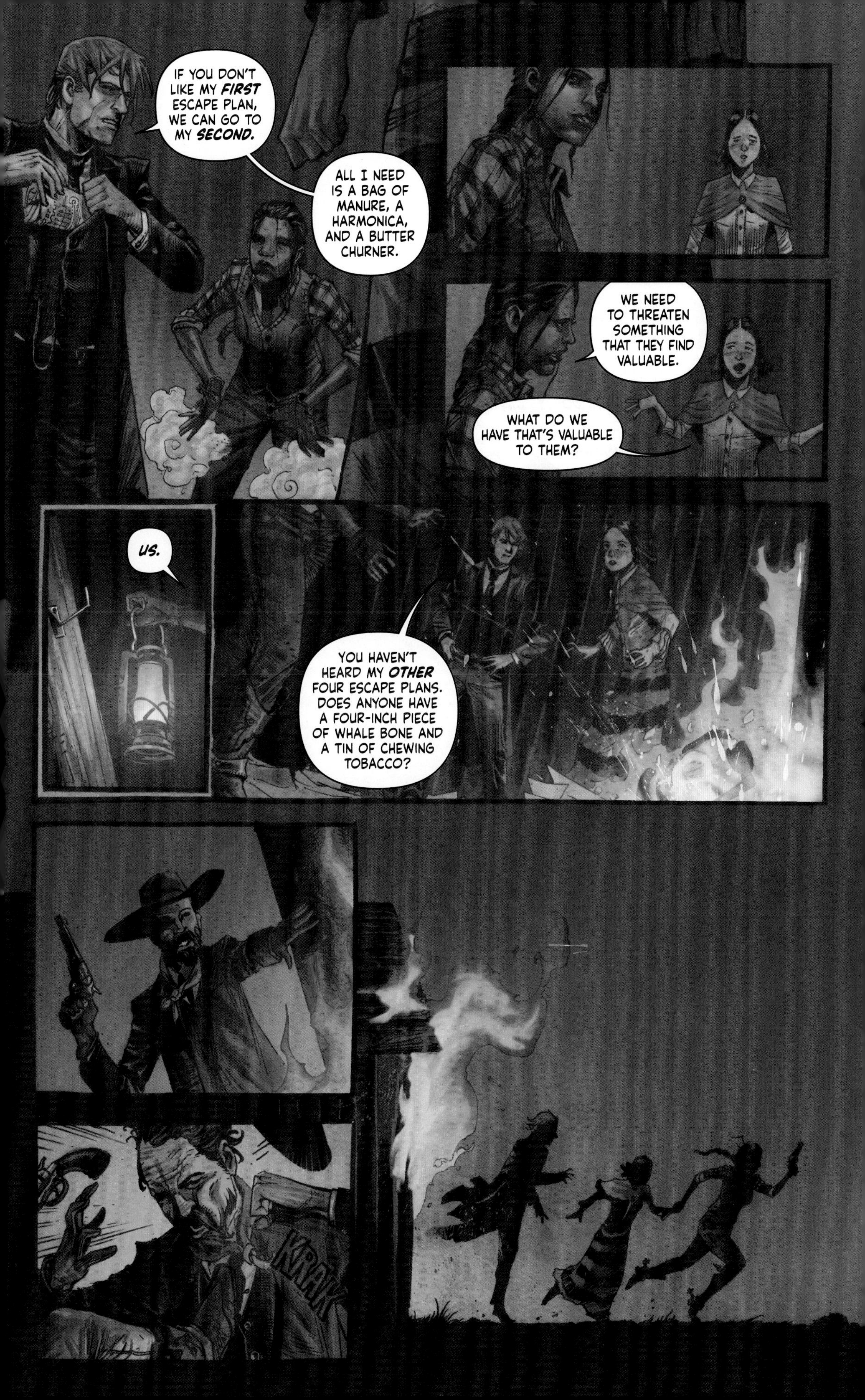
IF YOU DON'T LIKE MY FIRST ESCAPE PLAN, WE CAN GO TO MY SECOND.
ALL I NEED IS A BAG OF MANURE, A HARMONICA, AND A BUTTER CHURNER.
WE NEED TO THREATEN SOMETHING THAT THEY FIND VALUABLE.
WHAT DO WE HAVE THAT'S VALUABLE TO THEM?
US.
YOU HAVEN'T HEARD MY OTHER FOUR ESCAPE PLANS. DOES ANYONE HAVE A FOUR-INCH PIECE OF WHALE BONE AND A TIN OF CHEWING TOBACCO?
KRAK

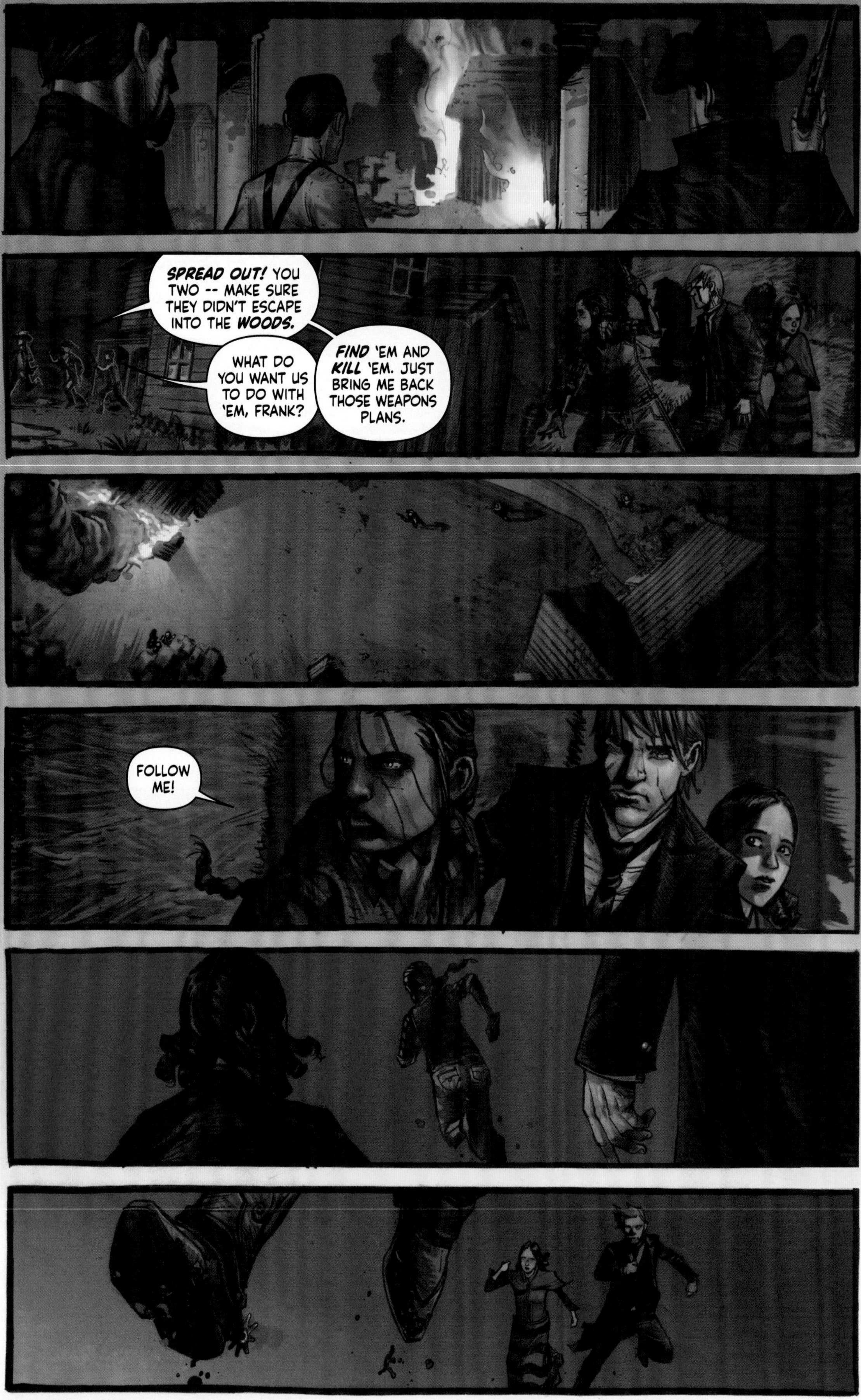
SPREAD OUT! YOU TWO -- MAKE SURE THEY DIDN'T ESCAPE INTO THE WOODS.
WHAT DO YOU WANT US TO DO WITH 'EM, FRANK?
FIND 'EM AND KILL 'EM. JUST BRING ME BACK THOSE WEAPONS PLANS.
FOLLOW ME!

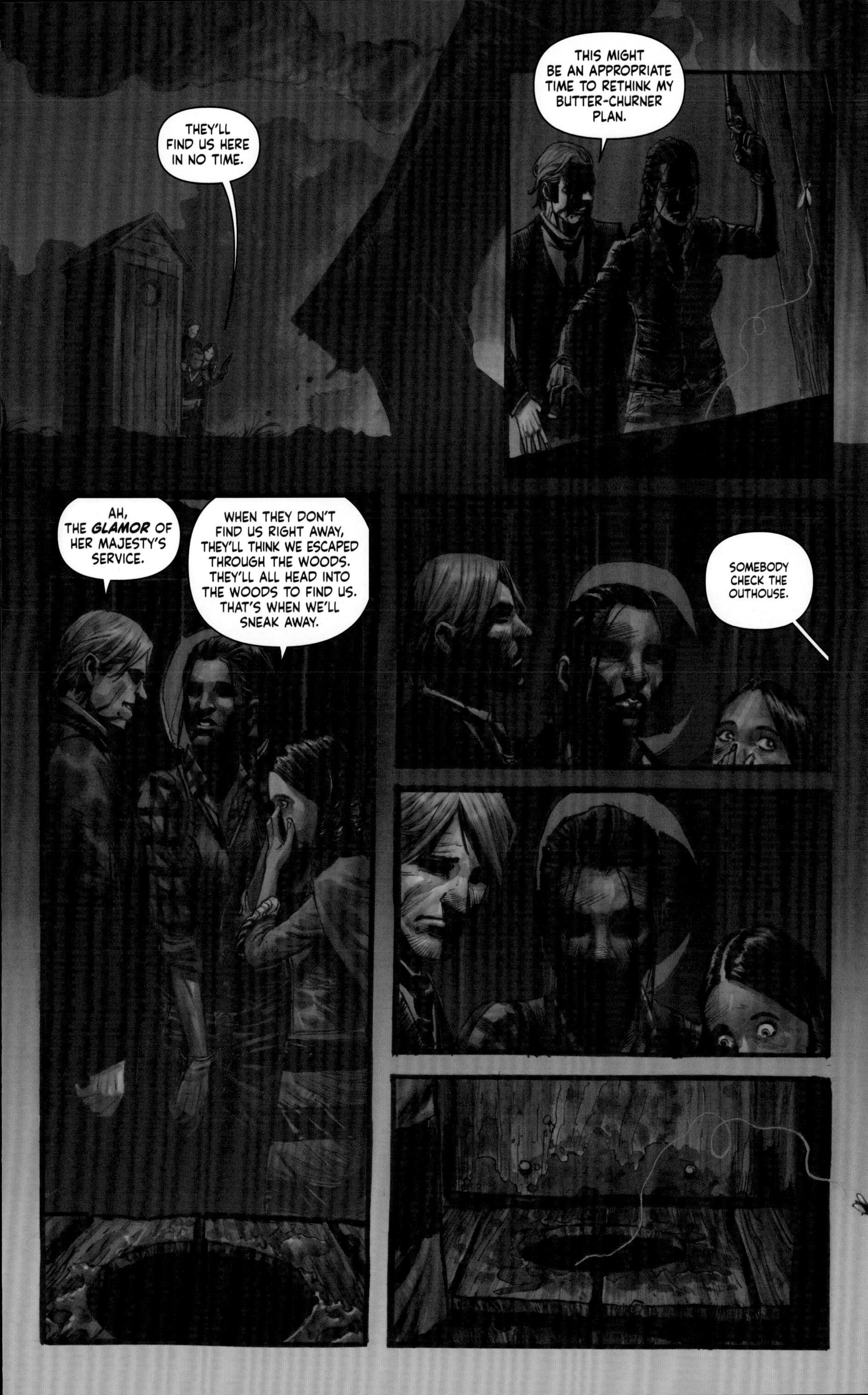
THEY'LL FIND US HERE IN NO TIME.
THIS MIGHT BE AN APPROPRIATE TIME TO RETHINK MY BUTTER-CHURNER PLAN.
AH, THE GLAMOR OF HER MAJESTY'S SERVICE.
WHEN THEY DON'T FIND US RIGHT AWAY, THEY'LL THINK WE ESCAPED THROUGH THE WOODS. THEY'LL ALL HEAD INTO THE WOODS TO FIND US. THAT'S WHEN WE'LL SNEAK AWAY.
SOMEBODY CHECK THE OUTHOUSE.

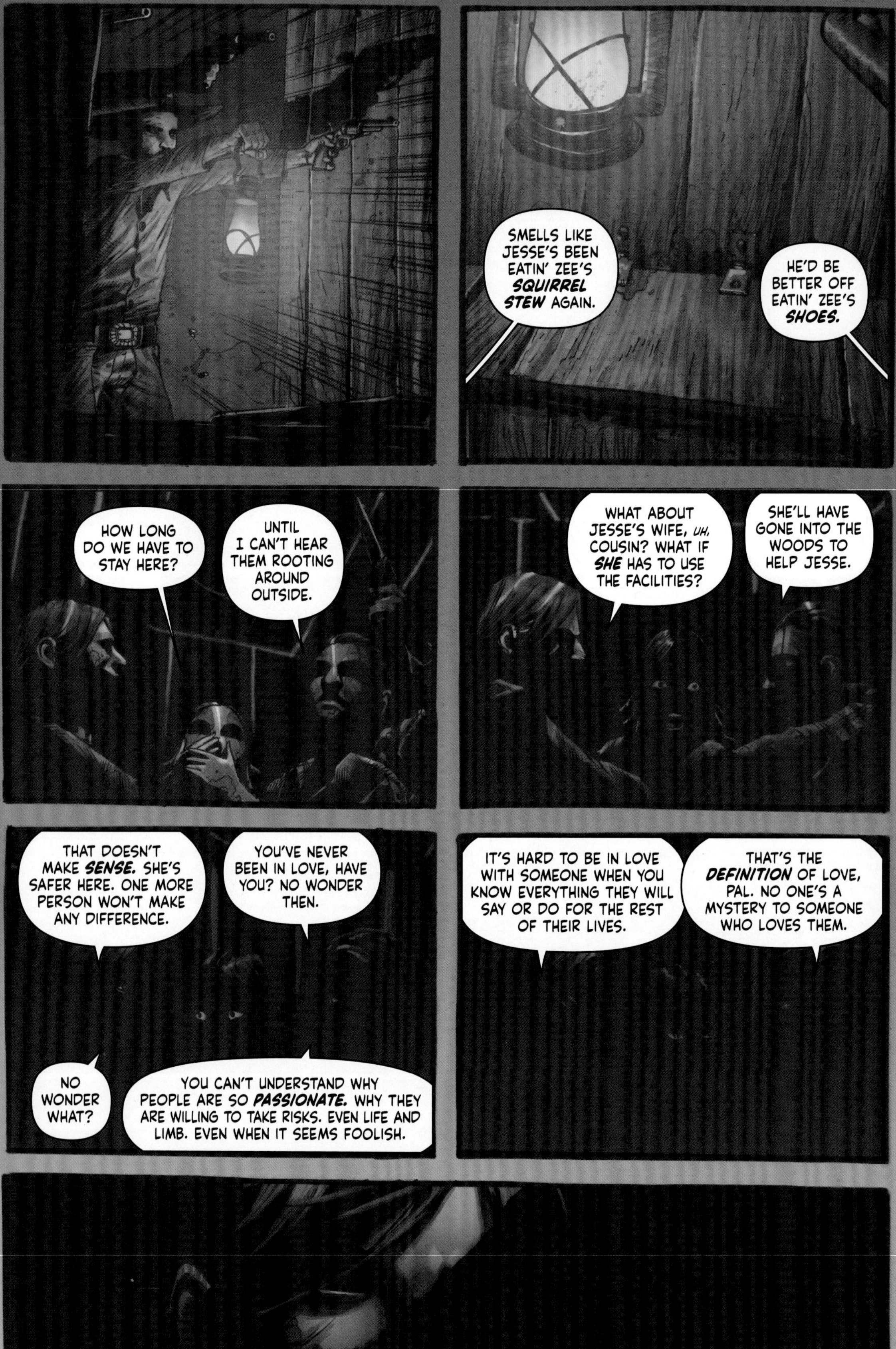
SMELLS LIKE JESSE'S BEEN EATIN' ZEE'S SQUIRREL STEW AGAIN.
HE'D BE BETTER OFF EATIN' ZEE'S SHOES.
HOW LONG DO WE HAVE TO STAY HERE?
UNTIL I CAN'T HEAR THEM ROOTING AROUND OUTSIDE.
WHAT ABOUT JESSE'S WIFE, UH, COUSIN? WHAT IF SHE HAS TO USE THE FACILITIES?
SHE'LL HAVE GONE INTO THE WOODS TO HELP JESSE.
THAT DOESN'T MAKE SENSE. SHE'S SAFER HERE. ONE MORE PERSON WON'T MAKE ANY DIFFERENCE.
YOU'VE NEVER BEEN IN LOVE, HAVE YOU? NO WONDER THEN.
NO WONDER WHAT?
YOU CAN'T UNDERSTAND WHY PEOPLE ARE SO PASSIONATE. WHY THEY ARE WILLING TO TAKE RISKS. EVEN LIFE AND LIMB. EVEN WHEN IT SEEMS FOOLISH.
IT'S HARD TO BE IN LOVE WITH SOMEONE WHEN YOU KNOW EVERYTHING THEY WILL SAY OR DO FOR THE REST OF THEIR LIVES.
THAT'S THE DEFINITION OF LOVE, PAL. NO ONE'S A MYSTERY TO SOMEONE WHO LOVES THEM.

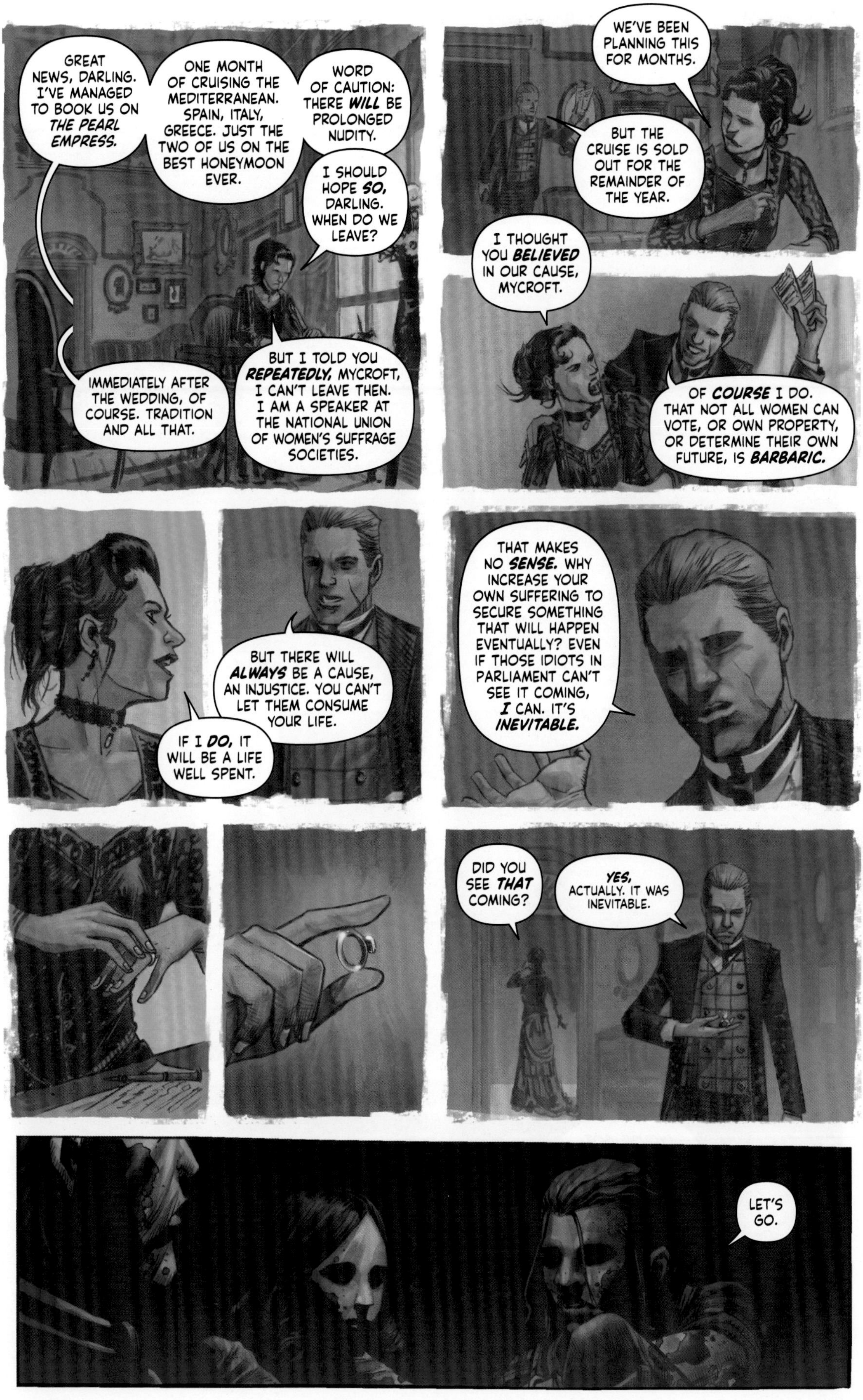
GREAT NEWS, DARLING. I'VE MANAGED TO BOOK US ON *THE PEARL EMPRESS.*
ONE MONTH OF CRUISING THE MEDITERRANEAN. SPAIN, ITALY, GREECE. JUST THE TWO OF US ON THE BEST HONEYMOON EVER.
WORD OF CAUTION: THERE ***WILL*** BE PROLONGED NUDITY.
I SHOULD HOPE ***SO,*** DARLING. WHEN DO WE LEAVE?
IMMEDIATELY AFTER THE WEDDING, OF COURSE. TRADITION AND ALL THAT.
BUT I TOLD YOU ***REPEATEDLY,*** MYCROFT, I CAN'T LEAVE THEN. I AM A SPEAKER AT THE NATIONAL UNION OF WOMEN'S SUFFRAGE SOCIETIES.
WE'VE BEEN PLANNING THIS FOR MONTHS.
BUT THE CRUISE IS SOLD OUT FOR THE REMAINDER OF THE YEAR.
I THOUGHT YOU ***BELIEVED*** IN OUR CAUSE, MYCROFT.
OF ***COURSE*** I DO. THAT NOT ALL WOMEN CAN VOTE, OR OWN PROPERTY, OR DETERMINE THEIR OWN FUTURE, IS ***BARBARIC.***
BUT THERE WILL ***ALWAYS*** BE A CAUSE, AN INJUSTICE. YOU CAN'T LET THEM CONSUME YOUR LIFE.
IF I ***DO,*** IT WILL BE A LIFE WELL SPENT.
THAT MAKES NO ***SENSE.*** WHY INCREASE YOUR OWN SUFFERING TO SECURE SOMETHING THAT WILL HAPPEN EVENTUALLY? EVEN IF THOSE IDIOTS IN PARLIAMENT CAN'T SEE IT COMING, ***I*** CAN. IT'S ***INEVITABLE.***
DID YOU SEE ***THAT*** COMING?
YES, ACTUALLY. IT WAS INEVITABLE.
LET'S GO.

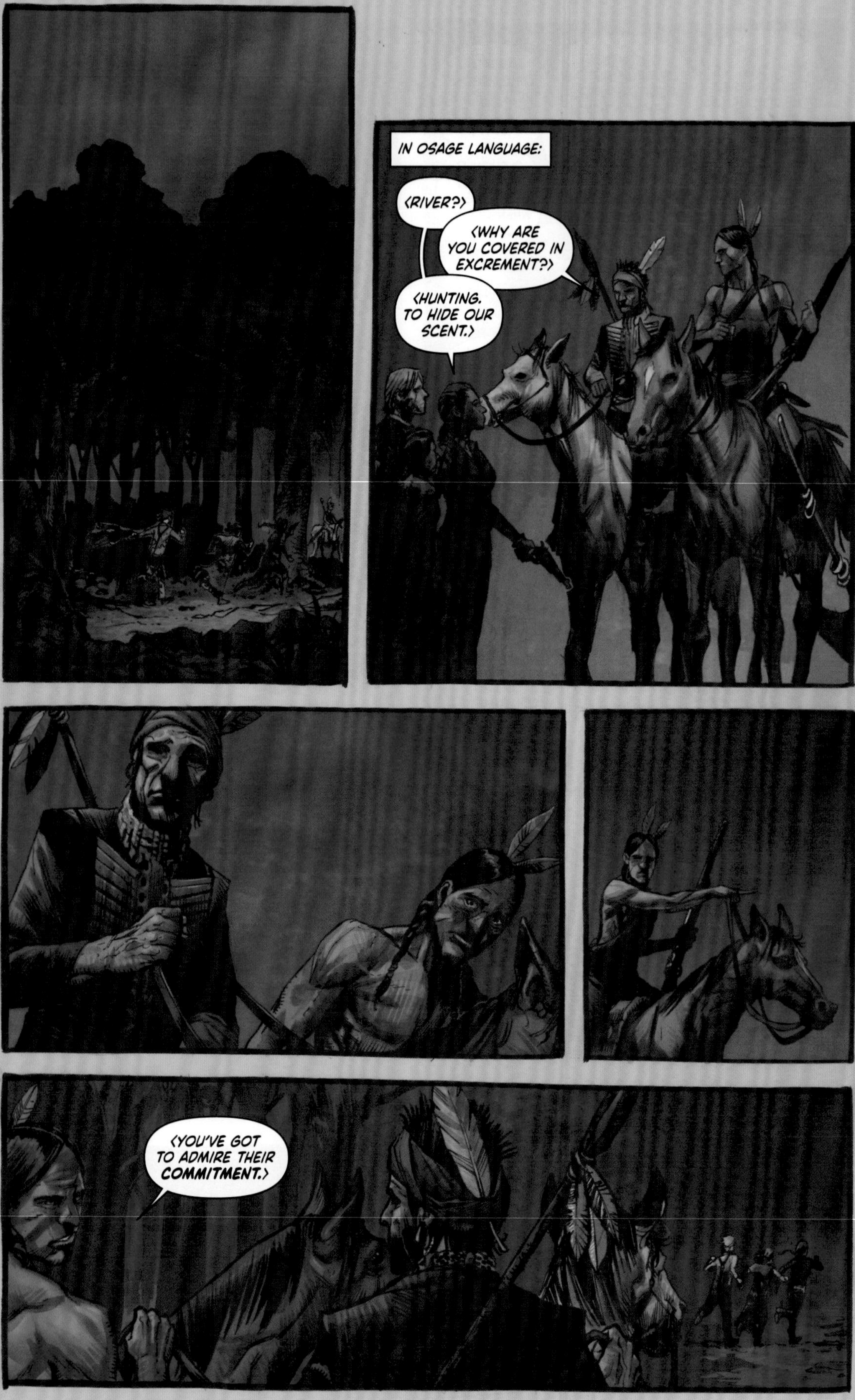
IN OSAGE LANGUAGE:
‹RIVER?›
‹WHY ARE YOU COVERED IN EXCREMENT?›
‹HUNTING. TO HIDE OUR SCENT.›
‹YOU'VE GOT TO ADMIRE THEIR COMMITMENT.›

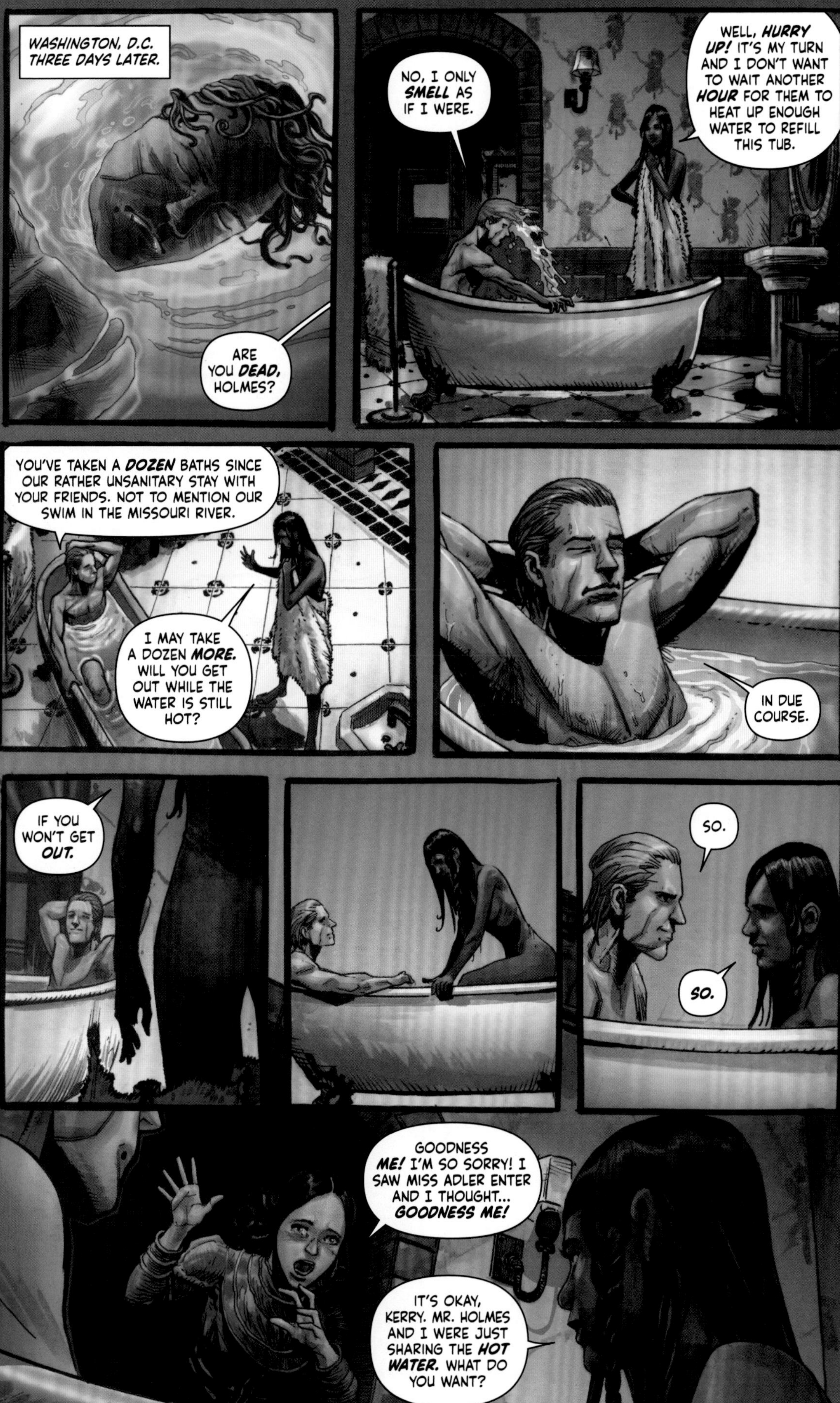
WASHINGTON, D.C. THREE DAYS LATER.
ARE YOU DEAD, HOLMES?
NO, I ONLY SMELL AS IF I WERE.
WELL, HURRY UP! IT'S MY TURN AND I DON'T WANT TO WAIT ANOTHER HOUR FOR THEM TO HEAT UP ENOUGH WATER TO REFILL THIS TUB.
YOU'VE TAKEN A DOZEN BATHS SINCE OUR RATHER UNSANITARY STAY WITH YOUR FRIENDS. NOT TO MENTION OUR SWIM IN THE MISSOURI RIVER.
I MAY TAKE A DOZEN MORE. WILL YOU GET OUT WHILE THE WATER IS STILL HOT?
IN DUE COURSE.
IF YOU WON'T GET OUT.
SO.
SO.
GOODNESS ME! I'M SO SORRY! I SAW MISS ADLER ENTER AND I THOUGHT... GOODNESS ME!
IT'S OKAY, KERRY. MR. HOLMES AND I WERE JUST SHARING THE HOT WATER. WHAT DO YOU WANT?

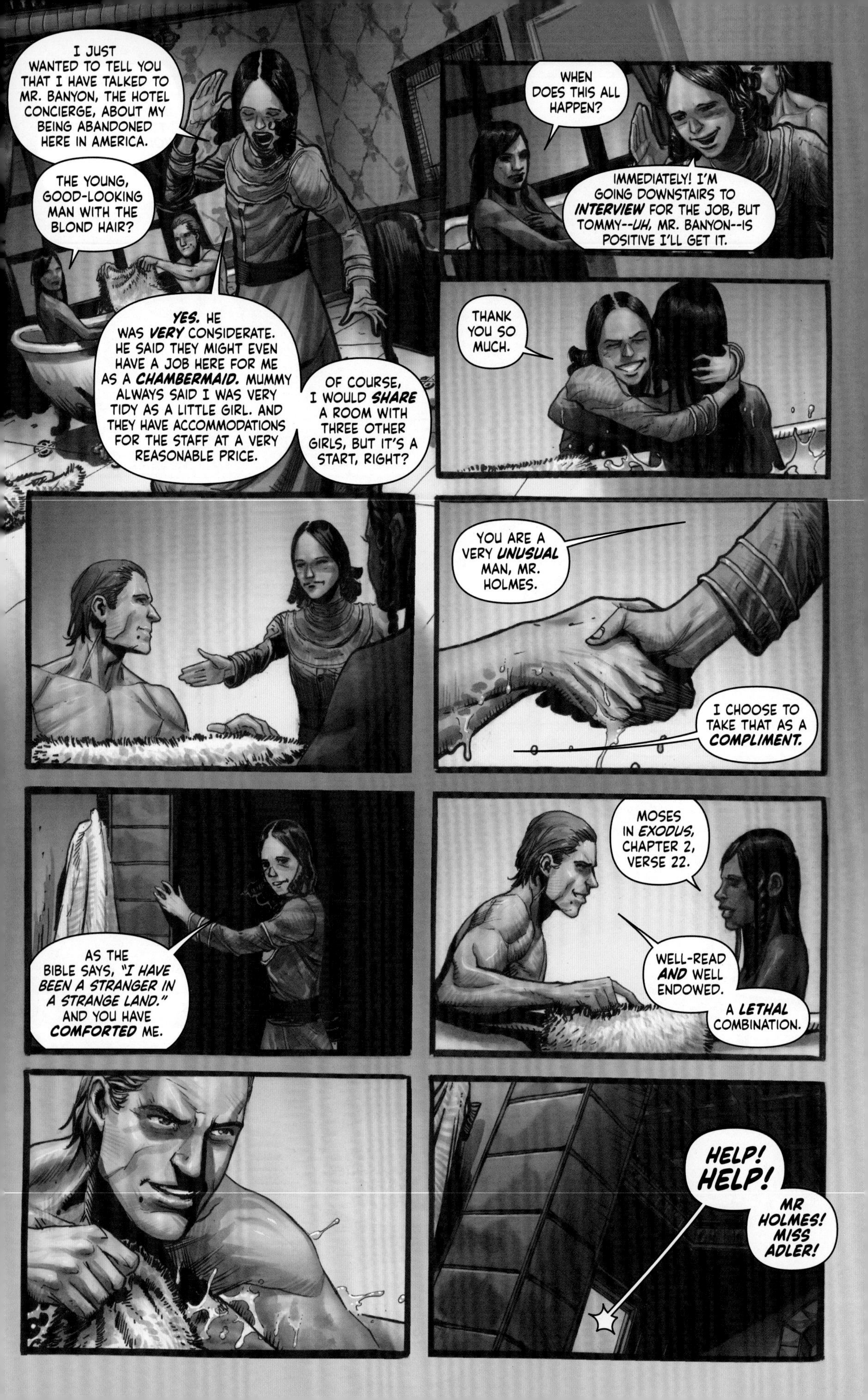
I JUST WANTED TO TELL YOU THAT I HAVE TALKED TO MR. BANYON, THE HOTEL CONCIERGE, ABOUT MY BEING ABANDONED HERE IN AMERICA.
THE YOUNG, GOOD-LOOKING MAN WITH THE BLOND HAIR?
YES. HE WAS VERY CONSIDERATE. HE SAID THEY MIGHT EVEN HAVE A JOB HERE FOR ME AS A CHAMBERMAID. MUMMY ALWAYS SAID I WAS VERY TIDY AS A LITTLE GIRL. AND THEY HAVE ACCOMMODATIONS FOR THE STAFF AT A VERY REASONABLE PRICE.
OF COURSE, I WOULD SHARE A ROOM WITH THREE OTHER GIRLS, BUT IT'S A START, RIGHT?
WHEN DOES THIS ALL HAPPEN?
IMMEDIATELY! I'M GOING DOWNSTAIRS TO INTERVIEW FOR THE JOB, BUT TOMMY--UH, MR. BANYON--IS POSITIVE I'LL GET IT.
THANK YOU SO MUCH.
YOU ARE A VERY UNUSUAL MAN, MR. HOLMES.
I CHOOSE TO TAKE THAT AS A COMPLIMENT.
AS THE BIBLE SAYS, "I HAVE BEEN A STRANGER IN A STRANGE LAND." AND YOU HAVE COMFORTED ME.
MOSES IN EXODUS, CHAPTER 2, VERSE 22.
WELL-READ AND WELL ENDOWED.
A LETHAL COMBINATION.
HELP! HELP!
MR HOLMES! MISS ADLER!

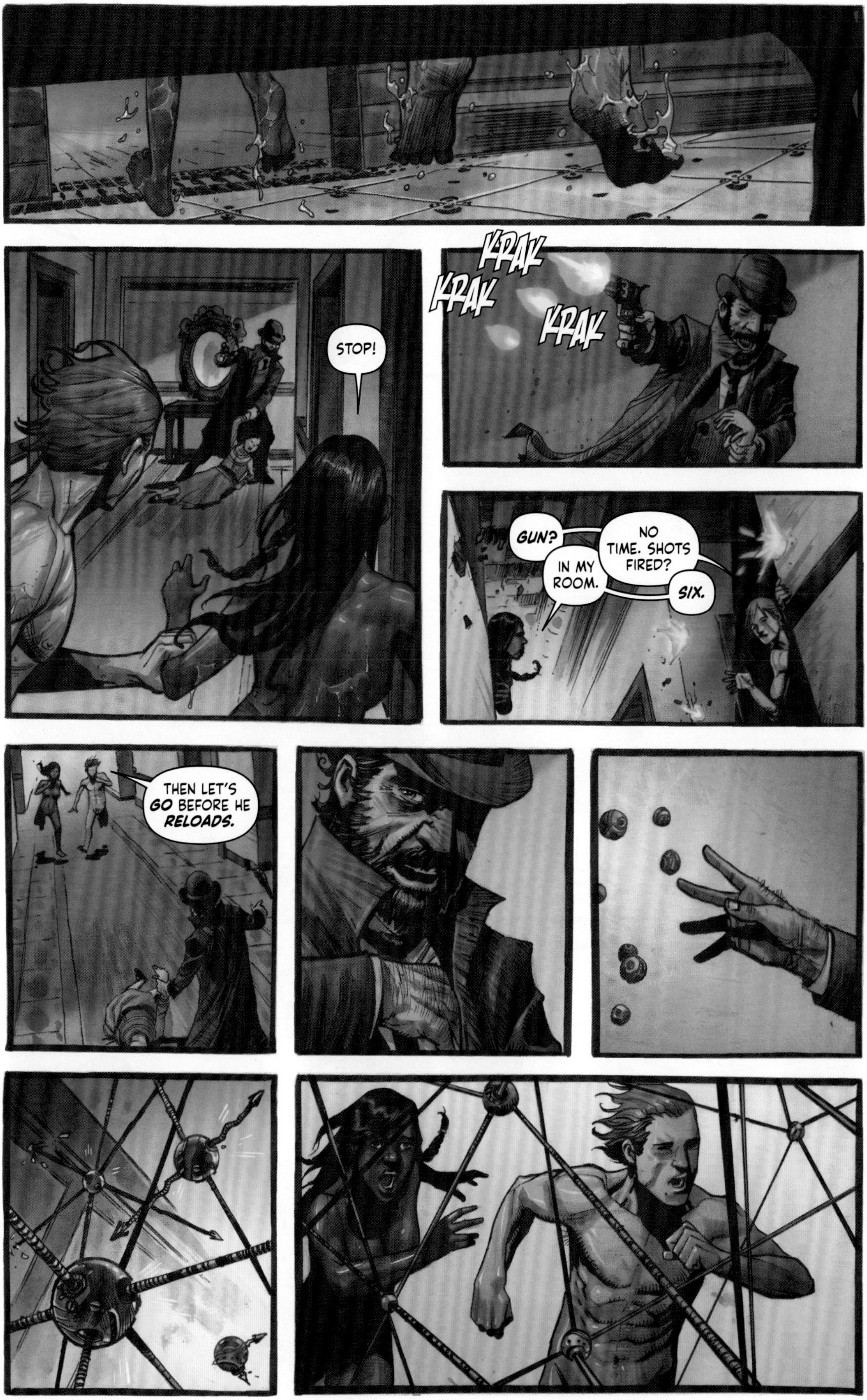
STOP!
KRAK
KRAK
KRAK
GUN?
NO TIME. SHOTS FIRED?
IN MY ROOM.
SIX.
THEN LET'S GO BEFORE HE RELOADS.

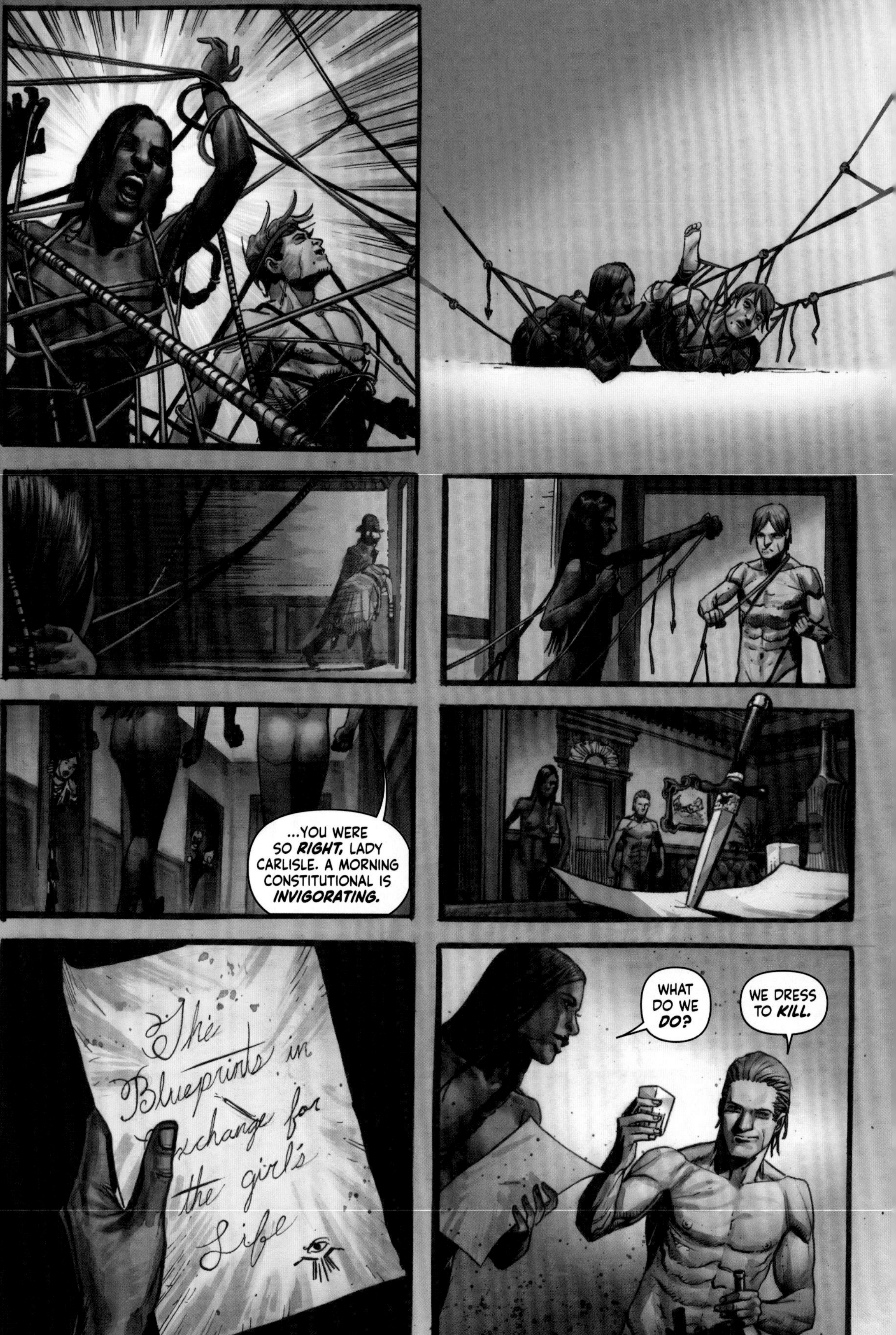
...YOU WERE SO RIGHT, LADY CARLISLE. A MORNING CONSTITUTIONAL IS INVIGORATING.
The Blueprints in Exchange for the girl's Life
WHAT DO WE DO?
WE DRESS TO KILL.

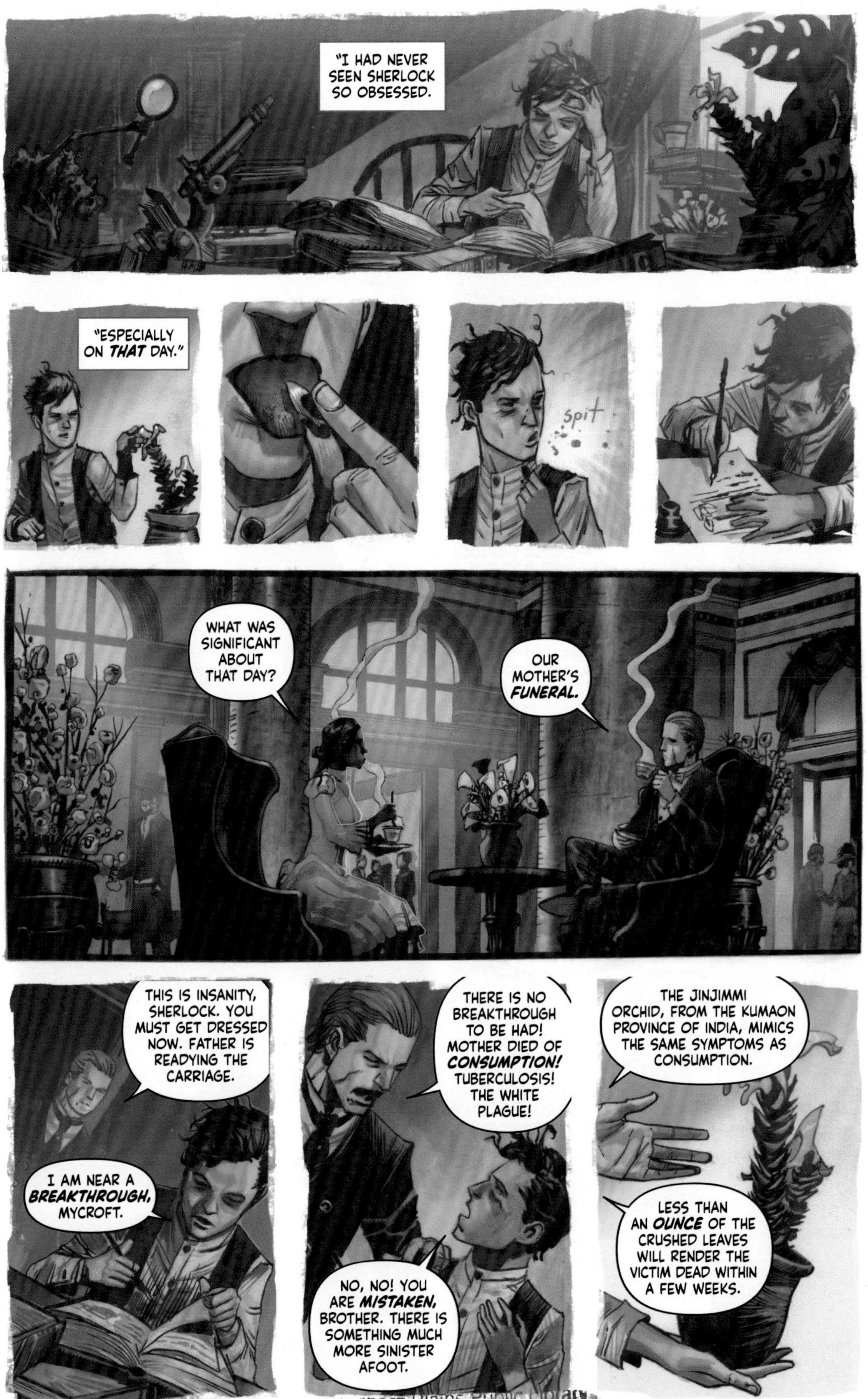
"I HAD NEVER SEEN SHERLOCK SO OBSESSED.
"ESPECIALLY ON THAT DAY."
spit
WHAT WAS SIGNIFICANT ABOUT THAT DAY?
OUR MOTHER'S FUNERAL.
THIS IS INSANITY, SHERLOCK. YOU MUST GET DRESSED NOW. FATHER IS READYING THE CARRIAGE.
I AM NEAR A BREAKTHROUGH, MYCROFT.
THERE IS NO BREAKTHROUGH TO BE HAD! MOTHER DIED OF CONSUMPTION! TUBERCULOSIS! THE WHITE PLAGUE!
NO, NO! YOU ARE MISTAKEN, BROTHER. THERE IS SOMETHING MUCH MORE SINISTER AFOOT.
THE JINJIMMI ORCHID, FROM THE KUMAON PROVINCE OF INDIA, MIMICS THE SAME SYMPTOMS AS CONSUMPTION.
LESS THAN AN OUNCE OF THE CRUSHED LEAVES WILL RENDER THE VICTIM DEAD WITHIN A FEW WEEKS.

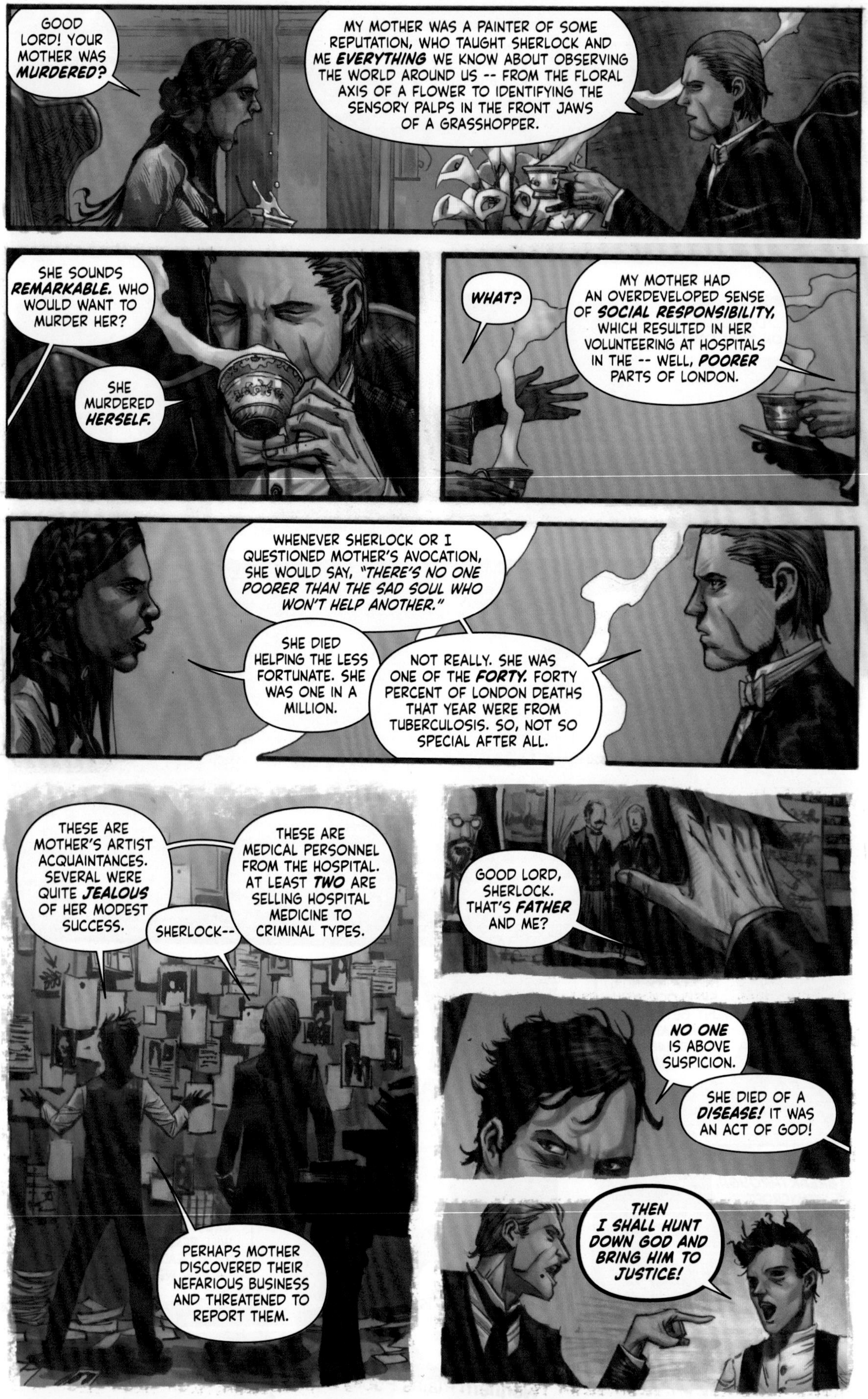
GOOD LORD! YOUR MOTHER WAS MURDERED?
MY MOTHER WAS A PAINTER OF SOME REPUTATION, WHO TAUGHT SHERLOCK AND ME EVERYTHING WE KNOW ABOUT OBSERVING THE WORLD AROUND US -- FROM THE FLORAL AXIS OF A FLOWER TO IDENTIFYING THE SENSORY PALPS IN THE FRONT JAWS OF A GRASSHOPPER.
SHE SOUNDS REMARKABLE. WHO WOULD WANT TO MURDER HER?
SHE MURDERED HERSELF.
WHAT?
MY MOTHER HAD AN OVERDEVELOPED SENSE OF SOCIAL RESPONSIBILITY, WHICH RESULTED IN HER VOLUNTEERING AT HOSPITALS IN THE -- WELL, POORER PARTS OF LONDON.
WHENEVER SHERLOCK OR I QUESTIONED MOTHER'S AVOCATION, SHE WOULD SAY, "THERE'S NO ONE POORER THAN THE SAD SOUL WHO WON'T HELP ANOTHER."
SHE DIED HELPING THE LESS FORTUNATE. SHE WAS ONE IN A MILLION.
NOT REALLY. SHE WAS ONE OF THE FORTY. FORTY PERCENT OF LONDON DEATHS THAT YEAR WERE FROM TUBERCULOSIS. SO, NOT SO SPECIAL AFTER ALL.
THESE ARE MOTHER'S ARTIST ACQUAINTANCES. SEVERAL WERE QUITE JEALOUS OF HER MODEST SUCCESS.
THESE ARE MEDICAL PERSONNEL FROM THE HOSPITAL. AT LEAST TWO ARE SELLING HOSPITAL MEDICINE TO CRIMINAL TYPES.
SHERLOCK--
PERHAPS MOTHER DISCOVERED THEIR NEFARIOUS BUSINESS AND THREATENED TO REPORT THEM.
GOOD LORD, SHERLOCK. THAT'S FATHER AND ME?
NO ONE IS ABOVE SUSPICION.
SHE DIED OF A DISEASE! IT WAS AN ACT OF GOD!
THEN I SHALL HUNT DOWN GOD AND BRING HIM TO JUSTICE!

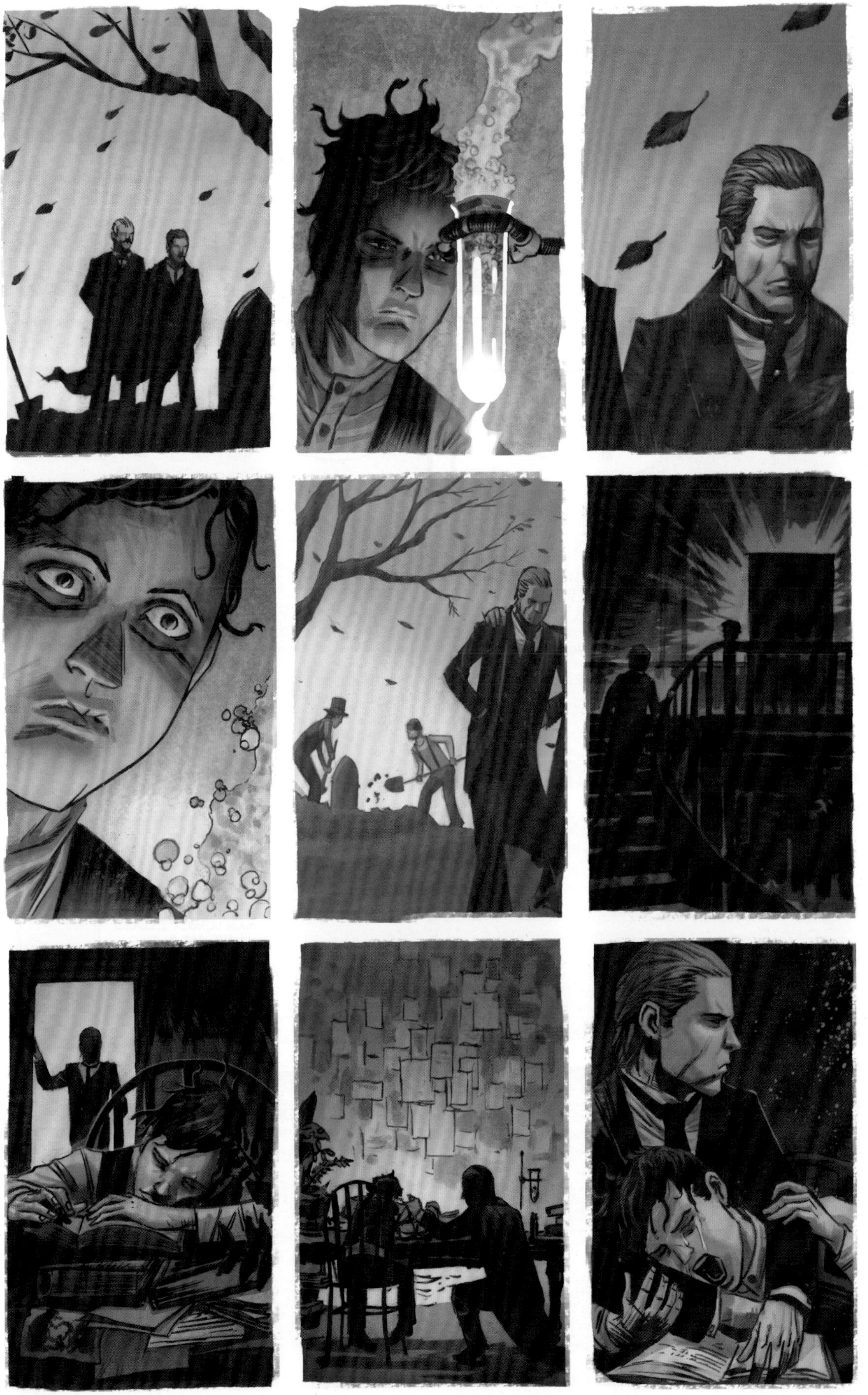

IS THIS YOUR WAY OF TELLING ME WHY YOU DON'T LIKE TO GET INVOLVED IN THE AFFAIRS OF PEOPLE?

NO GOOD DEED GOES *UNPUNISHED.* AS MY MOTHER COULD ATTEST, WERE SHE ALIVE.

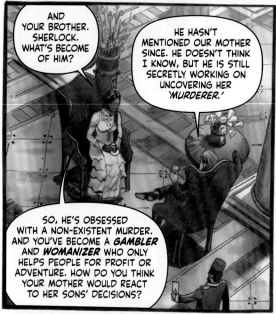

AND YOUR BROTHER. SHERLOCK. WHAT'S BECOME OF HIM?

HE HASN'T MENTIONED OUR MOTHER SINCE. HE DOESN'T THINK I KNOW, BUT HE IS STILL SECRETLY WORKING ON UNCOVERING HER *'MURDERER.'*

SO, HE'S OBSESSED WITH A NON-EXISTENT MURDER. AND YOU'VE BECOME A *GAMBLER* AND *WOMANIZER* WHO ONLY HELPS PEOPLE FOR PROFIT OR ADVENTURE. HOW DO YOU THINK YOUR MOTHER WOULD REACT TO HER SONS' DECISIONS?

MR. HOLMES, SIR. I WAS INSTRUCTED TO DELIVER THIS TO YOU.

ABOUT *TIME.* I DON'T KNOW HOW MUCH LONGER I COULD HAVE SAT IN THIS *RIDICULOUS* OUTFIT SIPPING TEA.

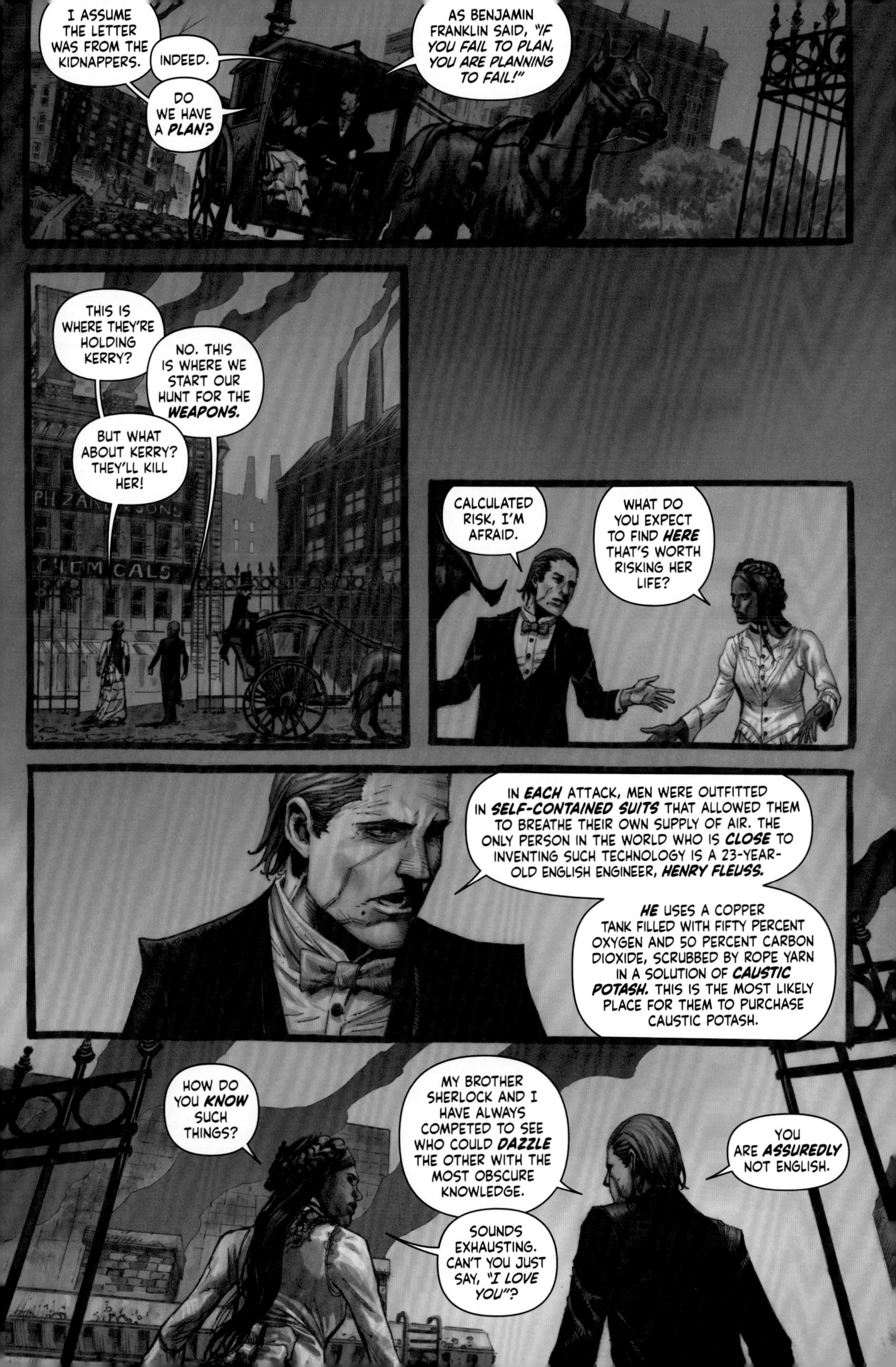

I ASSUME THE LETTER WAS FROM THE KIDNAPPERS.
INDEED.
DO WE HAVE A PLAN?
AS BENJAMIN FRANKLIN SAID, "IF YOU FAIL TO PLAN, YOU ARE PLANNING TO FAIL!"
THIS IS WHERE THEY'RE HOLDING KERRY?
NO. THIS IS WHERE WE START OUR HUNT FOR THE WEAPONS.
BUT WHAT ABOUT KERRY? THEY'LL KILL HER!
CALCULATED RISK, I'M AFRAID.
WHAT DO YOU EXPECT TO FIND HERE THAT'S WORTH RISKING HER LIFE?
IN EACH ATTACK, MEN WERE OUTFITTED IN SELF-CONTAINED SUITS THAT ALLOWED THEM TO BREATHE THEIR OWN SUPPLY OF AIR. THE ONLY PERSON IN THE WORLD WHO IS CLOSE TO INVENTING SUCH TECHNOLOGY IS A 23-YEAR-OLD ENGLISH ENGINEER, HENRY FLEUSS.
HE USES A COPPER TANK FILLED WITH FIFTY PERCENT OXYGEN AND 50 PERCENT CARBON DIOXIDE, SCRUBBED BY ROPE YARN IN A SOLUTION OF CAUSTIC POTASH. THIS IS THE MOST LIKELY PLACE FOR THEM TO PURCHASE CAUSTIC POTASH.
HOW DO YOU KNOW SUCH THINGS?
MY BROTHER SHERLOCK AND I HAVE ALWAYS COMPETED TO SEE WHO COULD DAZZLE THE OTHER WITH THE MOST OBSCURE KNOWLEDGE.
SOUNDS EXHAUSTING. CAN'T YOU JUST SAY, "I LOVE YOU"?
YOU ARE ASSUREDLY NOT ENGLISH.

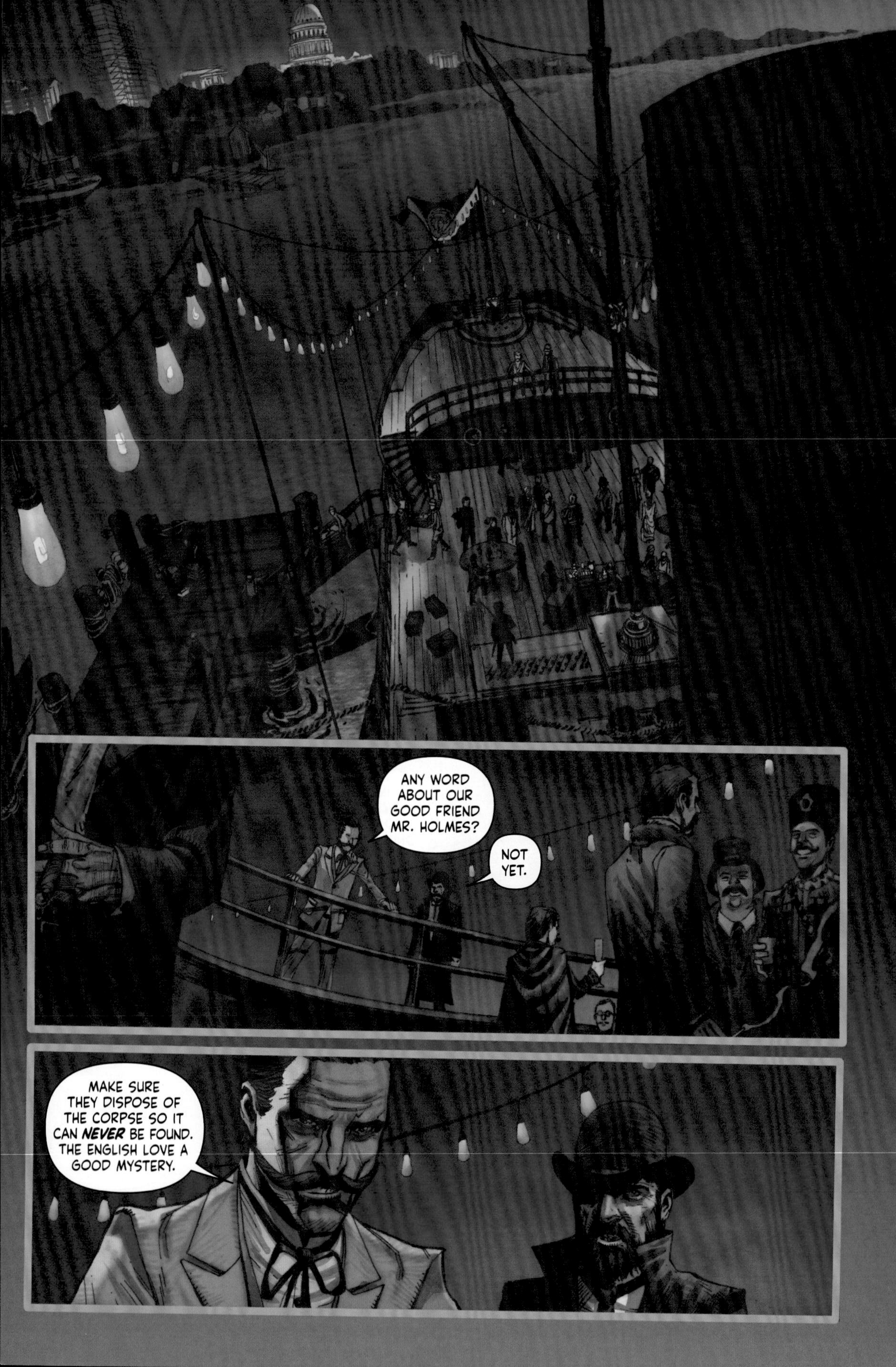
ANY WORD ABOUT OUR GOOD FRIEND MR. HOLMES?
NOT YET.
MAKE SURE THEY DISPOSE OF THE CORPSE SO IT CAN *NEVER* BE FOUND. THE ENGLISH LOVE A GOOD MYSTERY.

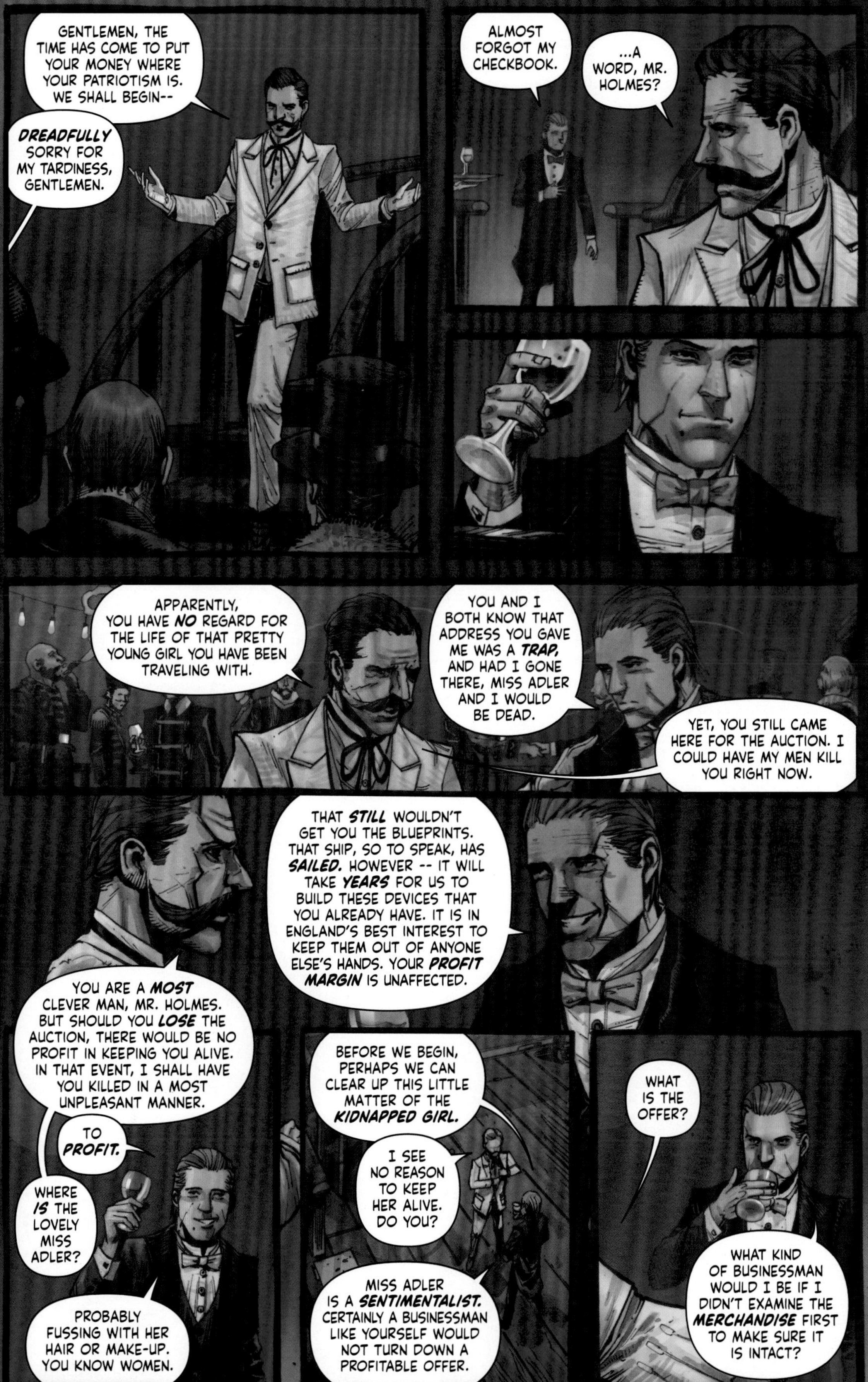
GENTLEMEN, THE TIME HAS COME TO PUT YOUR MONEY WHERE YOUR PATRIOTISM IS. WE SHALL BEGIN--
DREADFULLY SORRY FOR MY TARDINESS, GENTLEMEN.
ALMOST FORGOT MY CHECKBOOK.
...A WORD, MR. HOLMES?
APPARENTLY, YOU HAVE NO REGARD FOR THE LIFE OF THAT PRETTY YOUNG GIRL YOU HAVE BEEN TRAVELING WITH.
YOU AND I BOTH KNOW THAT ADDRESS YOU GAVE ME WAS A TRAP, AND HAD I GONE THERE, MISS ADLER AND I WOULD BE DEAD.
YET, YOU STILL CAME HERE FOR THE AUCTION. I COULD HAVE MY MEN KILL YOU RIGHT NOW.
THAT STILL WOULDN'T GET YOU THE BLUEPRINTS. THAT SHIP, SO TO SPEAK, HAS SAILED. HOWEVER -- IT WILL TAKE YEARS FOR US TO BUILD THESE DEVICES THAT YOU ALREADY HAVE. IT IS IN ENGLAND'S BEST INTEREST TO KEEP THEM OUT OF ANYONE ELSE'S HANDS. YOUR PROFIT MARGIN IS UNAFFECTED.
YOU ARE A MOST CLEVER MAN, MR. HOLMES. BUT SHOULD YOU LOSE THE AUCTION, THERE WOULD BE NO PROFIT IN KEEPING YOU ALIVE. IN THAT EVENT, I SHALL HAVE YOU KILLED IN A MOST UNPLEASANT MANNER.
TO PROFIT.
WHERE IS THE LOVELY MISS ADLER?
PROBABLY FUSSING WITH HER HAIR OR MAKE-UP. YOU KNOW WOMEN.
BEFORE WE BEGIN, PERHAPS WE CAN CLEAR UP THIS LITTLE MATTER OF THE KIDNAPPED GIRL.
I SEE NO REASON TO KEEP HER ALIVE. DO YOU?
MISS ADLER IS A SENTIMENTALIST. CERTAINLY A BUSINESSMAN LIKE YOURSELF WOULD NOT TURN DOWN A PROFITABLE OFFER.
WHAT IS THE OFFER?
WHAT KIND OF BUSINESSMAN WOULD I BE IF I DIDN'T EXAMINE THE MERCHANDISE FIRST TO MAKE SURE IT IS INTACT?

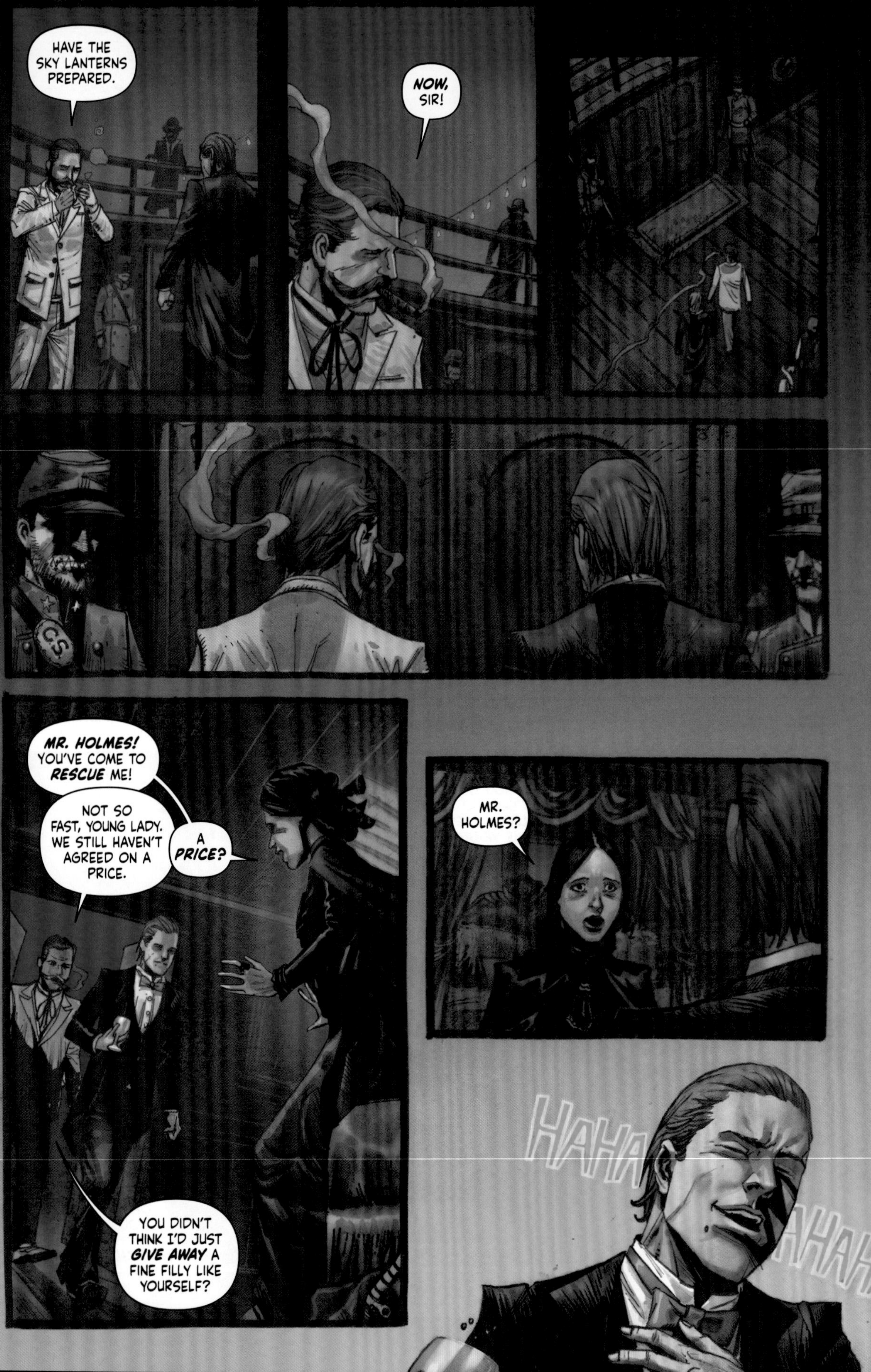
HAVE THE SKY LANTERNS PREPARED.
NOW, SIR!
C.S.
MR. HOLMES! YOU'VE COME TO RESCUE ME!
NOT SO FAST, YOUNG LADY. WE STILL HAVEN'T AGREED ON A PRICE.
A PRICE?
MR. HOLMES?
YOU DIDN'T THINK I'D JUST GIVE AWAY A FINE FILLY LIKE YOURSELF?
HAHA
HAHA

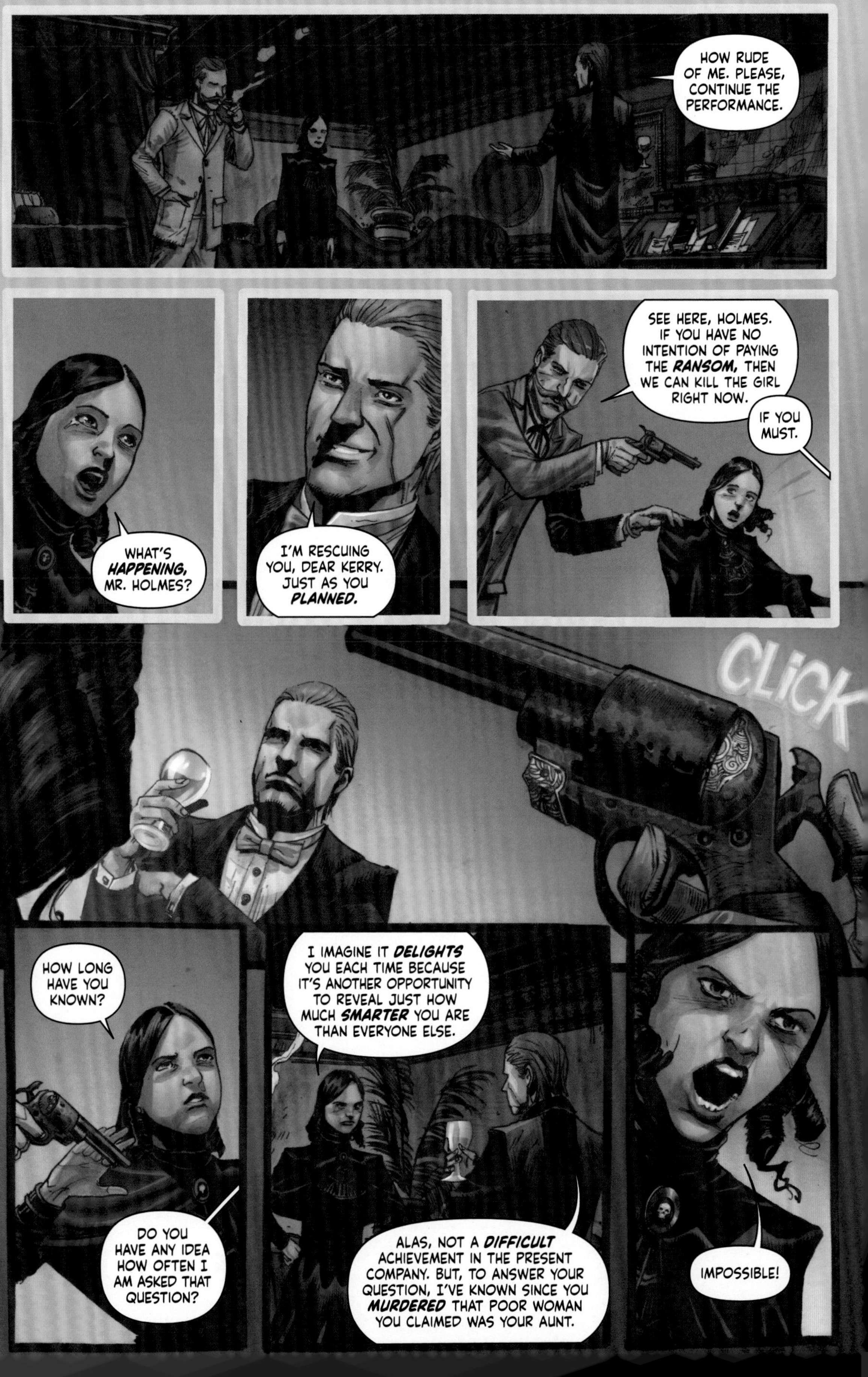

HOW RUDE OF ME. PLEASE, CONTINUE THE PERFORMANCE.
WHAT'S HAPPENING, MR. HOLMES?
I'M RESCUING YOU, DEAR KERRY. JUST AS YOU PLANNED.
SEE HERE, HOLMES. IF YOU HAVE NO INTENTION OF PAYING THE RANSOM, THEN WE CAN KILL THE GIRL RIGHT NOW.
IF YOU MUST.
CLICK
HOW LONG HAVE YOU KNOWN?
DO YOU HAVE ANY IDEA HOW OFTEN I AM ASKED THAT QUESTION?
I IMAGINE IT DELIGHTS YOU EACH TIME BECAUSE IT'S ANOTHER OPPORTUNITY TO REVEAL JUST HOW MUCH SMARTER YOU ARE THAN EVERYONE ELSE.
ALAS, NOT A DIFFICULT ACHIEVEMENT IN THE PRESENT COMPANY. BUT, TO ANSWER YOUR QUESTION, I'VE KNOWN SINCE YOU MURDERED THAT POOR WOMAN YOU CLAIMED WAS YOUR AUNT.
IMPOSSIBLE!

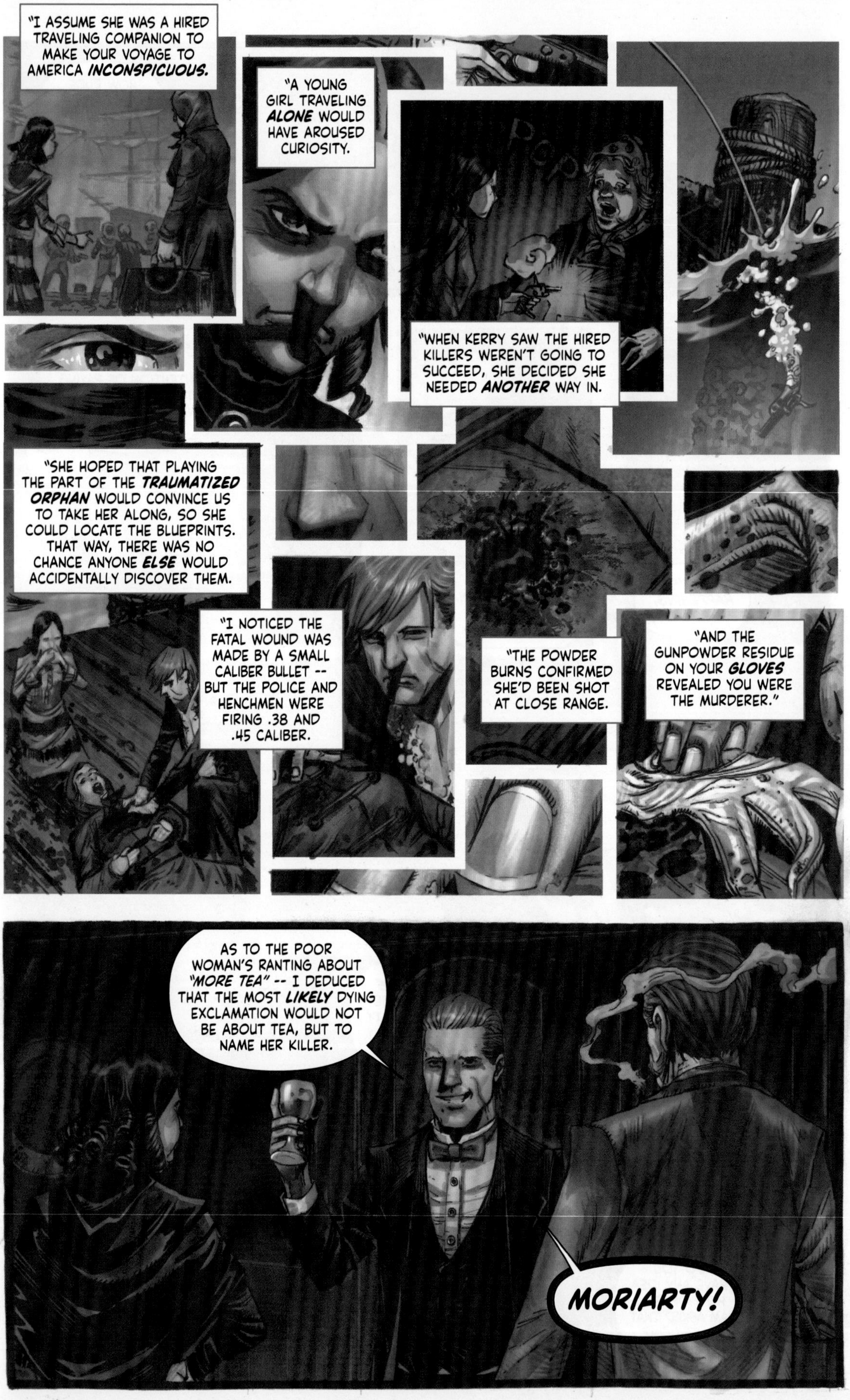

"I ASSUME SHE WAS A HIRED TRAVELING COMPANION TO MAKE YOUR VOYAGE TO AMERICA *INCONSPICUOUS.*
"A YOUNG GIRL TRAVELING *ALONE* WOULD HAVE AROUSED CURIOSITY.
"WHEN KERRY SAW THE HIRED KILLERS WEREN'T GOING TO SUCCEED, SHE DECIDED SHE NEEDED *ANOTHER* WAY IN.
"SHE HOPED THAT PLAYING THE PART OF THE *TRAUMATIZED ORPHAN* WOULD CONVINCE US TO TAKE HER ALONG, SO SHE COULD LOCATE THE BLUEPRINTS. THAT WAY, THERE WAS NO CHANCE ANYONE *ELSE* WOULD ACCIDENTALLY DISCOVER THEM.
"I NOTICED THE FATAL WOUND WAS MADE BY A SMALL CALIBER BULLET -- BUT THE POLICE AND HENCHMEN WERE FIRING .38 AND .45 CALIBER.
"THE POWDER BURNS CONFIRMED SHE'D BEEN SHOT AT CLOSE RANGE.
"AND THE GUNPOWDER RESIDUE ON YOUR *GLOVES* REVEALED YOU WERE THE MURDERER."
AS TO THE POOR WOMAN'S RANTING ABOUT *"MORE TEA"* -- I DEDUCED THAT THE MOST *LIKELY* DYING EXCLAMATION WOULD NOT BE ABOUT TEA, BUT TO NAME HER KILLER.
MORIARTY!

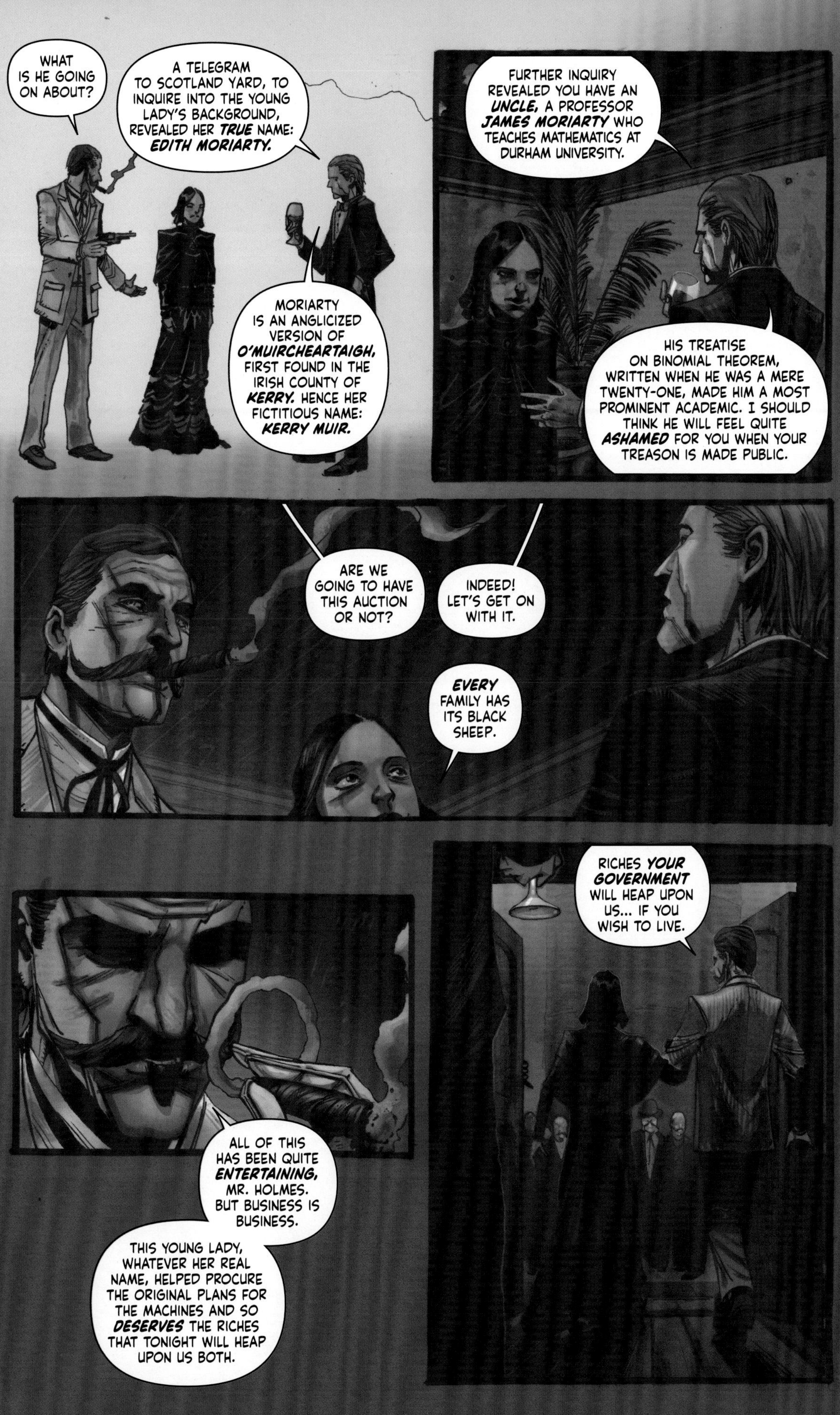
WHAT IS HE GOING ON ABOUT?
A TELEGRAM TO SCOTLAND YARD, TO INQUIRE INTO THE YOUNG LADY'S BACKGROUND, REVEALED HER TRUE NAME: EDITH MORIARTY.
MORIARTY IS AN ANGLICIZED VERSION OF O'MUIRCHEARTAIGH, FIRST FOUND IN THE IRISH COUNTY OF KERRY. HENCE HER FICTITIOUS NAME: KERRY MUIR.
FURTHER INQUIRY REVEALED YOU HAVE AN UNCLE, A PROFESSOR JAMES MORIARTY WHO TEACHES MATHEMATICS AT DURHAM UNIVERSITY.
HIS TREATISE ON BINOMIAL THEOREM, WRITTEN WHEN HE WAS A MERE TWENTY-ONE, MADE HIM A MOST PROMINENT ACADEMIC. I SHOULD THINK HE WILL FEEL QUITE ASHAMED FOR YOU WHEN YOUR TREASON IS MADE PUBLIC.
ARE WE GOING TO HAVE THIS AUCTION OR NOT?
INDEED! LET'S GET ON WITH IT.
EVERY FAMILY HAS ITS BLACK SHEEP.
ALL OF THIS HAS BEEN QUITE ENTERTAINING, MR. HOLMES. BUT BUSINESS IS BUSINESS.
THIS YOUNG LADY, WHATEVER HER REAL NAME, HELPED PROCURE THE ORIGINAL PLANS FOR THE MACHINES AND SO DESERVES THE RICHES THAT TONIGHT WILL HEAP UPON US BOTH.
RICHES YOUR GOVERNMENT WILL HEAP UPON US... IF YOU WISH TO LIVE.

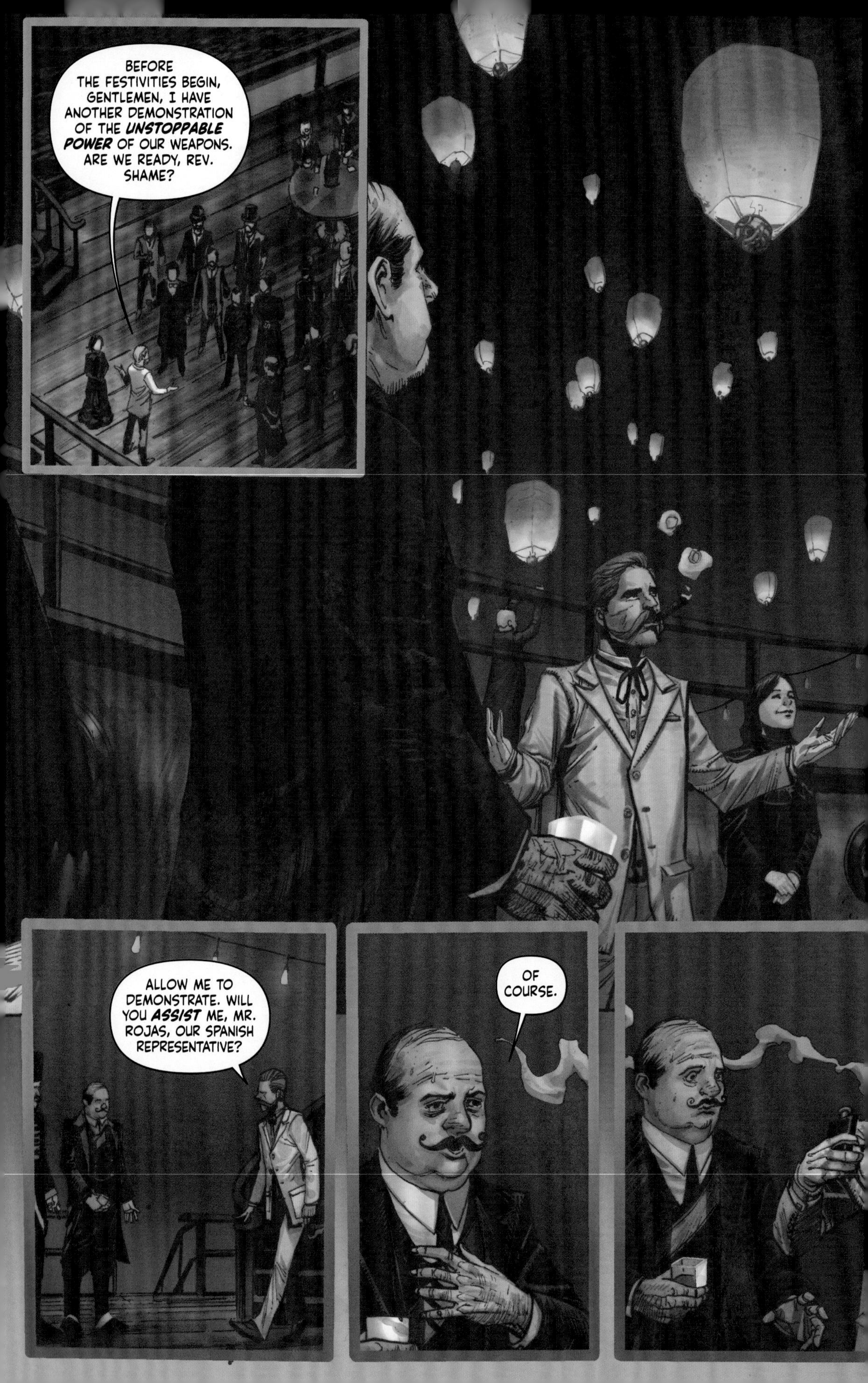
BEFORE THE FESTIVITIES BEGIN, GENTLEMEN, I HAVE ANOTHER DEMONSTRATION OF THE UNSTOPPABLE POWER OF OUR WEAPONS. ARE WE READY, REV. SHAME?
ALLOW ME TO DEMONSTRATE. WILL YOU ASSIST ME, MR. ROJAS, OUR SPANISH REPRESENTATIVE?
OF COURSE.

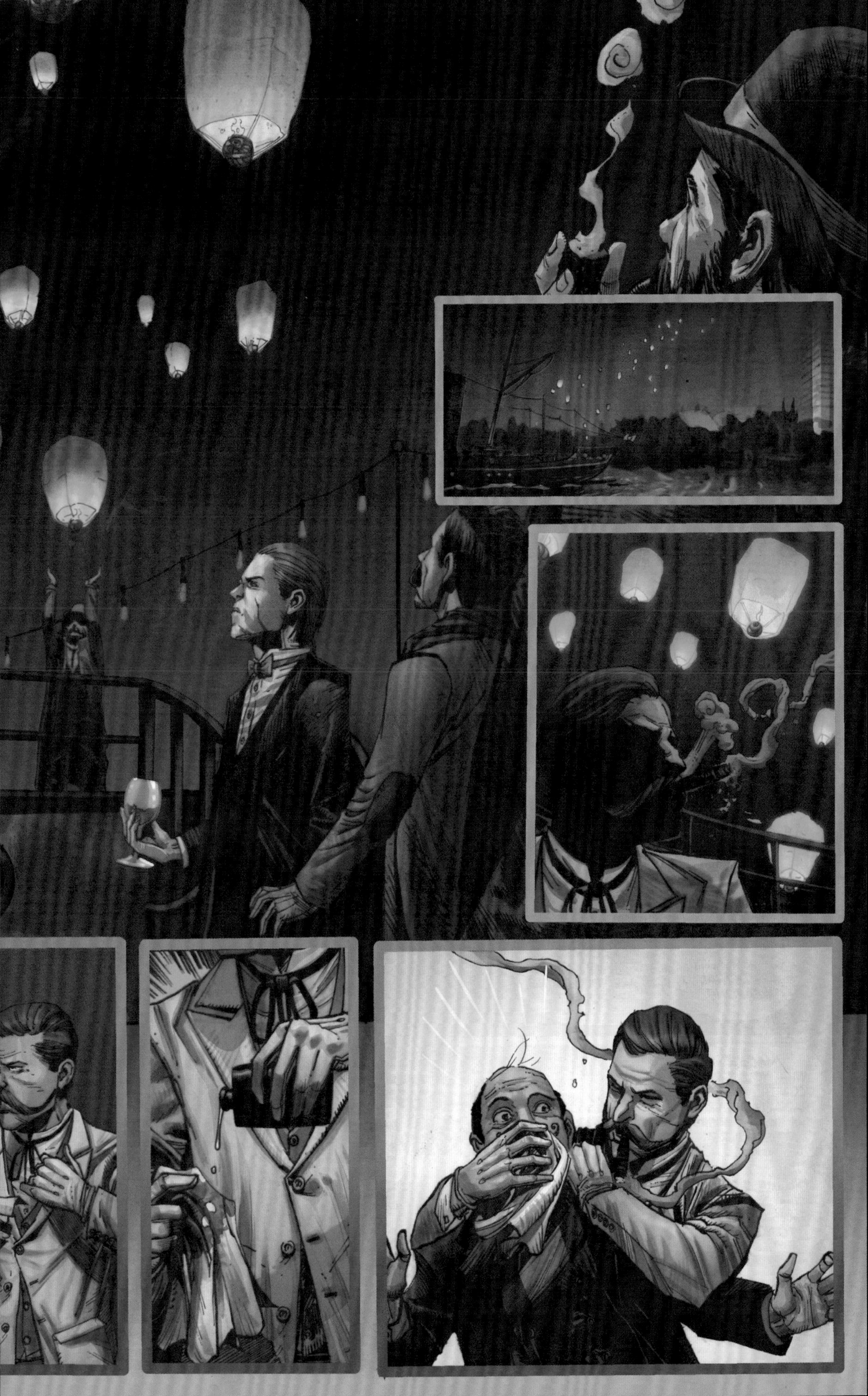

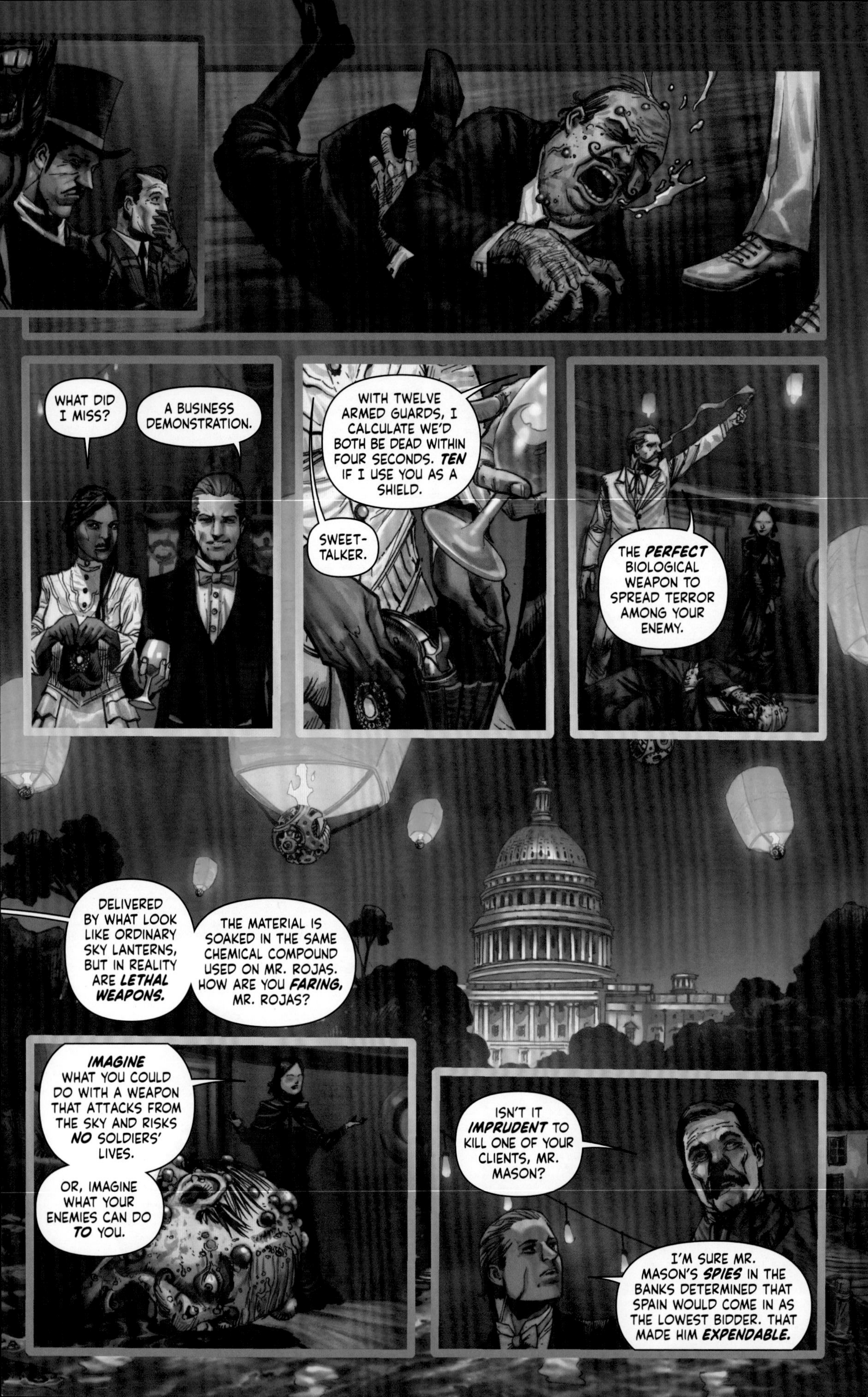
WHAT DID I MISS?
A BUSINESS DEMONSTRATION.
WITH TWELVE ARMED GUARDS, I CALCULATE WE'D BOTH BE DEAD WITHIN FOUR SECONDS. TEN IF I USE YOU AS A SHIELD.
SWEET-TALKER.
THE PERFECT BIOLOGICAL WEAPON TO SPREAD TERROR AMONG YOUR ENEMY.
DELIVERED BY WHAT LOOK LIKE ORDINARY SKY LANTERNS, BUT IN REALITY ARE LETHAL WEAPONS.
THE MATERIAL IS SOAKED IN THE SAME CHEMICAL COMPOUND USED ON MR. ROJAS. HOW ARE YOU FARING, MR. ROJAS?
IMAGINE WHAT YOU COULD DO WITH A WEAPON THAT ATTACKS FROM THE SKY AND RISKS NO SOLDIERS' LIVES.
OR, IMAGINE WHAT YOUR ENEMIES CAN DO TO YOU.
ISN'T IT IMPRUDENT TO KILL ONE OF YOUR CLIENTS, MR. MASON?
I'M SURE MR. MASON'S SPIES IN THE BANKS DETERMINED THAT SPAIN WOULD COME IN AS THE LOWEST BIDDER. THAT MADE HIM EXPENDABLE.

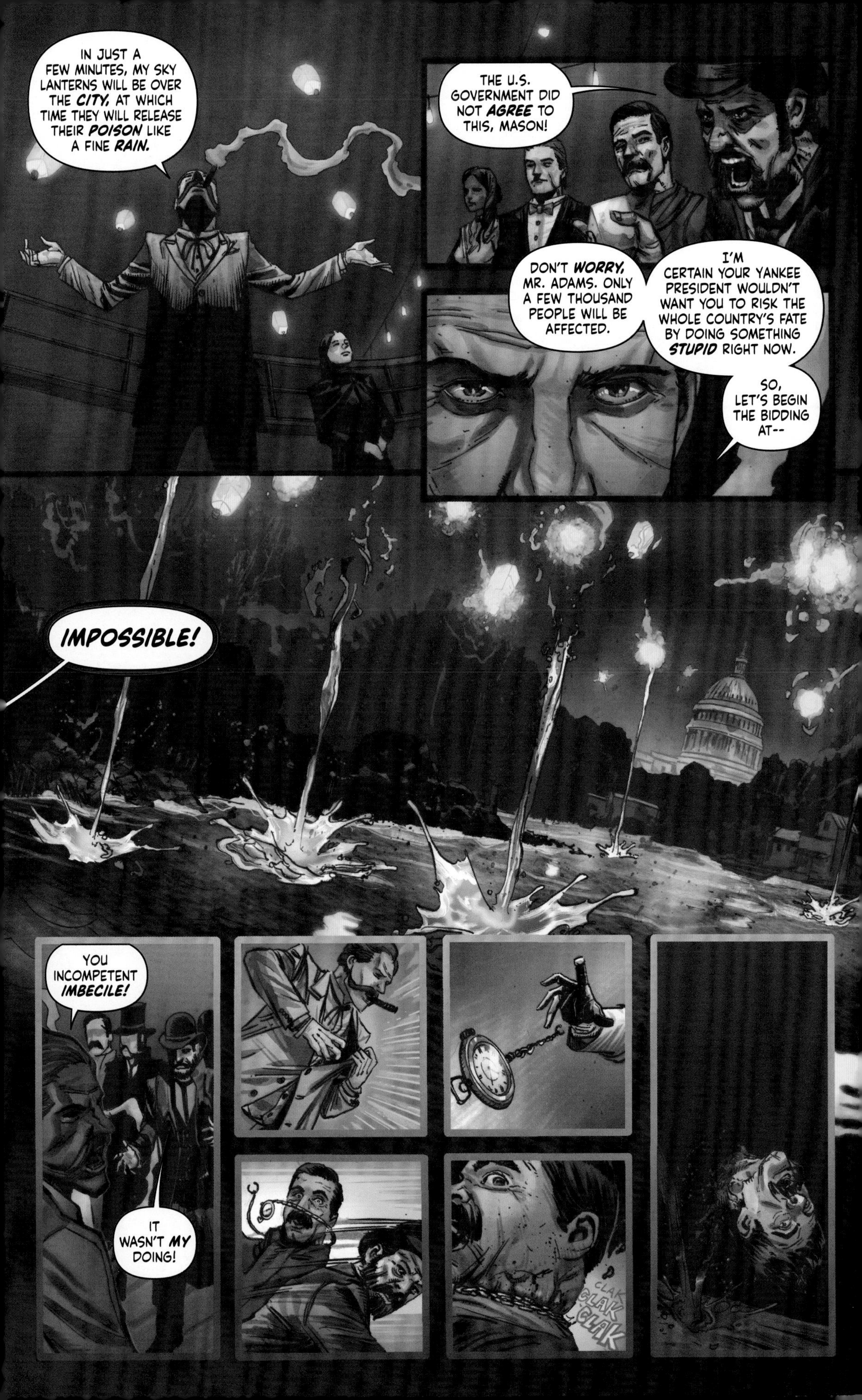
IN JUST A FEW MINUTES, MY SKY LANTERNS WILL BE OVER THE *CITY,* AT WHICH TIME THEY WILL RELEASE THEIR *POISON* LIKE A FINE *RAIN.*
THE U.S. GOVERNMENT DID NOT *AGREE* TO THIS, MASON!
DON'T *WORRY,* MR. ADAMS. ONLY A FEW THOUSAND PEOPLE WILL BE AFFECTED.
I'M CERTAIN YOUR YANKEE PRESIDENT WOULDN'T WANT YOU TO RISK THE WHOLE COUNTRY'S FATE BY DOING SOMETHING *STUPID* RIGHT NOW.
SO, LET'S BEGIN THE BIDDING AT--
IMPOSSIBLE!
YOU INCOMPETENT *IMBECILE!*
IT WASN'T *MY* DOING!
CLAK CLAK CLAK

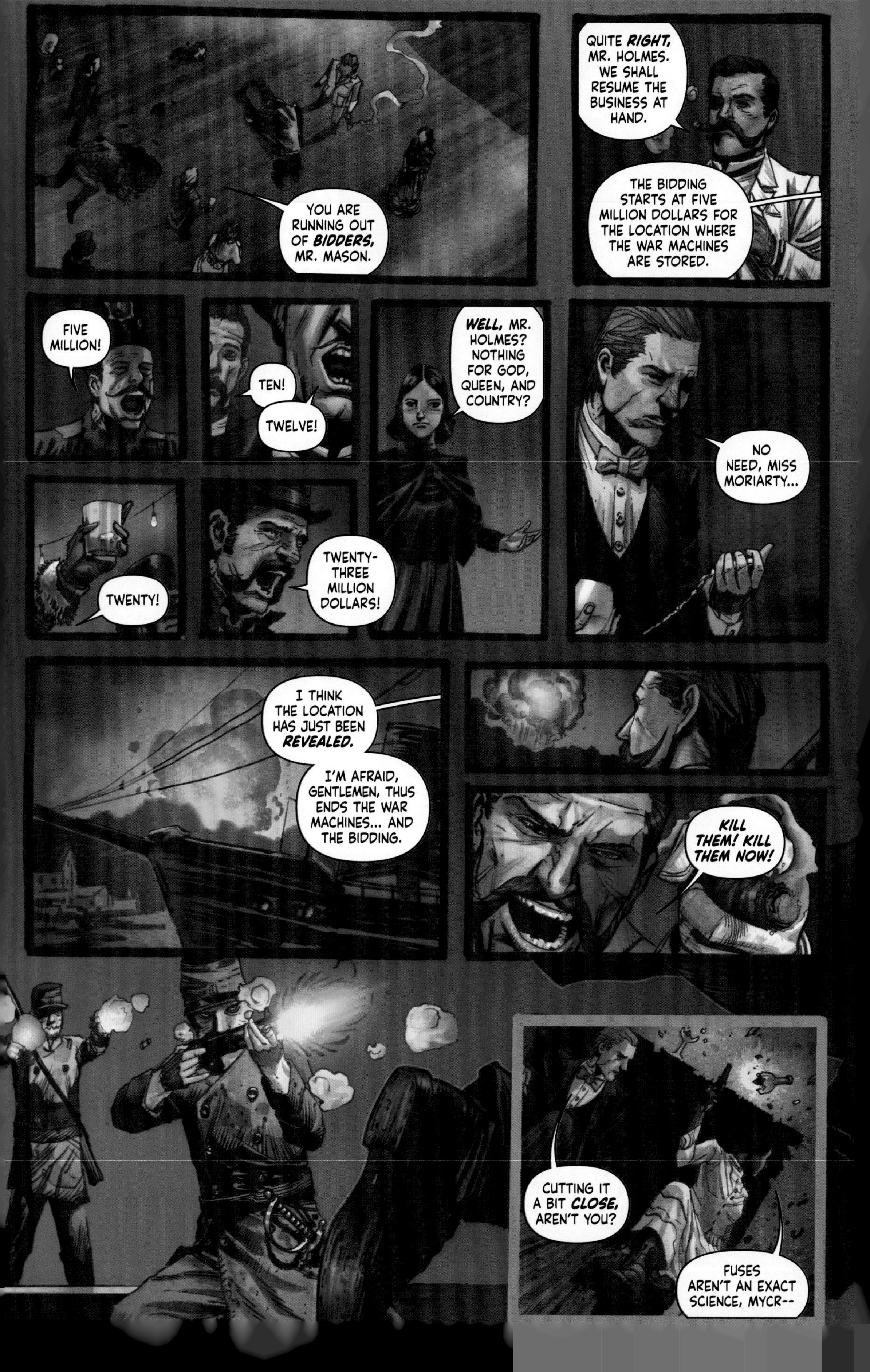
YOU ARE RUNNING OUT OF **BIDDERS,** MR. MASON.
QUITE **RIGHT,** MR. HOLMES. WE SHALL RESUME THE BUSINESS AT HAND.
THE BIDDING STARTS AT FIVE MILLION DOLLARS FOR THE LOCATION WHERE THE WAR MACHINES ARE STORED.
FIVE MILLION!
TEN!
TWELVE!
TWENTY!
TWENTY-THREE MILLION DOLLARS!
WELL, MR. HOLMES? NOTHING FOR GOD, QUEEN, AND COUNTRY?
NO NEED, MISS MORIARTY...
I THINK THE LOCATION HAS JUST BEEN **REVEALED.**
I'M AFRAID, GENTLEMEN, THUS ENDS THE WAR MACHINES... AND THE BIDDING.
KILL THEM! KILL THEM NOW!
CUTTING IT A BIT **CLOSE,** AREN'T YOU?
FUSES AREN'T AN EXACT SCIENCE, MYCR--

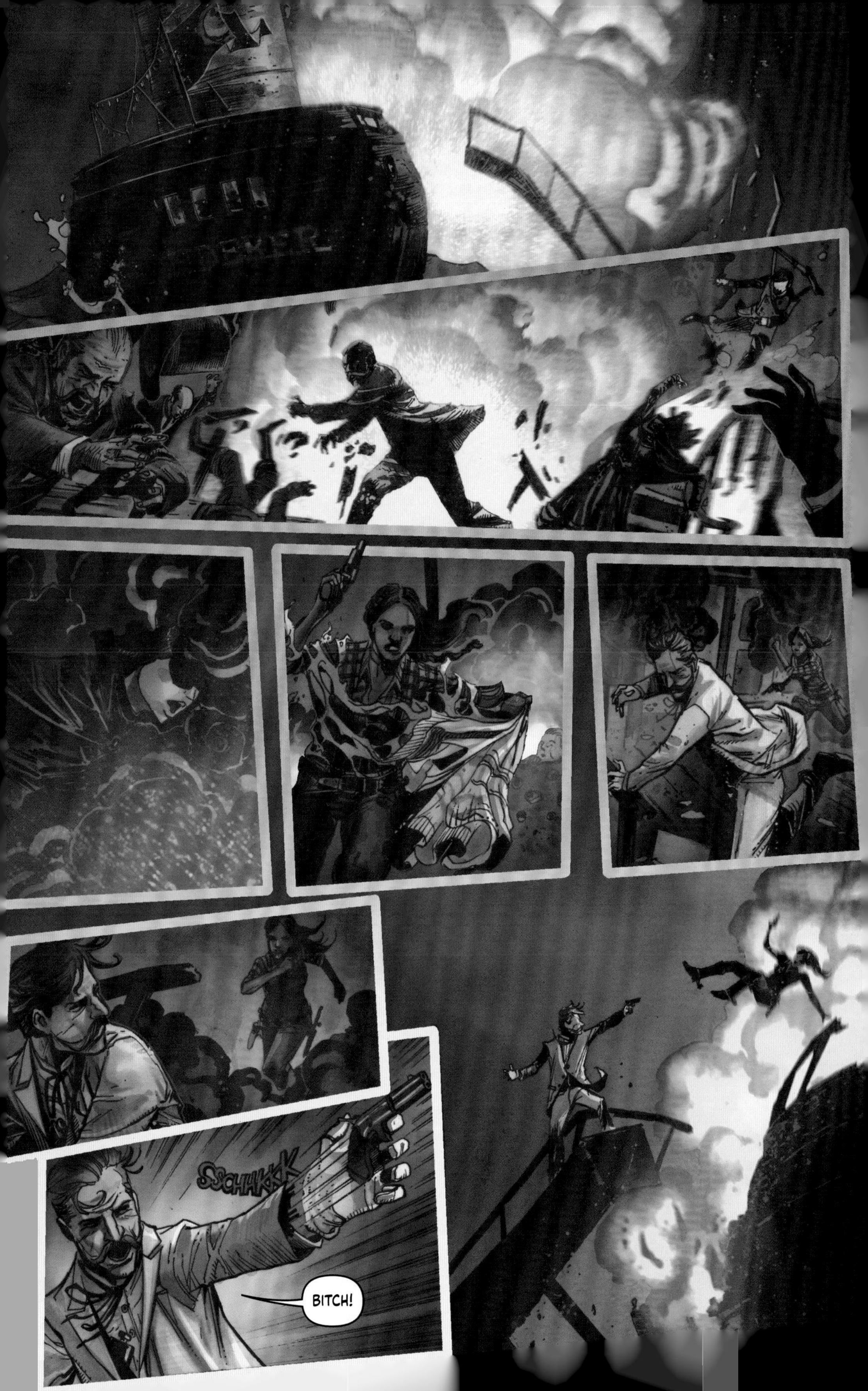
SSCHAKKK
BITCH!

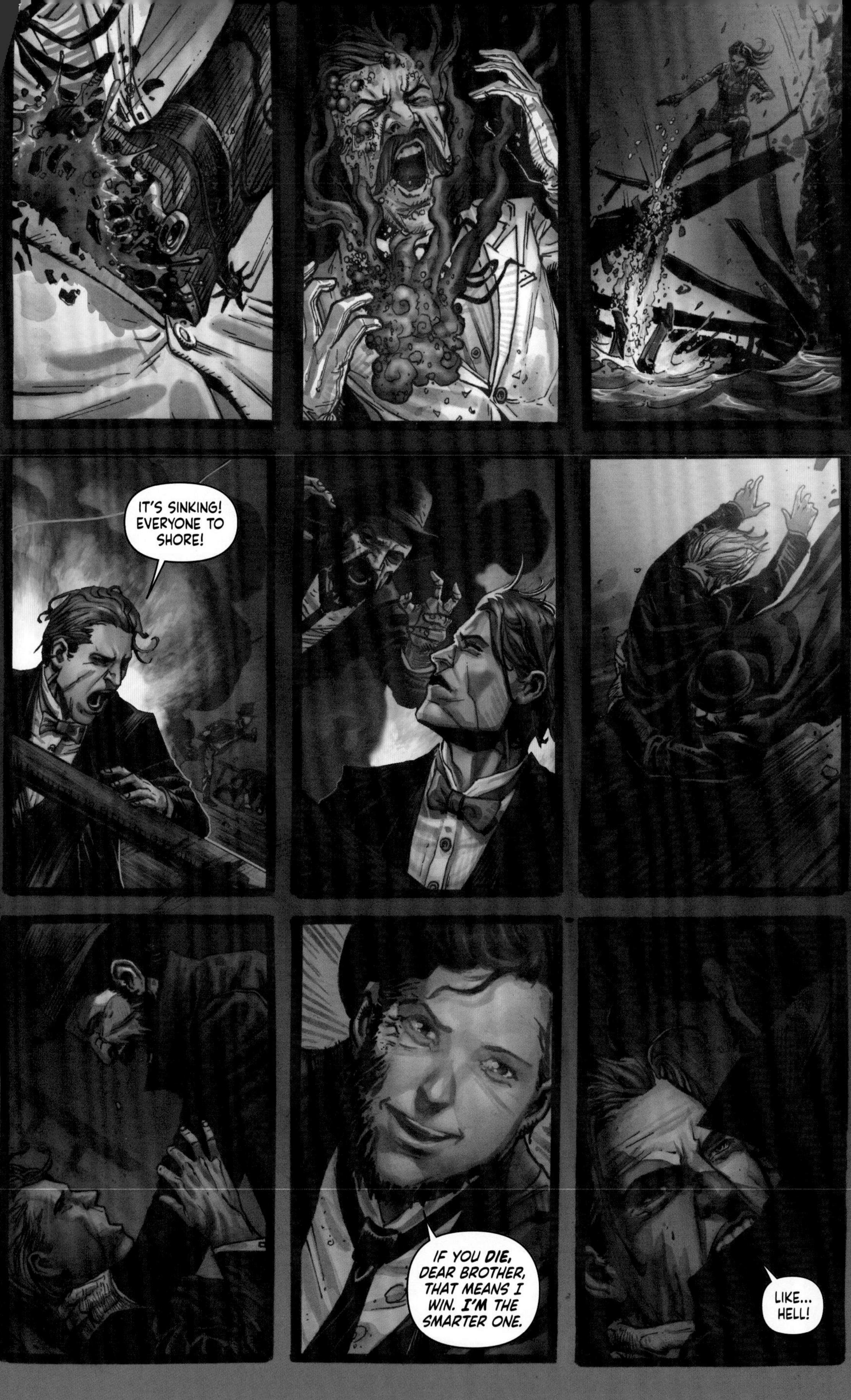

IT'S SINKING! EVERYONE TO SHORE!
IF YOU DIE, DEAR BROTHER, THAT MEANS I WIN. I'M THE SMARTER ONE.
LIKE... HELL!

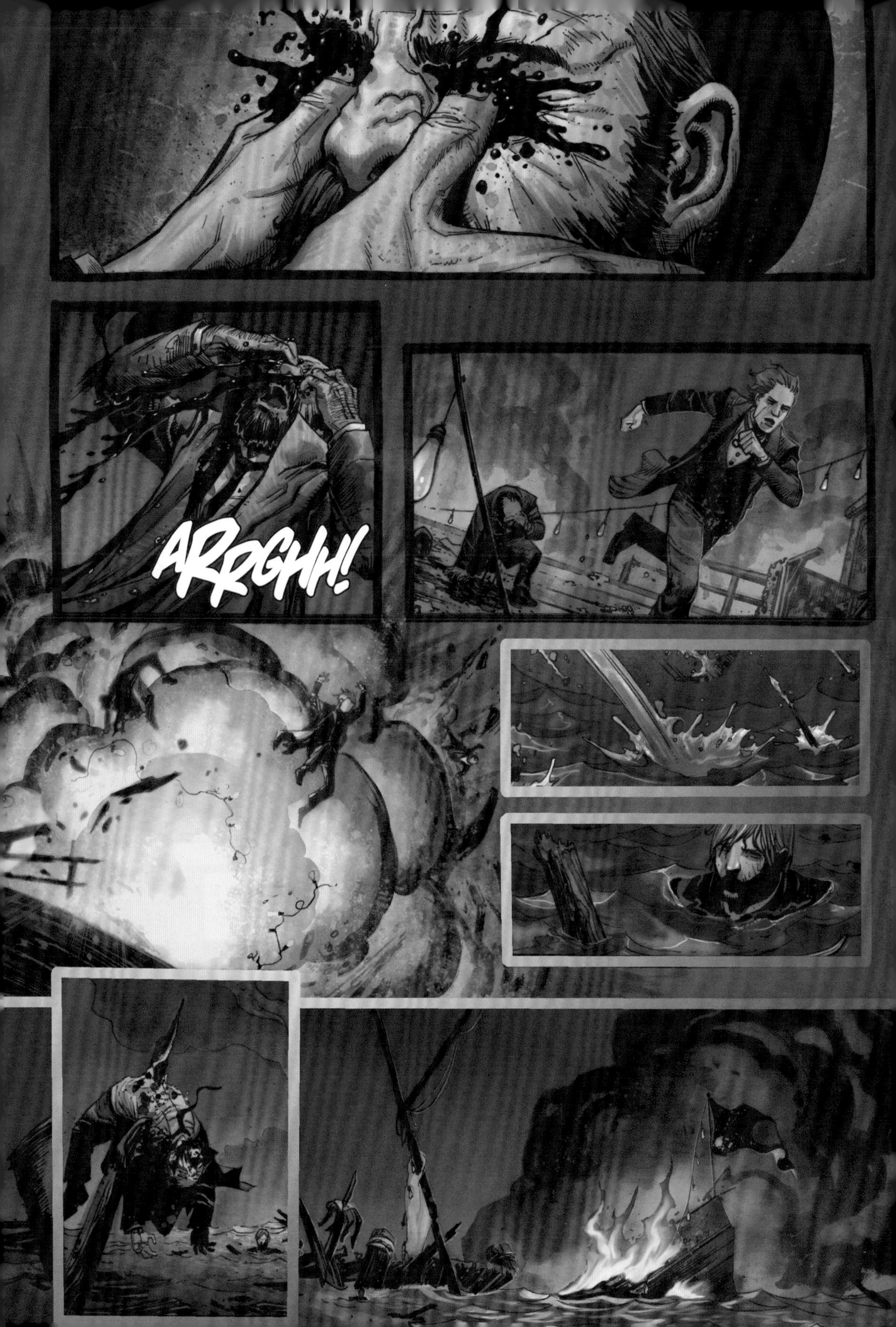
ARRGHH!

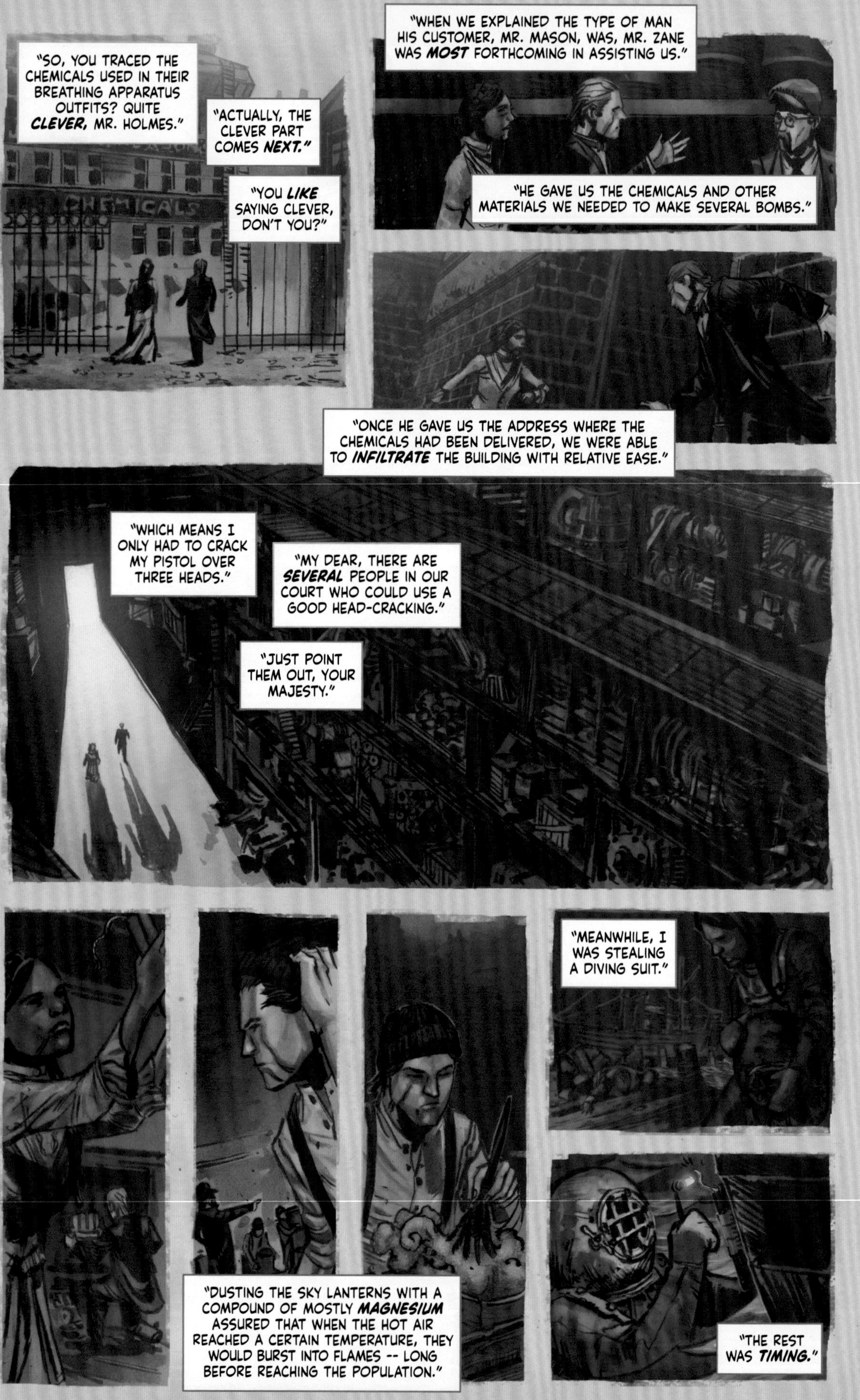
"SO, YOU TRACED THE CHEMICALS USED IN THEIR BREATHING APPARATUS OUTFITS? QUITE CLEVER, MR. HOLMES."
"ACTUALLY, THE CLEVER PART COMES NEXT."
"YOU LIKE SAYING CLEVER, DON'T YOU?"
CHEMICALS
"WHEN WE EXPLAINED THE TYPE OF MAN HIS CUSTOMER, MR. MASON, WAS, MR. ZANE WAS MOST FORTHCOMING IN ASSISTING US."
"HE GAVE US THE CHEMICALS AND OTHER MATERIALS WE NEEDED TO MAKE SEVERAL BOMBS."
"ONCE HE GAVE US THE ADDRESS WHERE THE CHEMICALS HAD BEEN DELIVERED, WE WERE ABLE TO INFILTRATE THE BUILDING WITH RELATIVE EASE."
"WHICH MEANS I ONLY HAD TO CRACK MY PISTOL OVER THREE HEADS."
"MY DEAR, THERE ARE SEVERAL PEOPLE IN OUR COURT WHO COULD USE A GOOD HEAD-CRACKING."
"JUST POINT THEM OUT, YOUR MAJESTY."
"DUSTING THE SKY LANTERNS WITH A COMPOUND OF MOSTLY MAGNESIUM ASSURED THAT WHEN THE HOT AIR REACHED A CERTAIN TEMPERATURE, THEY WOULD BURST INTO FLAMES -- LONG BEFORE REACHING THE POPULATION."
"MEANWHILE, I WAS STEALING A DIVING SUIT."
"THE REST WAS TIMING."

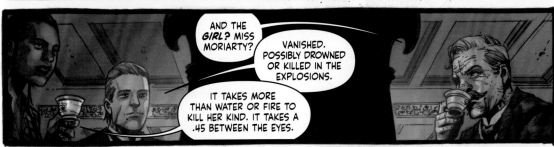

AND THE *GIRL?* MISS MORIARTY?

VANISHED. POSSIBLY DROWNED OR KILLED IN THE EXPLOSIONS.

IT TAKES MORE THAN WATER OR FIRE TO KILL HER KIND. IT TAKES A .45 BETWEEN THE EYES.

AND THE *BLUEPRINTS,* MR. HOLMES. WHERE ARE THE BLUEPRINTS FOR THOSE MACHINES?

SAFE.

WE PREFER THEM SAFE IN OUR HANDS, SIR.

I AM CERTAIN YOU *DO.* BUT I'VE DECIDED THE WORLD IS BETTER OFF WITH SOMEONE LIKE *ME* AS THE CARETAKER.

POSSESSION OF THESE BLUEPRINTS COULD PROVE VERY DANGEROUS.

UNLESS I PLACE A *PERSONAL AD* IN A REVOLVING SERIES OF NEWSPAPERS, *DAILY,* THE BLUEPRINTS WILL BE SENT TO THE HEADS OF EIGHT OF THE WORLD'S MOST POWERFUL COUNTRIES.

ARE YOU *BLACKMAILING* THE QUEEN OF ENGLAND, SIR?!

APPARENTLY.

YOU HAVE PROVEN YOURSELF A *MOST* RESOURCEFUL YOUNG MAN, MR. HOLMES. SUCH A MAN WOULD MAKE A *FINE* AGENT FOR ENGLAND.

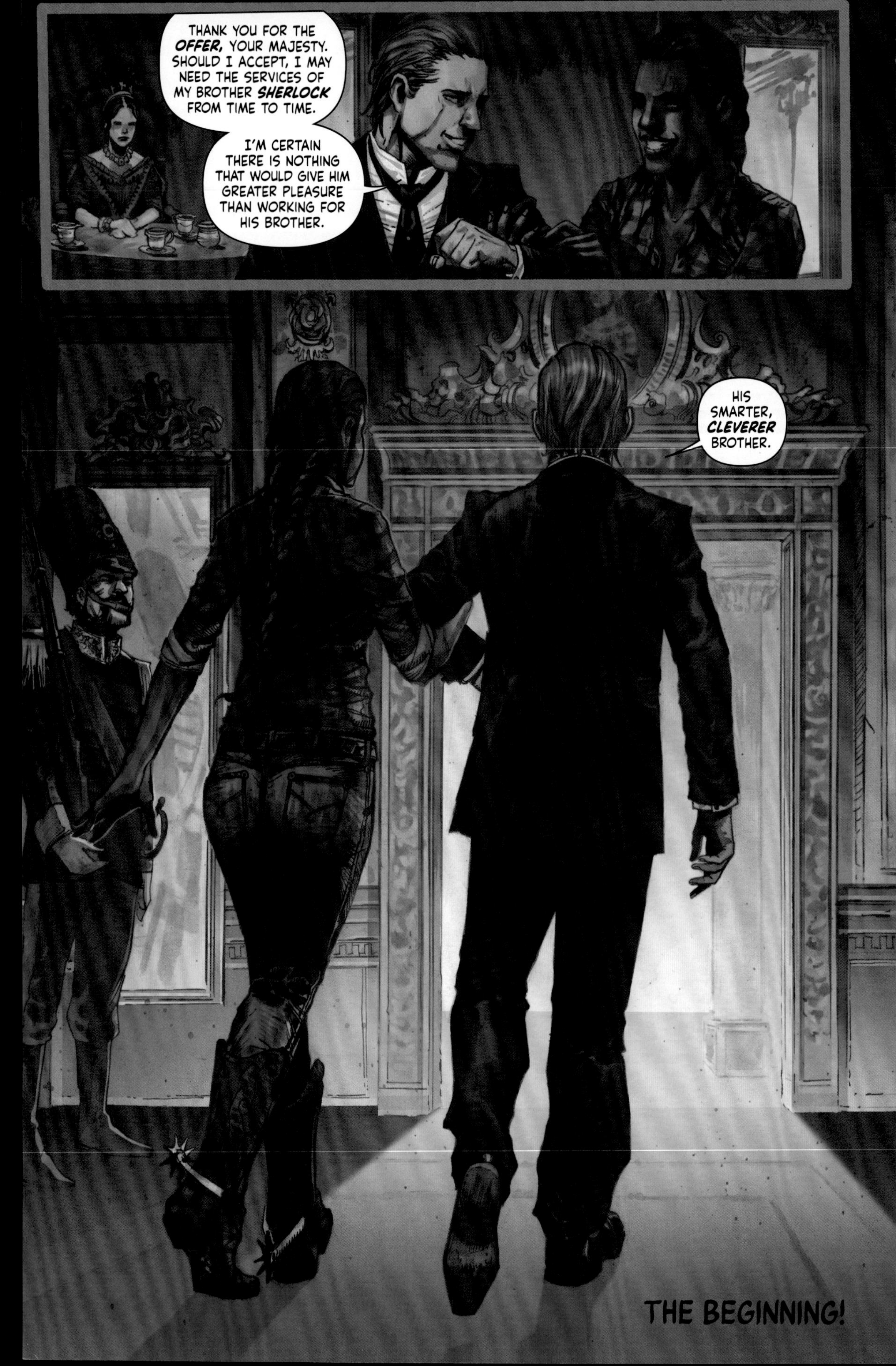
THANK YOU FOR THE **OFFER,** YOUR MAJESTY. SHOULD I ACCEPT, I MAY NEED THE SERVICES OF MY BROTHER **SHERLOCK** FROM TIME TO TIME.
I'M CERTAIN THERE IS NOTHING THAT WOULD GIVE HIM GREATER PLEASURE THAN WORKING FOR HIS BROTHER.
HIS SMARTER, **CLEVERER** BROTHER.
THE BEGINNING!

COVER GALLERY

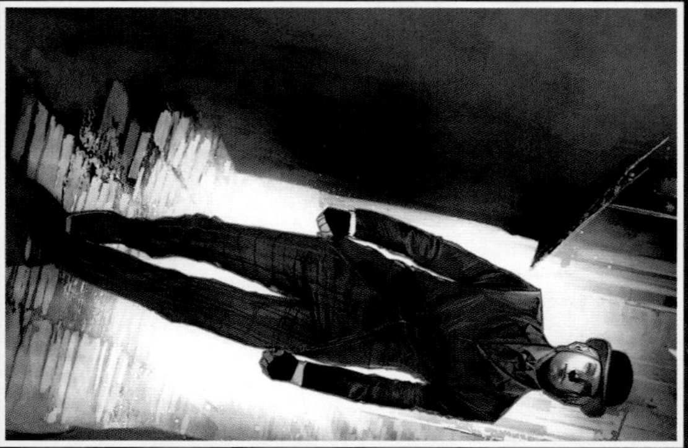

#1 COVER B – ROD REIS

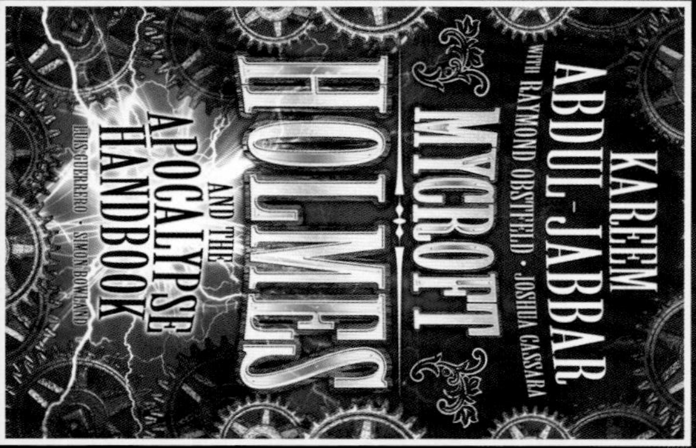
KAREEM
ABDUL-JABBAR
WITH RAYMOND OBSTFELD · JOSHUA CASSARA
MYCROFT
HOLMES
AND THE
APOCALYPSE
HANDBOOK
LUIS GUERRERO · SIMON BOWLAND

#1 COVER C – ROB FARMER

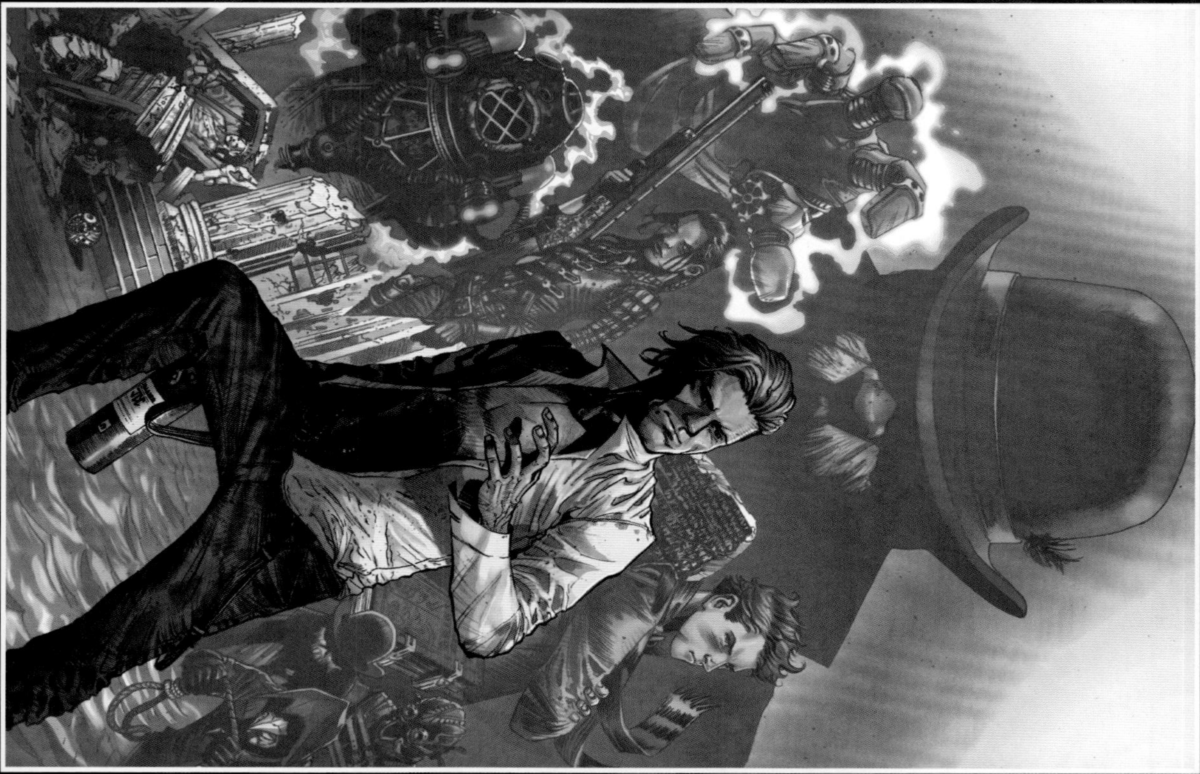

#1 COVER A – JOSHUA CASSARA & LUIS GUERRERO

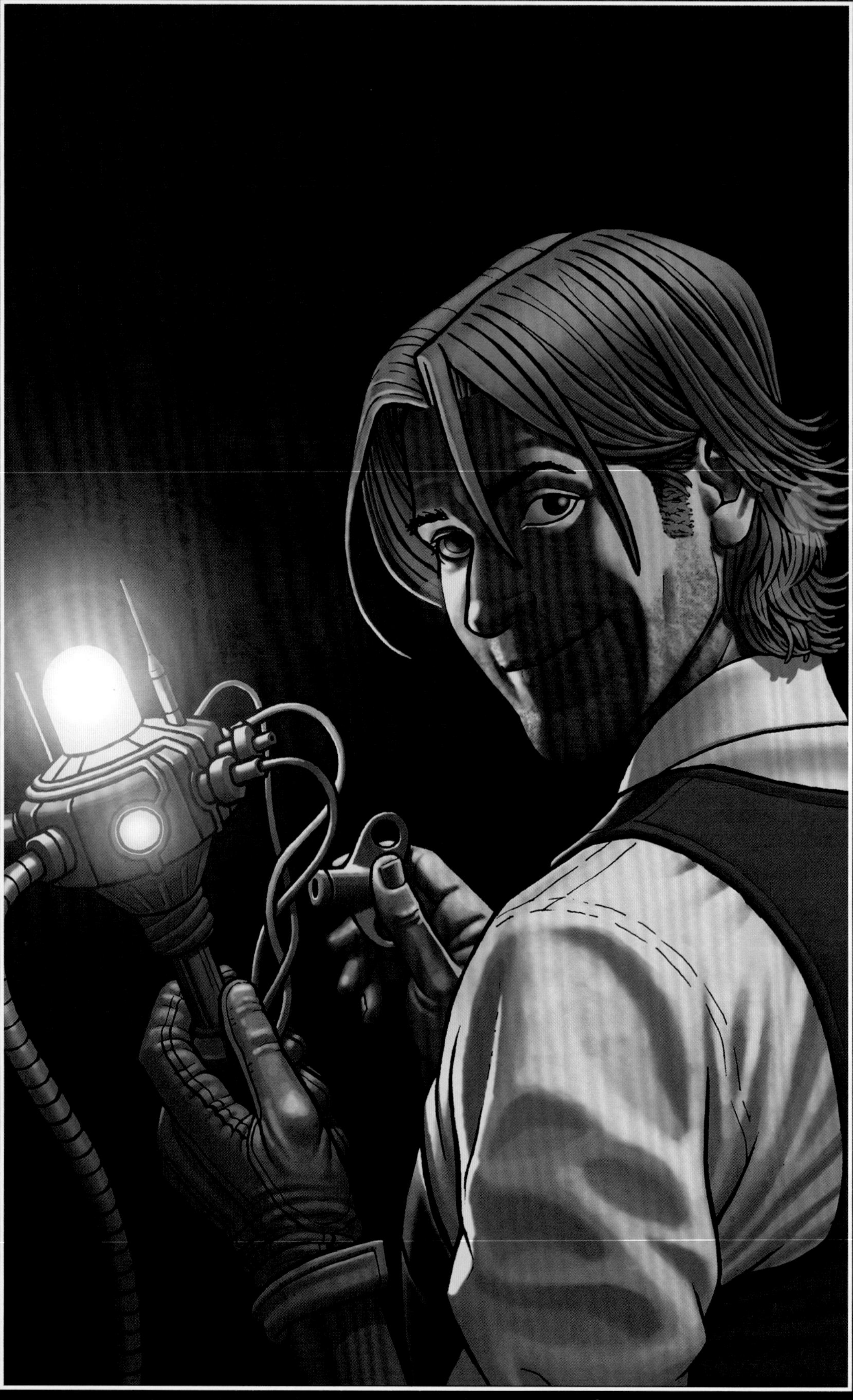

#1 COVER D
PAUL MCCAFFREY

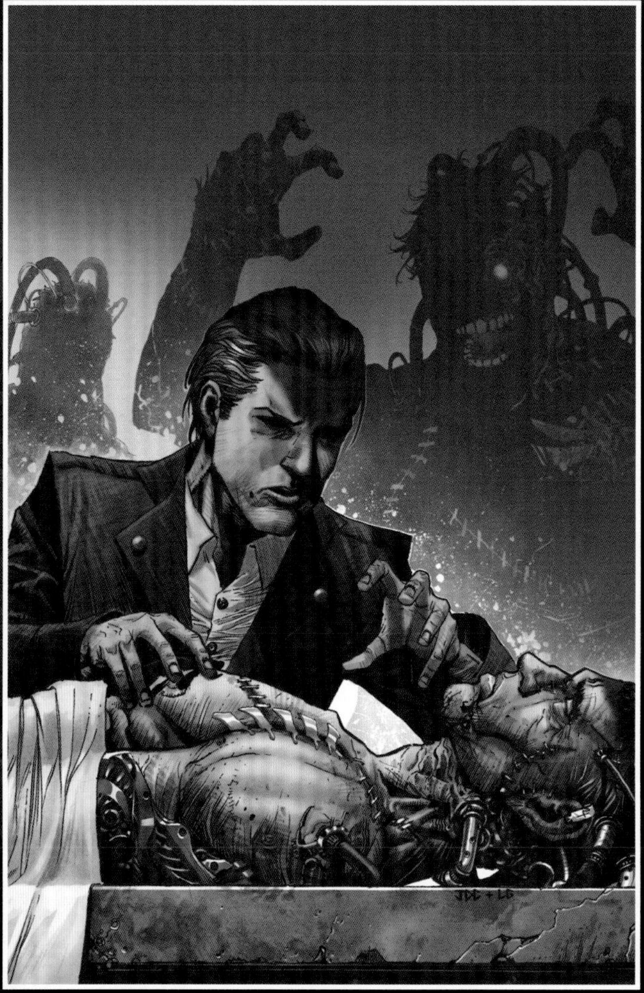

#2 COVER A – JOSHUA CASSARA & LUIS GUERRERO

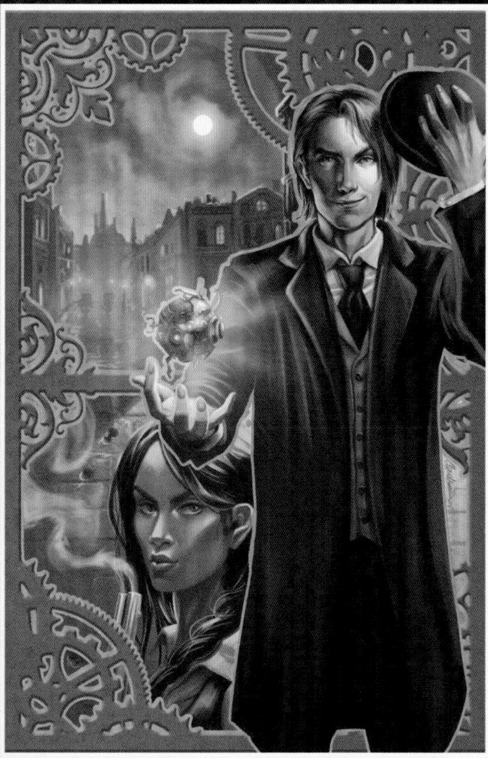

#2 COVER B – CLAUDIA IANNICIELLO

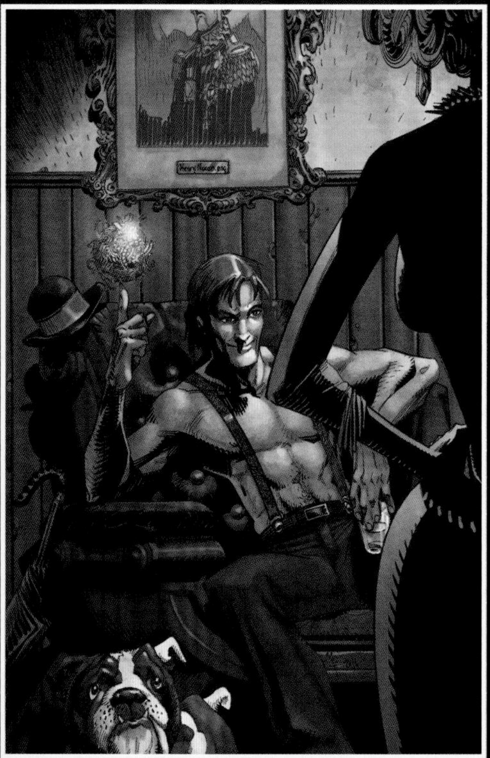

#2 COVER C – JOHN MCCREA & MIKE SPICER

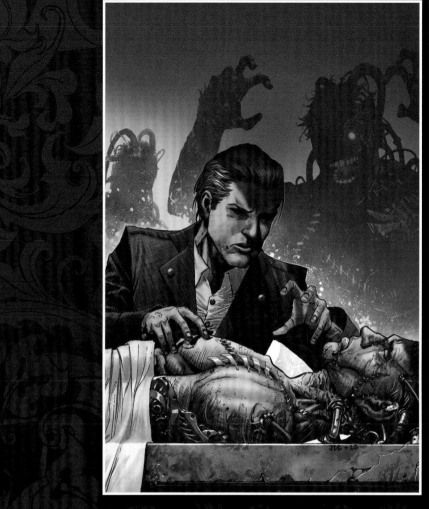

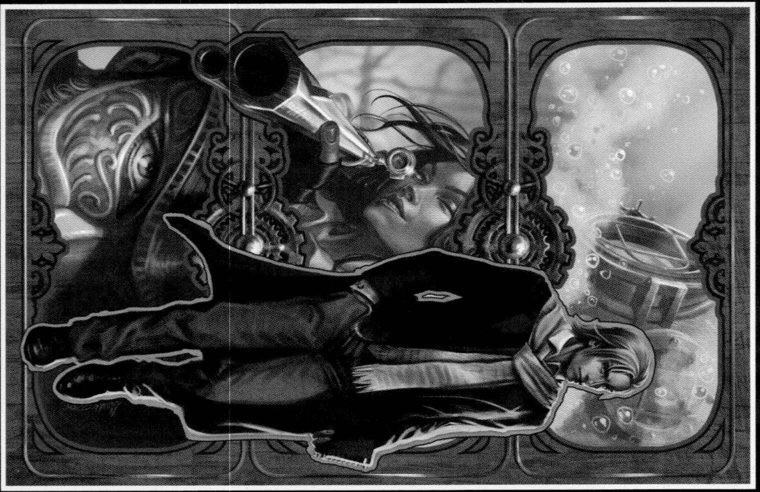

#3 COVER B – CLAUDIA IANNICIELLO

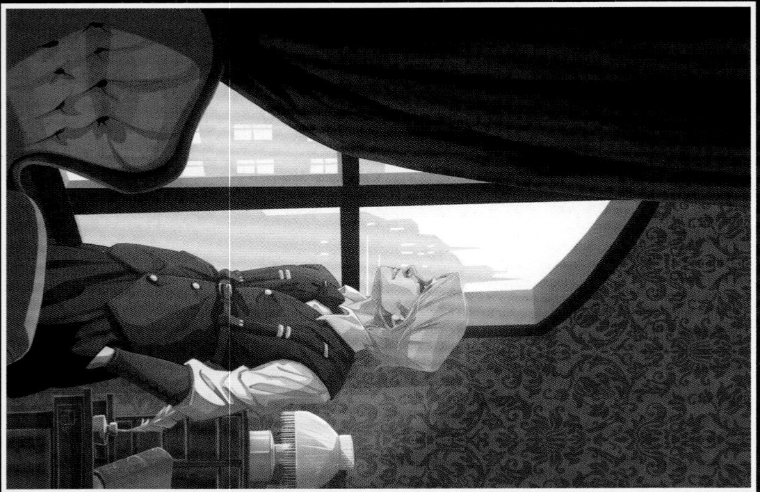

#3 COVER C – ARIANNA FLOREAN

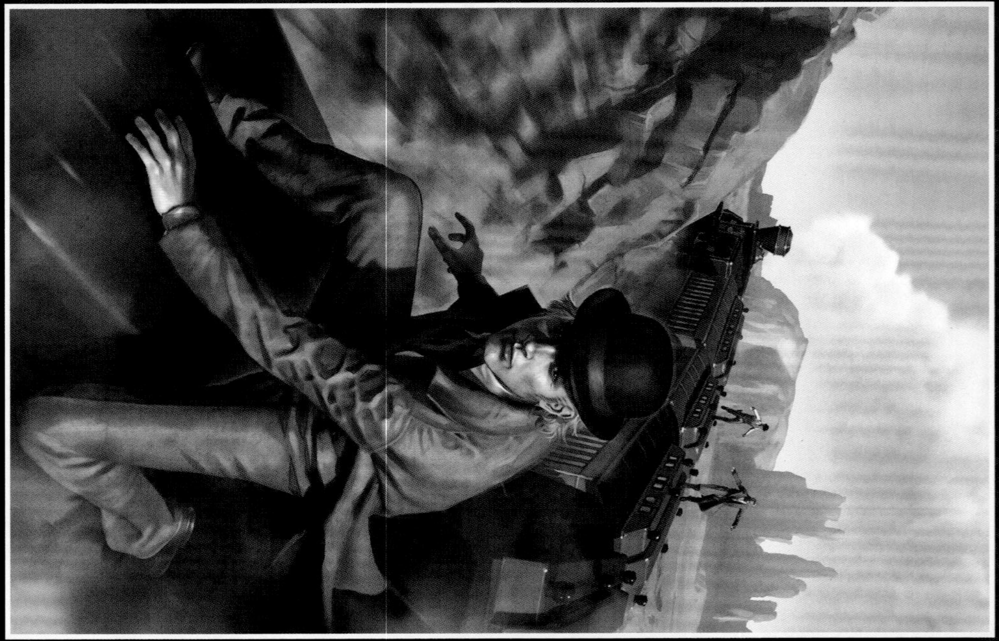

#3 COVER A – ALEX RONALD

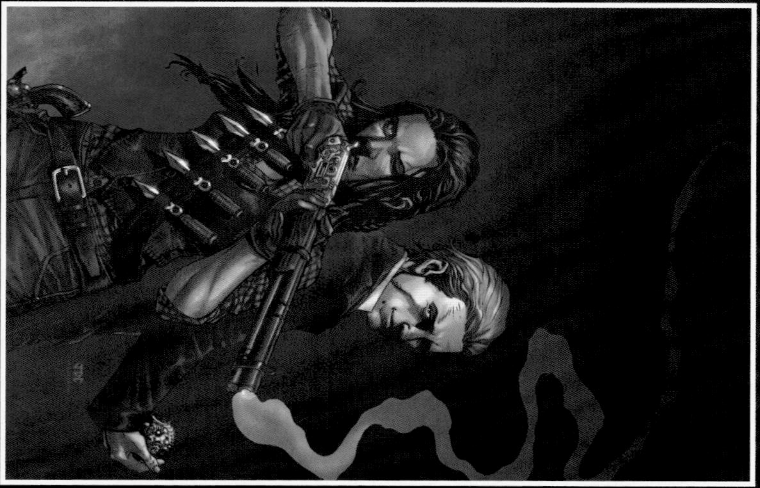

#4 COVER B – JOSHUA CASSARA & LUIS GUERRERO

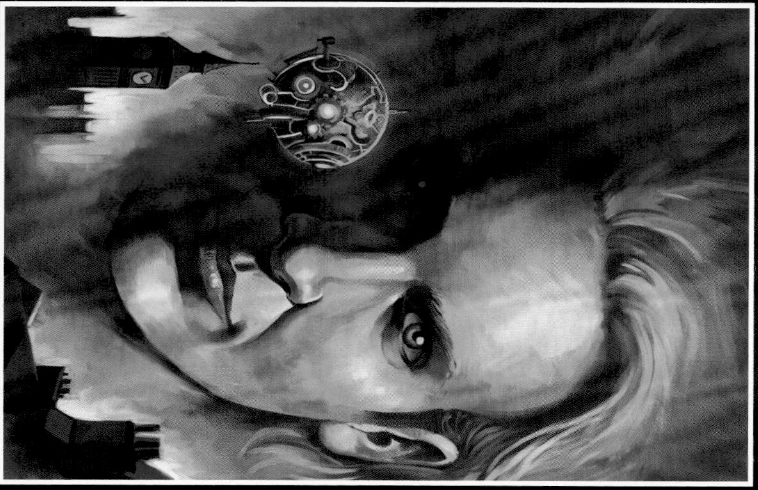

#4 COVER C – MARIANO LACLAUSTRA

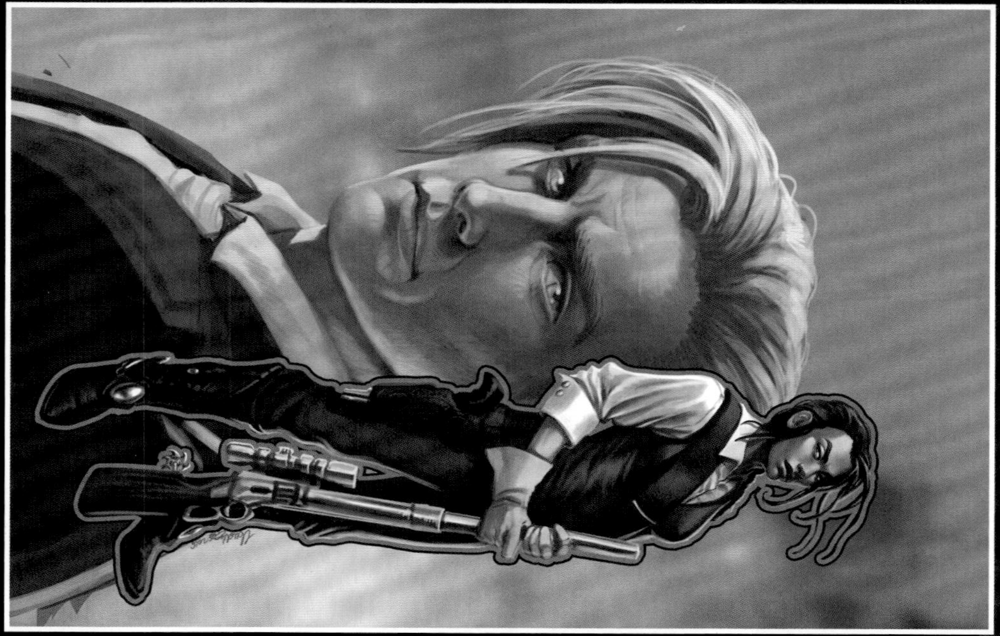

#4 COVER A – CLAUDIA IANNICIELLO

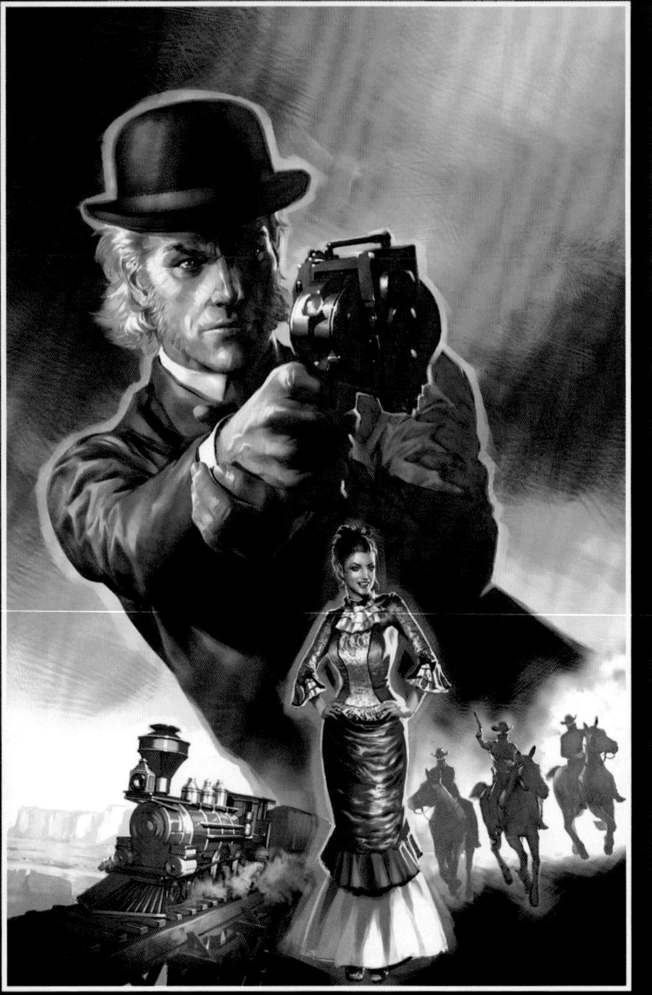
#5 COVER A – ALEX RONALD

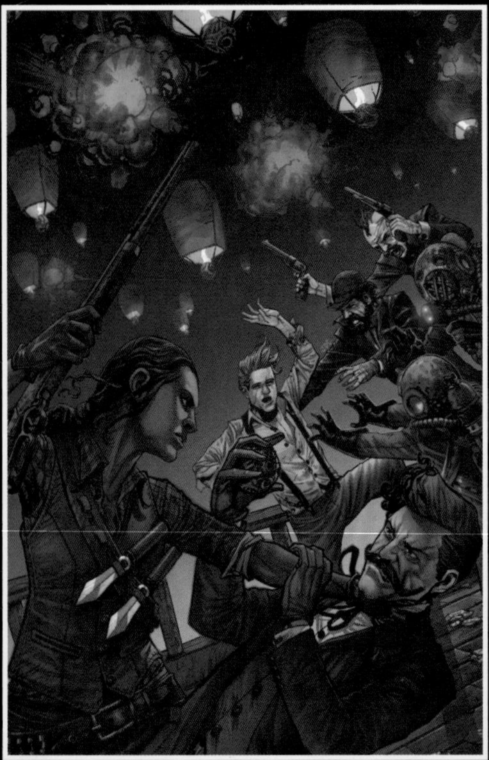
#5 COVER B – JOSHUA CASSARA & LUIS GUERRERO

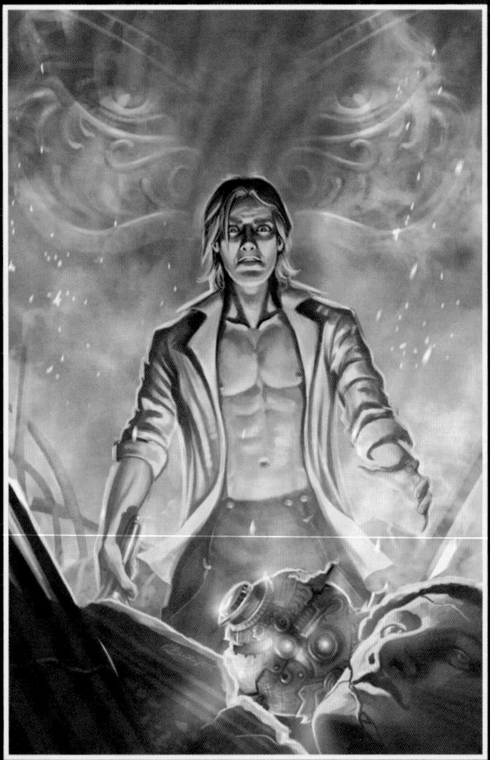

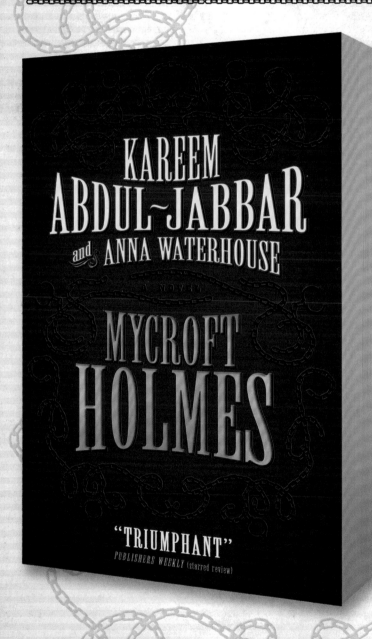

CREATOR BIOGRAPHIES

KAREEM ABDUL-JABBAR

Kareem Abdul-Jabbar is the NBA's all-time leading scorer and a six-time NBA champion. He is also one of a handful of influential and respected black men in America who has a national platform as a regular contributing columnist for *The Washington Post* and *Time Magazine*, where he shares his thoughts on some of the most socially relevant and politically controversial topics facing the nation today. After 50 years as an athlete, activist, and *New York Times* bestselling author, he offers his perspectives on how we can work together to solve some of these issues as a nationally recognized speaker who appears regularly on the lecture circuit. His new political book, *Writings on the Wall – Searching for a New Equality Beyond Black and White*, from Time Books, offers his personal perspectives on political issues facing America.

In 2012, Kareem was appointed to be the U.S. Cultural Ambassador by then Secretary of State Hillary Rodham Clinton. Currently he serves as the chairman of his Skyhook Foundation, whose mission is to "Give Kids a Shot That Can't be Blocked" by bringing educational opportunities to under-served communities through innovative outdoor environmental learning. Kareem's most recent projects include the HBO Sports documentary, *Kareem: Minority of One*, which debuted in 2015 as HBO's most watched and highest rated sports documentary. His debut novel *Mycroft Holmes* - a mystery novel and the first of an action/mystery series based on Sherlock Holmes's savvy older brother - was also released by Titan Books in 2015. This graphic novel collection, *Mycroft Holmes and the Apocalypse Handbook*, follows the success of that novel.

RAYMOND OBSTFELD

Raymond Obstfeld is an American novelist, screenwriter, and non-fiction writer of over fifty books. He teaches creative writing at Orange Coast College. His novels include the Edgar-nominated *Dead Heat* and the award-winning young-adult novel *Joker and the Thief*. He and co-author Kareem Abdul-Jabbar won the NAACP Image Award for their children's book *What Color Is My World* and were nominated for another NAACP Image Award for *Writings on the Wall: Searching for a New Equality Beyond Black and White*. He has also published two instructional books on writing, *The Novelist's Essential Guide to Crafting Scenes* and *Fiction First-Aid*.

JOSHUA CASSARA

Based in San Diego, Joshua Cassara is an artistic talent on the rise. As well as crafting the visual look and sumptuous storytelling of the world of *Mycroft Holmes*, his stunningly inked artwork has graced the pages of *The Troop* – a modern superhero adventure created and written by actor, screenwriter, and director Noel Clarke – and Marvel's *New Avengers*.

LUIS GUERRERO

Luis Guerrero's colors can be found in such diverse Titan Comics titles as *Doctor Who*, *Rivers of London*, *Warhammer 40,000*, and *The Troop*, where his creative partnership with Joshua began.

SIMON BOWLAND

Simon Bowland letters comics for Titan Comics, Marvel, DC, IDW, Dynamite, 2000AD, and many more, his characterful digital calligraphy bringing quick-witted dialogue and sound effects to the page.